"This wonderful book is artistic in every wi[...] reminder that we need to honor seasons in [...] calendar require, artfully punctuating life's significant moments. The book is deeply rooted in location, often southern France where Sylvie grew up. Thus it is incarnational in the best sense, as all good art should be. Two types of illustration permeate the book. First, the *santons*—figures for the crèche from Sylvie's native Provence— 'saintlets' which, unlike the haloed figures of classical art, are simply local personages: the baker, the farmer, the seamstress . . . and by implication, you and me. Second, there are marvelous botanical illustrations of plants and vegetables that go with each season, such as the bell flowers for Easter or the thornbush for passion week. This book is not just to be picked up each morning but to be savored all year. As Kevin, Sylvie's husband, puts it in his foreword, it is 'life changing.'"

William Edgar, author of *A Supreme Love: The Music of Jazz and the Hope of the Gospel* and professor emeritus of apologetics, Westminster Theological Seminary

"What then are we to do with this book so unlike any other? Shelve it all alone and give it pride of place? It is a work of art. Or might we slip it in a pocket to carry through the afternoon? Or better, allow ourselves to be carried by it through a calendar of seasons, instructed in the folkways of each one, in unexpected beauty and surprise? Might we allow this book to ask us questions, make us wonder, tell us new and ancient stories of other places, other times? And surely, if we listen, if we pay attention, we will see and learn. We will be charmed; we will be changed. For yes, this lovely book is just that fine."

Linda McCullough Moore, author of *The Book of Not So Common Prayer*

"Sylvie Vanhoozer's winsome and infectious compendium is about learning in practical and endearing ways to use our imaginations and behold Jesus becoming incarnate in the seasons of our days. But more profoundly, it is about letting our lives be transposed so we become characters in the story of God in Christ. Here you will find something for body, mind, and spirit to cluster round Christ's earthy throne of grace. This book will make your soul grow."

Samuel Wells, vicar of St. Martin-in-the-Fields, London

"My spiritual life has long been shaped by the liturgical calendar, but this book opened a cornucopia of new insights (and delights) for me. I was utterly charmed, a smile dancing on my face as I read each chapter. The adventure starts in Vanhoozer's native Provence with its distinctive Advent traditions, and from there she artfully shows us by her felicitous language and personal example how to incorporate the wisdom of her tradition where we each live and work. Along the way she helps us taste a culinary spirituality, inhabit an earthy theology, and practice a neighborly hospitality, all the while anticipating our eternal home with God."

Bobby Gross, author of *Living the Christian Year: How to Inhabit the Story of God*

"Opening Sylvie Vanhoozer's *The Art of Living in Season* is like stepping through the wardrobe on a great Narnian adventure! Everyday saints, like you and me, are invited on pilgrimage through the pages of this thoughtfully conceived, beautifully designed, and deeply moving book. Bring your gift, indeed, your very self, and follow Sylvie's story—as she invites us to journey with Christ through the Christian year. A marvelous resource for individuals, families, and congregations alike!"

Todd Wilson, cofounder of the Center for Pastor Theologians

"Sylvie Vanhoozer journeys with us as a pilgrim through the church year using the lens of the characters in a French crèche, rooted in the earthy everyday beauty of the natural world, a beauty she first learned to see during her childhood in Provence. She writes with grace, reverence, and a sense of wonder, weaving in cultural and historical background, her study of nature, and her own practice of living deeply into the rich meaning of each movement of the church year. Her accessible suggestions throughout the book serve as an invitation for all who hunger and thirst to live with intention in each sacred season of the year."

Michelle Van Loon, author of *Moments & Days: How Our Holy Celebrations Shape Our Faith*

"Fine wines are grown in historically acknowledged *terroirs*—that French word meaning a very specific mix of soil, grade, hours of sunlight, and harnessed minerals. The distance of ten feet can be the distance between a ten-dollar wine and a thousand-dollar wine. In this book, Sylvie Vanhoozer studies the *terroir* of everyday life and the complex interplay of each person's history, geography, personality, and God-call. Her protagonists? The small *santons* of French provincial life, miniature clay figures that are brought out each Advent and who represent ordinary people (us!) on pilgrimage to the Christ child. This book is a delightful blend of memoir, nature journal, and theological reflection on a unique tradition from southern France that invites us to root our own lives in the Nativity, such that it takes on the contours of our terroir and can become fine wine."

Julie Canlis, author of *Theology of the Ordinary*

"Sylvie Vanhoozer weaves an exquisite telling of what it is to live in the fullness of the seasons, both of nature and the church. From her opening description to closing benediction, a luminous beauty is present in every page. This is a book I want to read and live through again and again, all the year through."

Lancia E. Smith, publisher of Cultivating Oaks Press

"This tender, beautiful, and entirely original book does indeed offer an *art de vivre*, an art of living. The age-old wisdom embedded in the traditional seasons of the Christian year is brought to new life and made available to us in new ways."

Malcolm Guite, poet, theologian, and author of *Mariner: A Theological Voyage with Samuel Taylor Coleridge*

SYLVIE VANHOOZER

FOREWORD BY
KEVIN J. VANHOOZER

ILLUSTRATED BY
SYLVIE VANHOOZER

The ART
of
LIVING
in
SEASON

A YEAR *of*
REFLECTIONS
for
EVERYDAY
SAINTS

An imprint of InterVarsity Press
Downers Grove, Illinois

InterVarsity Press
P.O. Box 1400 | Downers Grove, IL 60515-1426
ivpress.com | email@ivpress.com

InterVarsity Press® is the publishing division of InterVarsity Christian Fellowship/USA®. For more information, visit intervarsity.org.

Scripture quotations, unless otherwise noted, are from The Holy Bible, English Standard Version, copyright © 2001 by Crossway Bibles, a division of Good News Publishers. Used by permission. All rights reserved.

While any stories in this book are true, some names and identifying information may have been changed to protect the privacy of individuals.

Interior illustrations: Sylvie Vanhoozer

The publisher cannot verify the accuracy or functionality of website URLs used in this book beyond the date of publication.

Cover design: David Fassett
Interior design: Daniel van Loon
Cover images: Sylvie Vanhoozer

ISBN 978-1-5140-0696-2 (print) | ISBN 978-1-5140-0697-9 (digital)

Printed in the United States of America ♾

Library of Congress Cataloging-in-Publication Data
Names: Vanhoozer, Sylvie P., 1959- author. | Vanhoozer, Kevin J. writer of
  foreword.
Title: The art of living in season : a year of reflections for everyday
  saints / Sylvie P. Vanhoozer ; foreword by Kevin J. Vanhoozer.
Description: Downers Grove, IL : IVP, [2024] | Includes bibliographical
  references.
Identifiers: LCCN 2023039513 (print) | LCCN 2023039514 (ebook) | ISBN
  9781514006962 (print) | ISBN 9781514006979 (digital)
Subjects: LCSH: Church year meditations. | Seasons–Religious
  aspects–Christianity. | Devotional literature.
Classification: LCC BV30 .V36 2024 (print) | LCC BV30 (ebook) | DDC
  242/.2–dc23/eng/20231026
LC record available at https://lccn.loc.gov/2023039513
LC ebook record available at https://lccn.loc.gov/2023039514
A catalog record for this book is available from the Library of Congress.

31 30 29 28 27 26 25 24 | 12 11 10 9 8 7 6 5 4 3 2 1

To KEVIN,

companion pilgrim of forty-three years, and

MARY AND EMMA,

who joined and graced our pilgrimage later on.

For everything there is a season, and a time for every matter under heaven.

ECCLESIASTES 3:1

CONTENTS

ஐ *Part One* | *11* ஐ
EVERYDAY SAINTS *in*
the SPECIAL SEASONS

~ *Part Two* | *117* ~
EVERYDAY SAINTS *in*
ORDINARY TIME

FOREWORD

KEVIN J. VANHOOZER

*T*he book you are about to read is life-changing, particularly if you have lived with its author for forty years, as I have. I can vouch that she practices what she preaches (and in this book gently, exquisitely preaches her practice). The art of living in season, as a subset of the art of living (*l'art de vivre*), indirectly addresses life's biggest questions.

Don't panic. This is not an academic treatise, but a reflection on lived experience, viewed through a wholly original lens: a southern French Christmas manger scene. To read this book is to enter into a thought experiment: What would it be like to follow the holy family and their entourage out of the manger, into everyday places, through the whole year and the various seasons of life? This is the story of a Christian pilgrim from Provence who does just that. Readers who embark on her journey will find a congenial, insightful, interesting, and enlivening companion along the ways of their own life journeys. I know I have.

I first met Sylvie in the north of France, in a small town outside Paris, but she immediately made it clear that she was from the south (Provence, so named because it was the first Roman province west of the Alps) and that she had no intention of leaving—and, if she did, it would certainly not be with an American tumbleweed. After she finished her studies, she would return to southern France, the better to walk the hills and cultivate her garden.

At the time I didn't fully appreciate what leaving her homeland would cost her. Well, I did—a little. Even before we were married, as a student in the cloudy north, she would sometimes get homesick. There were lavender-infused fragrances and bath oils labeled "Eau de Provence" that recalled the countryside, but I couldn't afford those. Instead, I got an empty glass dropper bottle, captioned it "Air de Provence," and added a label instructing the user to "Sniff twice every four hours when feeling homesick." We were married a year later. Brilliant!

I relate this story because it provides a crucial backdrop to the present book. Our age is one of increasing displacement, whether chosen, as it was for Sylvie, or forced, as is the case with refugees. Even people who don't leave their countries leave their homes. Life is a journey through time from place to place. How then should we live in places that are not our true homes? This is one of the central questions of the book.

Sylvie's willingness to leave everything to be a disciple of Jesus impressed me from the start. After becoming a Christian as an eighteen-year-old, she left home to attend a Bible institute against the wishes of her parents. Then, like Abram, she obeyed an even greater call: "Go from your country and your kindred and your father's house to the land that I will show you" (Genesis 12:1). It turned out that we had to go, repeatedly, from several countries: the United States, England, and Scotland. Can a disciple ever recover from homesickness? Where, and what, is "home"?

This book stems from Sylvie's attempts to make herself "at home" abroad. She is hardly the only person who has had to learn to live, perchance to flourish, in a non-native land. How does one do that? I'll let the following pages speak for themselves. Let me just say that it has to do with attending to, and embracing, your location. Sylvie came to see that the same God who created the hills of Provence made the dales of England and the Midwestern plains. All show signs of divine artistry, even if the style is different. It was through reading novels about life on the prairie and taking classes in botanical art that Sylvie came to see, know, and appreciate the Midwest's land, people, and flora. Taking time not simply to look at things but to *see* them is a kind of spiritual discipline.

Sylvie has taught me to pay attention as, together, we pass through the seasons of life, some familiar (spring and autumn), others new (losing one's parents). Each of us has now written books asking, in our own respective ways, what Christian discipleship means and looks like in the twenty-first century: Who am I, for Christ, today in this place? What can I do to help the people, plants, and communities in my place to flourish? If Jesus came so that we may have life, and that abundantly, what can I say or do here and now to enliven others? Every Christian should consider this question in all seriousness. There is nothing more important than being Christ's man or woman, a representative of his reign, now, in this place.

"What's an everyday saint to do?" The question appears as a refrain in every chapter. It is Sylvie's way of helping readers think about what it means to "seek first the kingdom of God and his righteousness" (Matthew 6:33). So come, join the pilgrimage. And as you do, practice the art of living in season. Learn how to be at home, in Christ, in ten thousand places, both strange and familiar.

Introduction

A SEED IS PLANTED

A CHILD'S CHRISTMAS IN PROVENCE

What if the whole of a life (yours,
say, or mine) is simply this—a tiny germ
of wheat sleeping in a bed of soil?

ABIGAIL CARROLL, *A GATHERING OF LARKS*

*E*very year throughout the South of France, in villages set amid hills dotted with olive trees and scented with thyme and juniper, enchanting little parables unfold—part of a unique tradition unknown to most outsiders. At Advent, *santons*—"little saints"—appear in the shoebox-sized manger scenes, or *crèches*, that are placed in the dining or living rooms of people's homes just as they have always done since the nineteenth century. These santons are clay figurines, just three inches tall, painted colorfully in period dress. Each carries a simple gift for the baby Jesus, products from their own *terroir*, that distinct local place that nurtures their growth. These crèche scenes do not so much represent the story of the Christmas night as restage it, setting the birth of Jesus in the terroir of the people of Provence. This is where my own story starts.

But it is only the beginning. For these little clay figures, which I recall from my own childhood home, have become part of popular culture, so much so that they have come to represent the people of Provence and their way of life. Yet always in the background lies the Christ child. He is an integral part of this scene as well. Many *Provençaux* may not talk about him, nor know much about him, yet he still belongs to the scene. He is every bit as essential to the crèche as the olive trees and villagers. His quiet presence hallows the land. He is what renders these clay figurines of plain villagers something special: he makes them little saints, set apart to serve him and his story. (For more details on the historical background of the santons—and pictures!—see my website www.theart oflivinginseason.com.)

Unlike other manger scenes, the Provençal crèche does not so much depict a static scene as provide a stage for a Christmas pageant. Action! For these little saints are on a mission, a *pilgrimage* to Bethlehem (now transported to Provence). A strong desire to see the baby Jesus urges the pilgrims on. They come because they want to present their gifts—not gold, frankincense, and myrrh (those come too, in due course)—but simpler gifts related to their everyday vocations: a baker brings baguettes, a weaver brings wool blankets, a farmer brings produce from his field, and so forth. The songs and stories that accompany these pilgrims make them very human, so like us. Each little saint is cast in a specific role; each has a story of their own, within the greater story of Christmas, and each comes with their own fears and foibles. When they finally find the *crèche*, they offer Jesus what they have: their gifts, yes, but their fears and foibles too. And they receive something back.

So, perhaps, do the larger saints, the twenty-first century children and adults who keep the crèche—call them *everyday saints*. For, thanks to this singular custom, Christmas in Provence is a story that involves not simply clay figures, but every son and daughter of Adam, the original clay figure. This is a story that invites ongoing participation, and not just at Advent. This is a story not just to believe in, but to live in, and to live out. To the one with eyes to see, the crèche is an invitation to step into Advent—and perhaps beyond it.

This is why, during my own years of pilgrimage from my homeland of Provence to new lands—California, the Mid-Atlantic, England, Scotland, the Midwest—I began to wonder: What if, once Christmas is over, I continued the pilgrimage, in spiritual company with the santons, through all the seasons of the year? What if I were to follow Jesus *outside* the crèche in order to keep on doing, throughout the year, what these little saints did in Advent and Christmas? Could I bring an offering to Jesus daily, in my place and time, as the santons did in theirs? Could joining their pilgrimage help me answer the question, "What am I doing here?" Could it help me get out of bed in the morning? It would take intentionality, a discipline of paying attention to the seasons in which I find myself: the seasons of the church that teach us about Christ's life and ministry, the seasons of nature that reveal the goodness of our Creator, the seasons of life that unfold God's plan for my story. Could I approach every new season, whether I was in Bethlehem, Provence, or somewhere else, with the wonder and expectation of Advent? If so, what would that look like?

Little did I know, as a child growing up in Provence, how transformative these little clay figures would later become in my life. Their story has become my story, an invitation to "come and see" the Christ child. I came, I saw, I followed. Over the years, I have become not a fixture in the crèche, but an everyday saint. Like the santons, I come to Jesus, and then, inspired by these little figures, I follow Jesus out of the manger, through all the seasons of life.

Unlike Narnia, where it was "always winter and never Christmas," Christ has come to our world and enters into our lives in every season.[1] I have therefore come to believe that it is "never winter, always Advent." I have learned to anticipate him in every new chapter of my life, so that each season is not only an adventure but, in its own way, *Adventish.*

The early seeds from my childhood traditions—sown in the crèche with its stories that embraced southern French village life—have finally grown roots in my new land for new generations. There is indeed a precious seed here, the germ of a new kind of life, which is well worth

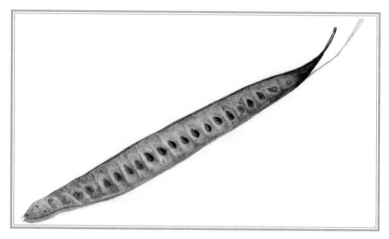

A seed pod full of promise

protecting, passing down, and transplanting in different contexts. Perhaps the Jesus who comes to us—in Bethlehem, Provence, or the heartland of America—makes every place and time special, as he makes Christmas special, gracing us again and again with the gift of his presence.

Our culture has trained us always to rush ahead toward the next big thing. But rushing ahead is not how everyday saints learn the art of living in season, the art of appreciating the possibilities of offering gifts to Christ in the particular time and place where God has planted us. I encourage saints on an everyday pilgrimage to relearn how to walk. Walking is wonderful exercise; everyone knows that. It is also the fundamental activity of the Christian pilgrim—a spiritual exercise. I therefore invite readers to walk, not run, through this book as you practice the gentle art of living in season. While I designed it to be used as a companion throughout the year starting at Advent, you can start in any season, or read it all at once, or in whatever way you find most useful.

My botanical artwork, in watercolor and colored pencils, will accompany us, encouraging the reader to reflect at a walking pace on the change of our natural seasons in the wild and in kitchen gardens. Scattered like seeds among the pages are the fruit of my own efforts at patient observation, a series of botanical illustrations, such as they are (my art, too, is on a pilgrimage). Keeping an artist's eye on the changing seasons of nature has become, for me, a spiritual discipline: watching and waiting for one advent after another.

As we walk together, each chapter will introduce you to a different santon and show you how each one uses his or her gift in season as an offering to the Lord of all seasons. To encourage you to take the time needed to observe and engage with each season in your place, I have included weekly reflections in each chapter. Think of them as stations in your pilgrimage, opportunities to watch and wait for the Lord's advent in your time and place. Each month I will ask you to Pause, Ponder, Pray, and Play Your Part. These reflective exercises will help you develop your own pilgrimage, the art of finding and following Jesus in every place and every season.

Let us now join the company of santons as we begin our journey through the church year, observing how they offer to the Lord what they can: their everyday skills, their everyday vocations, and their everyday lives. Let us learn from them the art of living for Christ as women and men for all seasons.

Part One

EVERYDAY SAINTS *in* *the* SPECIAL SEASONS

By "SPECIAL SEASONS," I mean those times of the year when the church celebrates important events in the life of Christ. They are holy days—set-apart times for paying attention. They punctuate the church year, providing order and rhythm to the church calendar.

Historically, setting apart certain days and weeks was one way for everyday Christians to become familiar with key events in Jesus' life on earth; they were part of the pedagogy by which laypeople learned Christ. With these events internalized, disciples could walk with Jesus through his story on a weekly and seasonal basis. The special seasons were ways that Jesus' followers could participate in Christ. They still serve as means of grace that help disciples hew to the story of the one who is "the way, and the truth, and the life" (John 14:6).

Church tradition has planted each episode of Jesus' story in a suitably appropriate season of nature; it makes sense to talk about fasting during the food-scarce winter. As Christians walked through the church year, the natural world around them illuminated Jesus' story. They walked through the seasons of nature and the church calendar alike as fellow pilgrims, members of the one holy catholic and apostolic church.

Centuries have passed, much has changed. Different countries have their own carols, Christmas treats, and stories. As a result, not every church today inhabits the church calendar in exactly the same way, though all churches observe at least some of the special seasons. Some churches are highly liturgical and observe the church calendar, well, religiously; others observe only Christmas and Easter. Still, the special seasons mark those times when the church remembers its foundation in the life of Jesus, her cornerstone. At minimum, they provide a sense of direction, identity, and purpose: a narrative template for the church year, a temporal frame for the art of living in season.

Why keep observing these age-old, analog traditions in our modern digital age, when people have their own personalized electronic calendar? Why celebrate special days? Because doing so still serves everyday saints. This truth is the burden of this book.

The rhythms of the church seasons hallow the seasons of nature. It is all too easy to become displaced, to lose one's bearings in a meaningless day-to-day sameness, where it is always a weekday and never Christmas. The special seasons are an antidote for this ennui, anchoring everyday saints in a passion play, a story that invites us in, as it has been doing for centuries, and asks us to "do this in remembrance of me" (Luke 22:19).

The special seasons train us in the way we should go:

Thus says the LORD:
"Stand by the roads, and look,
   and ask for the ancient paths,
where the good way is; and walk in it,
   and find rest for your souls." (Jeremiah 6:16)

In the land of my ancestors, the Christian year starts with the santons. This is no surprise: as crèche figures, the santons are obviously associated with the Christmas season. But if you examine these manger scenes more closely, you see not just the holy family, but also a collection of typical nineteenth-century French townsfolk, dressed in period clothing and furnished with appropriate props. To observe *this* Christmas scene is to enter a village suspended in time and space, abuzz with the news that Jesus is coming to Provence. To contemplate this crèche is to become aware that Christ may indeed arrive anywhere, anytime, to anyone. Yes, the original crèche belongs in Bethlehem, but

I suggest these santons have much to teach us about how Jesus continues to come to us, in our own times and places.

Strictly speaking, the French manger scene is inaccurate. Jesus did not in fact come to Provence in the nineteenth century! But the point is not to put Jesus into nineteenth-century Provence, but to learn how to put nineteenth-century Provence, or any time and place, into Jesus and his story. This is the real lesson and purpose of the special seasons: to help us learn how to put our own times and place, mine and yours, into his.

This, then, is how the crèche of my childhood Christmases in Provence has come to be—for me, my family, and hopefully for you too—parable of how to follow Jesus in *every* time and place.

In this book I propose to accompany these little saints as they make their pilgrimage through the church year. At times we will sing and laugh with them, at other times we will argue and grieve with them. They are not perfect, and neither are we—and that is all right. The purpose of the journey is to become mature in Christ, to fit our lives and stories into his.

We thus embark on a pilgrimage, following the rhythm of a calendar that is punctuated not by the usual cultural holidays, but by holy days that celebrate the gradual unfolding of the extended Christmas story, starting with Advent and moving on from one season of Jesus' life to the next, all the way to Pentecost. We will lean into Jesus' story in order better to follow him faithfully and fittingly, in ways that are in accordance with the Scriptures and appropriate to our cultural situations. In so doing, we will learn to cultivate the mind, and heart, of Christ. For, as Jesus said to the first disciples, so he says to us: "Come, follow me" (Matthew 4:19 NIV).

We're coming!

Chapter 1

ADVENT

THE ART OF WATCHFUL WAITING

The LORD is good to those who wait for him,
to the soul who seeks him.
It is good that one should wait quietly
for the salvation of the LORD.

LAMENTATIONS 3:25-26

We may not receive visits from winged angels proclaiming that God has
a message for us, but God still speaks to us. Our task as those who would
hear is to do all in our power to listen to God's voice speaking to us.

BETH A. RICHARDSON, *CHILD OF THE LIGHT*

WHERE CHURCH CALENDAR AND NATURE MEET

The first Sunday of Advent is the official start of the Christian year. It's a day marked not by parties and fanfare but by the quiet atmosphere of fading autumn days moving into early winter, when nothing much grows anymore in the land of the santons, whether countryside or kitchen garden. Hedges and vineyards barely hold on to leaves that are slowly fading, while the rolling hills and patchwork fields of my childhood are blanketed in a faint mist that invites repose. Advent, a time of prayerful expectation mixed with a quiet joy of anticipation, similarly invites inner stillness. It is as if nature begins her own Advent, waiting quietly for the season of growth and new life ahead. Christians replay the story of watching and waiting that started millennia ago, when the people of Israel looked forward to the Messiah's coming. Christians know he has come, yet they continue to wait, watchfully.

ADVENT COMES TO PROVENCE

In the land of my ancestors, Advent is when people bring their precious seasonal figurines out of storage, not forgetting the miniature barn with its stone walls and red roof, seemingly taken straight out of the Provençal countryside. According to the ancient carols, Advent marks the season when the shepherds went on their peculiar pilgrimage to Bethlehem. In similar fashion, and in a way that is entirely in keeping with the season, another "holy pilgrimage" starts, this time with real people. Children, parents, and grandparents ramble into the quiet hills to gather material with which to decorate the manger scene. This walk is so special it even has its own name: *La promenade de l'Avent* (Advent walk).[1]

By gathering native plants, moss, twigs, and so forth to provide a landscape for the manger scene, we root the crèche, and Jesus himself, in our terroir, our own patch of earth—the same earth, in fact, from which the santons figurines themselves were made, rendering the entire endeavor remarkably organic.[2] The Advent walk brings plants and people, and a special season of the church year, together in an intimate, unique, and interrelated way.

During these Advent walks, the elders speak softly to the young ones, initiating them into the deep mysteries of their storied place. Thyme is a "manger herb" because, according to legend, Joseph gathered grass and hay from the roadside with which to line the manger and, as soon as the baby's head touched the manger, the grass turned into fragrant herbs—one of which was thyme. Children learn to identify the native thyme by smell when they rub it between their fingers. They watch in wonder as the thyme sprigs they gathered, inserted into the manger scene, transform into olive trees like the ones that dot their land. They learn that the juniper they collected preserves the scent of the hills and stays green in the crèche throughout the season. Each plant that makes its way into the scenery of the crèche is an integral part of the soil in which the children themselves have their own roots. The Advent walk helps inoculate them from what Wendell Berry calls the "characteristic diseases" of the century, namely, "the suspicion that they would be greatly improved if they were someplace else."[3]

Upon their return home, young and old gather around the crèche and deck it out with their local treasures, re-creating a model version of their homeland with the herbs and scents they know so well. Each person has something to place in the scene, a small gift that, in a way, hints at the season of giving ahead. One may even catch a glimpse of a season further ahead in the story, when individual santons will become a fellowship of saints, sharing the gifts with one another they have been given by their risen Lord. With a little imagination, one might say that what ultimately grows out of the crèche gathering is a local church.

Juniperus virginiana

Juniper leaves and berries

In my family's Christmas crèche, simple brown paper and bark become hills, creases simulate paths, stones stand like ancient boulders along the way. Only when the scene is finally ready do we place the figurines. At first, the holy family is nowhere in sight, nor are the Magi—it is not yet their season. In the beginning of Advent, the crèche keepers have only *prepared* a place for the baby with the materials of their land. Afterward, however, the younger members of the family tend the crèche daily, adding and moving the little saints about, creating the impression of a bustling village. Now the baker and the miller seem to be in conversation; now the dairy maid comes out of the barn with a jug of milk; now an old man approaches the well with his earthen jars.

Meanwhile, the shepherds are abiding on those makeshift hills with their sheep (also little figurines), grazing on the freshly gathered moss. Shepherds are a familiar sight for anyone who lives in Provence. They are the first visitors to the crèche, just as they are in the Gospels. In the crèche, some shepherds are standing, others are sitting. All are watching and waiting.

THE SEASONAL SANTON

The first little saint we encounter as we set out on our pilgrimage through the seasons is, appropriately enough, a shepherd—*pastre* in the

WEEK 1 ∾ *Pause*

"Instructions for living a life:
Pay attention. / Be astonished. / Tell about it."[4]

Plants are mentioned by name throughout the Bible. They clearly matter to God, their Creator, who made each one for a particular place and people. We read about lilies, roses, great cedars, firs, olive trees, vines, rue, and myrtle. In the land of my ancestors, the Advent walk helps us locate our place and plants (and even the baby Jesus) in the Great Story, and in Provence.

> Whether or not you have a manger to decorate, go on an Advent walk in a nature reserve, botanic garden, country path, or city garden. Take slow, measured steps so that you can observe what's around you, and then try to name the native plants of your locale. (You can use an app like Seek to help you—but then put the phone away!) If you have children, involve them in this treasure

Provençal tongue, hence *pastorales*, the traditional Christmas plays that begin with the angels' announcement to the shepherds keeping watch in their fields by night. The plays follow Luke's Gospel in depicting the shepherds as the first ones to spread the news. The shepherd santon comes dressed in a traditional woolen cape (the wool sheared from his sheep, of course) that turns into a blanket to stave off the cold outdoor nights. The shepherd santon carries his gift for the baby Jesus on his shoulders—like Abel, he offers up his most precious possession, a lamb.

Le berger (the shepherd)

hunt. Gather some local flora to "plant" (i.e., contextualize) the Christmas story in your own place, and in your home.

- If you already have a manger scene, try to keep to the church calendar instead of rushing the holy family to the manger before their time. Keep the Magi closeted until the proper time (do you know when that is?). Advent watching and waiting can be spiritually formative, both as a teaching tool and a way to enter the season.
- Invite a neighbor over for coffee and show them your manger (they're great conversation starters!). She may ask you, "Why don't you have the baby Jesus in your manger?" How would you answer that question? Can you explain what makes the special seasons special? Think about the etymology of *holiday* (a "holy day"). Why should certain days be set apart? What should we do on them?

SHEPHERDS IN PROVENÇAL CULTURAL TRADITION

In Provence, people still regard shepherds with quiet respect. These *pastres* belong to the land, and to the landscape, as they have for generations. They figure in our popular stories (not just the pastorales) and they frequently appear in our songs, thanks to Nicolas Saboly, a seventeenth-century French poet and composer. Himself a descendant of shepherds, Saboly was the composer of the first Provençal carols, called *noëls*.

Saboly's beloved carols retell the biblical story of the first Christmas and the angelic announcement to the shepherds, with additional imaginative flourishes thrown in to add local color and detail. The noëls eventually became part of the regular repertoire of folk songs of Provence, part of the year-round culture.[5]

The shepherds were the first recorded people, apart from Mary and Joseph, to bear witness to Jesus' birth. And, according to the folk songs, the shepherds began spreading the news about the baby in the manger even as they made their way to see him. More than any other group, then, it is the shepherds who usher in Christmas: "How beautiful are the feet of those who bring good news!" (Romans 10:15).

The lyrics of Saboly's carols are down-to-earth, even comical at times, reminding us that these shepherds, while playing a special part in Jesus' story, are just as human as the rest of us. This becomes clear as they make their way to the child Christ: "It's such a long way. We're going to freeze in this wind! Our shirts, our trousers are full of holes. . . . Holes can't keep out the cold. . . . How are we going to manage? . . . I'm afraid we're going to die!"[6] This is a remarkably realistic picture of the ordinary cares and concerns that are part and parcel of an everyday saint's pilgrimage. On the other hand, Saboly's carols depict place and time somewhat confusedly. It is hard to tell whether the shepherds are on a long, drawn-out journey or whether everything happens in a single night, whether they are headed to Bethlehem or to some remote village in Provence. One might wonder as they wander: Is this an Advent walk or a lifelong pilgrimage? *Oui!*

Before the angels appear to them, the shepherds are minding their own business, up in the hills, watching the sheep, often in humble isolation, perhaps with a dog as a sole companion. Advent aside, the shepherds were always watching and waiting for something: wolves, wild boars, even highway robbers—anything that might threaten their flock. In the meantime they spend their days, weeks, and months on their own. To be a shepherd is to learn to embrace solitude.

Their solitary vocation evokes respect from the villagers, who in contrast (and by definition) are part of a small community that provides ready-made company. Solitude is no easy accomplishment, especially for a gregarious Mediterranean people. Blaise Pascal said that the root cause of human misery is our inability to sit quietly in our rooms alone.[7] Yet not everyone who sits alone feels alone; solitude is not the same as loneliness. An everyday saint seeks solitude, an inner quietness, in order to keep watch and wait for God's unexpected advents. As Bible teacher Jan Johnson reminds us: "To take time for silence and solitude means we assume that God wants to speak to us and relate to us in a personal way. . . . we learn to converse with God and hear God—first in solitude, then in all of life."[8] Such is the purpose of the Advent walk: to prepare the way of the Lord in one's own most particular place—our heart. Advent watching and waiting is a spiritual exercise for which the shepherd serves as our model and teacher.

Alone in the hills, away from the world below, the shepherd develops the art of attentiveness: concern for his charge, alertness to the land, and fondness for the stars above. The Northern Star is known to the French as *l'étoile du berger* ("the shepherd's star"). I cannot help wondering if it was the shepherds' natural attentiveness that led the angels to appear first to them that first Christmas night. Why else were they the first to hear the good news? Perhaps they saw the angels because they had already been practicing their solitary watchful waiting in the fields while "keeping watch over their flock by night" (Luke 2:8).

MY OWN PILGRIMAGE

I have often recalled those shepherds while taking my own quiet Advent walks, "wondering as I wandered out under the sky" across Yorkshire moors, Grantchester meadows, Edinburgh city parks, Wisconsin woods, and Midwest prairie paths, a permanent resident transplant in foreign lands. As my travels and the passing of time took me farther and farther away from my native land and beloved hills, I came to realize that something was amiss in my crèche. Even though I was careful to include herbs from Provence, dried and carefully stored from year to year, I sensed there was something out of place.

It was on one of these quiet Advent walks that it finally dawned on me: just as the traditional plays brought the story of Christ into Provence with all its local color, so I too had to bring it into my new place—or rather, I had to incorporate my place into the story of Christ. I therefore decided to bedeck my crèche with plants and shrubs from the surrounding terroir: heather when we lived in Scotland, white pine and prairie grass when we moved to Illinois. The only criterion was that it had to be local. I am here, and "here" is wherever God plants me for a particular season of my life; "here" is where he wants me to live,

WEEK 2 ⁊ *Pray*

"Be still, and know that I am God." Psalm 46:10

- Imagine yourself a shepherd, sitting quietly, not talking to God, but just watching and waiting and listening. Find a place where you will not be disturbed. Turn off your cell phone, quiet the voices in your head. Then, for five or six minutes, tell God that you are listening. Ask him to show you how to welcome him into your place this Advent. Then wait. This is his time to talk. This too is prayer.
- Try to do this every day this week. That's how habits are formed. Can you do it for ten minutes? Fifteen? The point is to be intentional about making time for quiet listening. Those who listen also watch and wait.
- God will speak, in his own way, and his own time, if you are attentive—not just now, but throughout the day. Have you heard him?

grow, and welcome the child Christ. The manger scene must therefore reflect my current place, as the Provençal crèche does in and for the land of my ancestors. As one book about the santons puts it: "If we can localize the nativity, we make it contemporary such that it is no longer an exotic mystery but a familiar event."[9] *Exactement.* I have accordingly made a mental shift. I now see my *new* place (wherever God happens to put me) less as a foreign land than a *holy land*, a place set apart in which I can continue to adore the Word become flesh. It was this insight—that Christ

Indiangrass from the prairies

could be reborn, as it were, here, there, and everywhere—that made me realize that I too could belong here, there, and everywhere. I am "here," far from Provence, a real-life little saint in a new crèche, eager to know, and love, my new environs: the vast prairie with its varied grasses waving over a snow-covered expanse; the white oaks of Illinois lifting their heavy limbs toward the sky; the native juniper, greening and scenting the manger throughout the season. Like the santons who populate my crèche, I found the grace to welcome Christ where I am.

THE ART OF EATING IN SEASON

The kitchen table is another place to practice watching and waiting, this time for the advent of each season's crops. Ideally, the everyday saints' food, like the rest of their lives, is organically connected to the local terroir. After all, God created us as embodied beings, and we can only be in one place at a time. Like prayer, watching and waiting for particular foods to ripen can be a way of sharpening awareness of our perpetual dependence on God, in our place, in and out of season. Advent watching and waiting reminds us, and our children, to be grateful for the created world around us, and to thank the Giver of all good gifts.

Advent is also a season that invites everyday saints to use restraint. For, at least in the northern hemisphere, Advent is a time when the garden begins its annual hibernation. Acknowledging the decreasing harvest is part and parcel of the art of living in season. Eating during Advent means reserving part of the harvest for the next feast: Christmas. Living in correspondence to the season of Advent may require fasting rather than feasting, regardless of the impression that supermarkets give, where it is always Christmas, never winter.

For wise everyday saints, local vegetables are de rigueur: cabbages, spinach, legumes (chickpeas in Provence, red beans in Illinois)—the staples of simple soups and stews. Nothing fancy, but nonetheless tastefully prepared. This too is a way of respecting the seasons, the land, and the Lord who created and ordered them.

Swiss chard and thyme

Those who live in sync with the rhythms of the land know that Advent marks the last of Swiss chard, a Mediterranean staple.[10] It is the last gasp of autumn, the last bright green leafy vegetable before the earth enters into the grave of winter. Chard is nothing for a gourmand to write home about, yet it is dressed by nature in festive colors, with its swirly red garland crisscrossing the bright green leaf. In Provence, cooks traditionally pair it with thyme gathered from the hills, embellished in a béchamel sauce, grilled with croûtons, drizzled with olive oil—perhaps garnished with crumbled bacon when it is dressed in its Sunday best.

Advent is not only about putting off good things until tomorrow, but it is a season of preparation. In the land of my ancestors, some families take little breaks, sampling a few Christmas specialties like nougat and mulled wine when they gather with neighbors to admire each other's crèche on Sundays, which according to the church calendar are minor feast days (they're sometimes called "little Easters"). During the rest of the week, however, they learn the virtue of watchful waiting, preserving rather than consuming the contents of the larder.

WEEK 3 ✎ *Play Your Part*

"We remember the fish we ate in Egypt that cost nothing, the cucumbers, the melons, the leeks, the onions, and the garlic." NUMBERS 11:5

The Bible mentions food by specific names throughout the Old and New Testaments—sorrel, cinnamon, honey, gum, wheat, milk, pistachio nuts, almonds, and grapes, to name but a few.

- Can you name five foods that are harvested or stored by local farmers in your local place during this particular season? Hint: read the "country of origin" at the supermarket or, even better, track down a farmers' market in your area.
- Procure some seasonal ingredients, then produce a seasonal dish. Then talk about it at the table as a way of introducing the discipline of eating in season. We won't find manna on our doorsteps, as the Israelites did, but we can learn to trust God to provide while waiting for the next harvest.
- In the passage cited above, Israel complained to God because of the food they did not have anymore. Can you focus, and help others at your table (family and small groups) to focus, on what God has provided, rather than complain about what is no longer available, even as you practice seasonal restraint?

END OF SEASON

Our Advent walk is approaching the threshold of Christmas. In the words of the angel who opens one of the pastorales: "The *Mistral* [a strong cold wind from the north] who is a friend of the Good Lord, decided to prepare the stage by cleansing the sky that night, leaving not a single cloud, so that every star might shine brightly on God's little one."[11] It is a beautiful thought, nature's way of preparing for a special season. The whole of creation, which has been watching and waiting, now welcomes the child Christ, just as the shepherd-poet David had said: "The heavens declare the glory of God, / and the sky above proclaims his handiwork" (Psalm 19:1). *Now*, the Christmas stage is set. The house is ready. The Guest may enter!

WHAT'S AN EVERYDAY SAINT TO DO?

The shepherds in the old carols faced dark mountain paths, biting cold, little food, and the prospect of brigands taking what little they had, yet they continued to search for the child Christ until they found him in a barnyard, lying between a cow and donkey. A contemporary everyday

WEEK 4 ⮜ *Ponder*

"Most of us grew up saying prayers, reading prayers, or listening to others praying. Few of us were challenged to be prayer. There is a difference between a person who says prayers and a prayerful person. It is the difference between something we do and someone we are."[12]

- ❧ Reflect on the last few weeks: Have you come to see the importance of watching and waiting? Have you learned how? Have you found a dwelling place in your life for the Lord? Think about what it looks like to watch, wait, and welcome Christ in your place.
- ❧ As you begin to listen to God speak throughout the day, note that "devotion" is not just an event at a set time, but an attitude of attentiveness and expectation to maintain throughout the day.

saint might well ask, "What dark paths will I have to take, and what hidden dangers and unknown assailants will I meet on my way to Christ?"

Everyday saints, shepherds or not, should know the seasons of the place where they are planted. They should go on quiet Advent walks, whether in hills, through prairies, or along riverbanks—anywhere away from the distractions of a stressful world, crowded shops, and hectic schedules that tempt them to rush to Christmas before its due season. The art of living in Advent involves remembering: 'tis *not yet* the season (of Christmas). Everyday saints who pay attention to the seasons will use Advent to prepare inwardly the way of the Lord, pondering in their hearts, like Mary, the mystery of the one who came down from heaven to be here—not Bethlehem (or Provence), but *here*: let it be to me, *here*, according to your word (Luke 1:38).

What does this season of Advent really mean for *me*? Much as I love my crèche, Advent is about more than searching the hills for herbs to adorn a model manger. The real art of living in the season of Advent is about learning how to welcome Jesus in my place this Christmas, and in the coming year—and not just in the "official" manger scene, but in all

🕊 Imagine Advent as the first chapter of a great story in which you are invited to come along. Imagine you are one of those little saints on a pilgrimage to find Christ. Can you see the story of your life as one of holy pilgrimage? You don't have to leave your place. You just have to be Adventish: prayerfully expecting and preparing to meet Christ where you are.

🕊 Can you imagine prayer becoming so naturally enmeshed in your daily life that your whole life might end up being prayer? Might praying continually (1 Thessalonians 5:17) be the art of watchful waiting, the art of living in Advent?

the scenes of my everyday life: home, neighborhood, workplace, church, and heart. Everyday saints need time to prepare a fitting welcome for their Lord. This is the reason for the Advent season: to watch and wait, in solitude and attentiveness, for God's active presence, so that as we make our own pilgrimage we can say with David:

> I will not give sleep to my eyes
>   or slumber to my eyelids,
> until I find a place for the LORD,
>   a dwelling place for the Mighty One of Jacob.
>   (Psalm 132:4-5)

Chapter 2

CHRISTMAS

THE ART OF GIVING

What can I give Him, poor as I am?
If I were a shepherd, I would bring a lamb;
If I were a Wise Man, I would do my part;
Yet what I can give Him: give my heart.

CHRISTINA ROSSETTI, "IN THE BLEAK MIDWINTER"

Then the people rejoiced because they had given willingly, for
with a whole heart they had offered freely to the LORD.

1 CHRONICLES 29:9

WHERE CHURCH CALENDAR AND NATURE MEET

Our Advent search in solitude was only a preparation for the special season that heralds a new beginning. *Noël* (Lat. *natalis* "related to birth" and, by extension, "new") heralds the good *news* at the heart of Christmas: a *new* age has been set in motion by a *new* turn of events in God's mysterious plan to rescue humanity. The Son of God enters into human history in the unexpected and thoroughly counterintuitive form of a *newborn*. In the words of C. S. Lewis: "The rightful king has landed, you might say landed in disguise, and is calling us all

Bright Christmas berries

to take part in a great campaign of sabotage."[1] In a culture that cultivates consuming, Christmas is a season for learning a subversive practice: giving without return. The traditional twelve days of Christmas celebration already hint at a new order of things. While in nature the land stops giving, the people give more generously than ever—alms to those who lack food, warm clothes for the homeless, toys for the young.

Outdoors, the earth prepares to sleep; field work stops. Nature bustles outdoor laborers indoors. Plants produce red berries, "as red as any blood." The berries remind us of the baby's fate: to die "for us and our salvation," and to suffer "to do poor sinners good," in the words of one carol.[2] Red berries reminds us that Christmas is after all only one season in the story of redemption, the *new*ness of new life. Europeans think of holly, but having learned the lesson of the Advent walk, I hunt down holly's local counterparts: American yew, viburnum, wintergreen and winterberry bushes. Fittingly, the symbol is there for all who have eyes to see, even those who are far from Bethlehem or Provence. Meanwhile, evergreens stay green in the bitter cold, a reminder that nature is not dead, only dormant. Nature will awaken; spring *will* spring again.

CHRISTMAS COMES TO PROVENCE

As we have seen, in the land of the santons the carols speak of Bethlehem as if it were in Provence. The way the Provençaux tell the Christmas story, when the angels proclaimed to the shepherds in the hills, all the inhabitants of the neighboring countryside heard something too—rumors of a wondrous divine birth and, for some reason they cannot fathom, they felt a sudden urge to undertake what the carols call a "pilgrimage." This was despite the bitter cold and dangers of paths riddled with brigands and wild animals. One pastorale hints that these inklings or prompts originate with God who is in high heaven, directing the earthly pageant down below.[3]

In the world behind the crèche, those keeping watch over the manger are biding their time, waiting for the right moment, late on Christmas Eve, to place the figure of the baby Jesus between his parents. Other little saints in the surrounding countryside also begin to inch their way toward the manger, helped along by eager little fingers. Eventually, the children reluctantly retire to bed, leaving the little saints to journey on into the night, only to discover, the next morning, a marvel: the figurines have all arrived at the manger after their nightlong journey! This is the signal for which the children have been watching and waiting.

Gift-giving time is upon them, in the crèche, and in the home. *Joyeux Noël!* As the santons lean in with their gifts, so close to Jesus that one can barely see the baby, the families beyond the manger act out a similar scene with their own children.

THE SEASONAL SANTON

Those santons whose gift is music set the tempo as we enter the scene. The Christmas story opens with "a multitude of the heavenly host praising God and saying, 'Glory to God in the highest!'" (Luke 2:13-14). And yet, in traditions the world over, the angels do not simply *say* but *sing* the words, and they are typically portrayed in paintings (and Christmas cards) with musical instruments. It's no surprise, then, that the way the Provençaux tell the story of Jesus' birth incorporates music played on traditional Provençal instruments, carved out of local wood by some little saint, perhaps a luthier, a craftsman with a special vocation; he does not make music himself, just the instruments others use to make music.[4]

Le tambourinaire (the drummer)

The musicians play a crucial part in the traditional Christmas plays of Provence. They follow hard on the heels of the angels and shepherds, leading all the little saints who set off to see the baby in Bethlehem like so many pied pipers. Like the virgins of ancient Israel, they adorn themselves "with tambourines / and shall go forth in the dance of the merry-makers" (Jeremiah 31:4). The *tambourinaire* is a well-known santon figure who plays the drum with one hand and the *galoubet* (a three-holed flute) with the other.

MUSICIANS IN PROVENÇAL CULTURAL TRADITIONS

Probably one reason why Christmas angels are always represented with instruments (trumpets, harps, and more) is that words are not enough to express the joy of this awesome moment. Music steps in when mere words stop short, failing to communicate the glory. Words need music to amplify the message; music needs words to clarify it. In the traditional carols, the music comes with lyrics. The singers express what every little saint in the crèche is thinking. The pastorales are, for lack of a better term, Christmas musicals with a twist: the characters wonder about their gifts, and what their lives are for. If this is the Son of God, then what can I bring him? Desperate for ideas, they ask their neighbors: What are *you* giving him?

The answers are simple, consistent with the common and comical style we encountered in Advent with our shepherds. In the traditional noëls, most villagers decide to bring something from their daily table fare.[5] But then, something like the miracle of the loaves and fishes takes place: their meager donations of bread, honey, eggs, goat cheese, grapes, cake, fresh fish, and stews in cooking pots eventually become a veritable feast laid at the feet of Jesus, mirroring the feast that is being prepared beyond the crèche around family tables. Meanwhile the village women, who are used to dealing with the practicalities of new births, bring up the necessity of fresh "diapers": Is anybody else thinking of straw for the baby? A woman, presumably a midwife, brings a wooden cradle with fresh linens. The noëls allow the characters to give voice to these minor concerns. By song's end, each little saint has come up with an idea of what he or she has to offer the infant King.

As the pilgrim-villagers gradually make their way toward the manger down through the hills of thyme and juniper, across the fields, and over rivers, they eventually meet fellow pilgrims at various crossroads, making the company of little saints larger and larger—and louder and louder as they come singing and dancing. The full-size everyday saints who watch the procession sing the songs as well. Some may identify with their miniature counterparts who ask, "What can I bring him?"

This may simply be another way of asking, "What is my role in the story of Christ?"

Nicholas Saboly, who composed early noëls in the 1600s, used his music to express life's questions in song as a way of helping the carolers think about how to live out their faith in their own places. The question had to do with the meaning of existence, but this was not existentialism. Rather, it was the question Christina Rossetti poses in her Christmas carol: "What can I give Him, poor as I am?"[6] Saboly's gift was to use his music not simply for entertainment but also edification. He wished to rekindle people's devotion to Christ in their everyday by expressing in his lyrics how they might use their gifts for Christ in their home of Avignon. Jesus is the center and the soul of Saboly's carols, but he comes wrapped in Provençal swaddling clothes to remind the people that their gifts are very much enmeshed with everything else they do and love. Provençal author Frédéric Mistral, who rediscovered Saboly and transcribed his songs in the 1800s, wrote about him in glowing terms: "As for men like Saboly, there is no more need to talk about their lives than you would a nightingale, or a cicada: their life is in their songs, for they spend their lives singing."[7]

The *tambourinaire* and companion musicians represent the gift of song. Their songs have become part of the local culture, reminding us that music is not just for special occasions like Christmas but adorns the everyday. For there is something to sing about not just during Christmas season, but all along the everyday saint's pilgrimage: celebrations of life and death, marriage and anniversary, entering and leaving school, and, of course, worship. The everyday saint adapts her music to her mood and situation, for there is a musical language for every emotion and season: from winter mourning, when darkness lurks in the background and the Spirit groans within us, to springtime celebration, when the poured-out Spirit breathes new life. Music accompanies everyday saints throughout their daily walk, when they whistle while they work, or when they sing from the rooftops—or rather, balconies—to shout down a pandemic.

MY OWN PILGRIMAGE

Listening to Saboly's noëls over the years has given me a deeper appreciation of music as a gift that makes the everyday saint's earthly pilgrimage a little easier. As he says: "We sing a little song on the pipe and the drum to keep our spirits up along the road."[8] Saboly, like King David, used his musical gifts as an offering to God. How can I do what he did in *my* place? I don't play a musical instrument, but there may be some other gift I can offer to encourage the world-weary travelers who accompany me.

WEEK 1 ∽ *Ponder*

"What can I give Him, poor as I am?
If I were a shepherd, I would bring a lamb."[9]

❧ If you were to continue Christina Rossetti's poem for yourself, what would you write? "If I were a shepherd, I would bring a lamb; if I were a Wise Man, I would do my part; . . . if I were a handyman, I would give my services, but I am a . . . [my role], and so I give my . . . [the gift, or gifts I bring]." What kind of little saint are you? What is your role in the story of Christ? Are you a musician santon, a cook santon, a teacher santon, or another kind of santon?

❧ If you can't think of an obvious gift, spend time in prayer and discernment, and ask the Lord: What do I have that I can I bring you? Perhaps the answer will be something practical, like making a meal for someone. Or perhaps you have the gift of encouragement. Remember that Jesus receives the gifts we give to others as if we were giving them to him: "And then the King will answer them, 'Truly, I say to you, as you did it to one of the least of these my brothers, you did it to me'" (Matthew 25:40).

❧ Would it change your daily perspective on your work if you realized that it (whether remunerated or not) is part and parcel of the role you have in the Great Story of the Christ?

Some people are fortunate to discern their gifts at a young age. My husband and daughters found their respective passions (for theology, music, and poetry) early on. Others, like me, are amateurs who ply their hand at several things, passing through seasons of vocations. Between seasons, we wonder: Now what? Oh, what can I give him now, in this new situation? I have had many positions over the years; a few even came with a salary. At other times, however, I responded to a perceived need, playing on the floor with toddlers, standing at the sink, welcoming students, caring for elder parents—without pay. Later still, I took up botanical art as a way of getting to know my place from the ground up, the garden where God had transplanted me. This too, is vocation: being an amateur who does something for the love of it, which can also be an expression of our love for God and neighbor.

When our daughters were very young, they saw how the little saints gave back to the God who gave to them. We, their parents and caretakers, were also first givers: of pocket money (allowance) that they saved for months in anticipation of giving something back to the givers. When they finally had chosen their gifts, they partook of Adventish joy by wrapping, unwrapping, and rewrapping them repeatedly in their anticipation of the joy of giving, a joy that seemed to exceed the prospect of imagining what was in their own Christmas stockings. Giving back was their first joyful response to our love for them. The physical present was but a tangible expression of what was in their hearts, a way of showing that, as Reuben Job and Marjorie Thompson put it, "a thankful life is naturally a generous life, desiring ways to give something back to God, however small the gesture may seem."[10]

One lesson I have learned on my pilgrimage, though modest, is nevertheless important: what matters is not only what I do (the gift) but the spirit in which I do it (the giving). The point, I think, is not technical precision, remuneration, or professionalism. A gift is still a gift even when it is not expertly wrapped. The Christmas season is not a competition—thou shalt not compare gifts! What matters, whatever gift we have to offer, is that we bring it to the Lord and lay it at his feet, a spontaneous response to his gift to us. This is what our seasonal tutor, the *tambouri-naire,* teaches us: the joy is in the giving. As C. S. Lewis rightly reminds us: "All our offerings, whether of music or martyrdom, are like the intrinsically worthless present of a child, which a father values indeed, but values only for the intention."[11] The shepherd, like Abel, gave a lamb; the wise man did his part; and I, what can I give him? Rossetti was right: I can give him my heart—all that I am.

THE ART OF EATING IN SEASON

In Provence, the manger is not the only Christmas scene. We also set the table, the stage for the Christmas feast. Three candlesticks appear on Christmas Eve to remind families that Christmas ultimately tells the story of the triune God. Next, the traditional "thirteen desserts" (*les treize desserts*[12]) take center stage, a *summa* composed entirely of local ingredients. These include the last fruits and nuts of the season: fresh fruit (winter pears, preferably bright red), dried and preserved fruit, a local nougat confection made of honey from the flowers of nearby hills, and a loaf of olive oil bread. The precise selection varies slightly from village to village, depending on the local terroir, but there *must* be thirteen (to represent Jesus and the twelve apostles), and the thirteenth must always be bread—bread that, like Jesus' body, will be not sliced but broken. And, of course, the food is taken with a glass of mulled wine (Jesus' blood shed for you) at the family table. These elements obviously anticipate a chapter yet to come in the gospel story, and another supper. In Provence, the Christmas Eve feast celebrates both Christmas and Good Friday, our Lord's incarnation and Passion—paired gifts of God for the people of God.

One of the thirteen desserts is a dish of dates, specifically, dates imported from Palestine, a tangible reminder that Jesus' story, though marvelous, is no imaginary tale, but rooted in the semi-arid climate of the Holy Land. The dates therefore provide an important footnote to the slightly embellished Provençal telling of the Christmas story: this is *history*! It is also *His story,* and to serve these traditional Christmas

Ripe Christmas pears

foods is to invite everyday saints to enter the story of Jesus, and to keep it going, in rhythm with the seasons—natural and liturgical—to come.

END OF SEASON

In Yvan Audouard's version of the pastorale, the Lord is so pleased with Mary's successful delivery that he spontaneously showers the pilgrims with gifts, which the narrating angel says are not *des grands miracles* (big miracles) but rather "little kindnesses," which I like to think of as *des petits miracles* (little miracles).[13] God-made-man is the "big" miracle, of course, yet these smaller miracles are, in the pastorales, what move the story forward. For these smaller miracles are prompts, deep within the characters' humble hearts, that export them out of their own mundane stories and import them into a greater story, in which they feel

WEEK 2 ✐ *Play Your Part*

"Yet what I can I give Him: give my heart."[14]

One of the lessons everyday saints learn from musicians is that their vocation is a gift to others. Can you think about ways of pursuing your own vocation this week that will be a gift to others?

- Ask yourself not simply "What should I give to God and neighbor?" but perhaps more importantly "How should I give?" We know that "God loves a cheerful giver" (2 Corinthians 9:7). What do you think it means to give Jesus your heart: Is this something we do once, or did once for all at the start of our pilgrimage, or do we need to keep doing it? Can the little Christmas musician help us be cheerful givers in every season?

- What about motives? Little saints, musically or otherwise gifted, may be tempted to forget who should occupy the center stage of their lives. Ask the Lord to give you contentment being not the star of the story, just part of the supporting cast of everyday saints.

- I hope Mistral could say about me something similar to what he said about Saboly: "As for women like this everyday saint, there is no more need to talk about her life than you would a nightingale, or a cicada: her life is in her songs, her words, her cakes, her open home, her classroom ... for she spends her life giving—'for she has given freely and wholeheartedly to the Lord' (1 Chronicles 29:9)."[15] What would you want Mistral, or more importantly, the Lord, to say about you?

compelled to give . . . what, exactly? Well, thanks and praise, by offering to the Lord what they do best—and surely this is no "petit" miracle!

WHAT'S AN EVERYDAY SAINT TO DO?

Everyday saints, musicians or not, know how to adapt their songs and lyrics (their words and deeds) to fit the season. They know that Christmas —the tabernacling of God in flesh—is only the beginning of the baby's story, and of those who have been reborn, as babes in Christ. Discipleship is about how to offer ourselves to Christ, throughout the seasons.

Everyday saints learn from the *tambourinaire* how to use their own gifts, musical or not, to glorify and enjoy him who gifted them in the first place. They learn how to be an instrument of Christmas joy and peace for their companions with whom they have embarked on a *lifelong* pilgrimage. To give of oneself—to die to oneself daily, like the apostle Paul (1 Corinthians 15:31)—is to take part in Lewis's "great campaign of sabotage" of the old order. Whether in churches, schools, the public square, or the privacy of their own homes, everyday saints learn to offer up to Christ everything they are, have, and can do, presenting their bodies "as a living sacrifice, holy and acceptable to God" (Romans 12:1). What can I give him? A heart for all seasons.

Chapter 3

EPIPHANY

THE ART OF WELCOMING THE STRANGER

Being a blessing as a stranger and practicing hospitality
to the stranger are rooted in an overarching narrative
central to the biblical message and the Christian life.

DAVID I. SMITH AND BARBARA CARVILL,
THE GIFT OF THE STRANGER

In your offspring shall all the nations of the world be blessed.

GENESIS 22:18

WHERE CHURCH CALENDAR AND NATURE MEET

With Epiphany, the season that lasts from January 6 through Ash Wednesday, we find ourselves in a story of mysterious strangers entering and exiting our manger scene—stage east.[1] From a place far, far away come wise men who saw a celestial phenomenon they felt compelled to follow: "his star" (Matthew 2:2). Their search led to the little child born to be King, to whom they presented royal gifts as he lay on a throne of hay, the only available accommodations for his parents, far from home.

The Magi gave the baby Jesus gifts fit for a king: gold to signify royalty, incense to signify divinity, and myrrh, a perfumed resin sometimes used

A blooming anthurium

for anointing the dead—an ominous foreboding perhaps of the child's eventual fate. The wise men then return to their own lands and we see them no more. According to tradition, it was the Magi who first presented Christ to the world by spreading abroad the news of their discovery.

Epiphany (Gk. *epiphaneia*, "appearance," "manifestation") is the season marking Christ's being made known to the nations (the Magi were Gentiles, not Jews). Epiphany is therefore crucial to the gospel because it announces the fulfillment of the promise God made to Abraham centuries before: "In you all the families of the earth shall be blessed" (Genesis 12:3). The coming of the Magi marks the beginning of a new age, a new King, and a new kingdom without borders.

Meanwhile, in nature, winter has dug in its heels for the long haul. All is calm, hidden under a thick blanket of snow as pristine as the new baby still in the manger. In our crèche, the stage is set for the appearance of other plants, like the Magi, from faraway places: poinsettias and anthurium from Central America, amaryllis from South Africa. Outside, nature appears to be hibernating, but inside we welcome these botanic visitors from afar.

EPIPHANY COMES TO PROVENCE

Today, those strangers "from the east" appear in Christmas scenes the world over, including Provence. By the third century, they had morphed from Magi to monarchs, and tradition described them as three in number. Five centuries later, they received names. Eventually, they received a special spot on the calendar: Kings' Day (*le jour des rois*). According to one tradition, young Gaspard (Caspar) was an olive-skinned Semite, Melchior had white hair with white skin, and Balthazar was dark-skinned and middle-aged. Together, the three symbolized all the ethnicities of the known world for whom Jesus had come. The Magi are a crucial part of the story, for they represent the recipients of the "great joy that will be for all the people" (Luke 2:10).

In the land of my ancestors, Epiphany marks the day to take down the Christmas décor. That is, everything but the crèche in its promising greenery—*that* remains central for a few more weeks. Over the past few days, since Christmas, the little saints have gradually spread out and moved away from the crib. The villagers have an everyday life: there are goats to milk, bread to bake, babies to feed. On January 6, however, the scene once again comes to life. Little hands make sure the clay figures of the three kings make their entrance, accompanied by servants, musicians, and camels with rugs from the East laden with mysterious boxes piled high. You can almost smell the new scents wafting around them. None of the crèche's inhabitants have ever seen such a sight as this! These strangers from afar remind one and all that indeed something wonderful has happened here, in their very own village, of all places, something of global significance! Perhaps they were already beginning to forget the little miracles, their hopes buried under a foot of newly fallen snow. Yet now, three pilgrims with eyes that read the sky—strangers, no less!—have confirmed the news anew: *surely this was the Son of God!*

As the wise men reach the manger, the entire population of santons crowd the crèche once more, as do the everyday saints who have set up the miniature scene. The little saints will mill around the manger for a few more days, lost in wonder, love, and praise. And then, suddenly, it is over: the Christmas season now only a memory, truly in the past. The onlookers will disperse. And yet the crèche remains a while longer in our houses. Epiphany is a season, after all.

Attentive everyday saints know that the story continues. Christmas is not a one-off miracle, only the first act of an ongoing story, a story that continues outside the crèche and beyond national borders. Jesus will not be boxed away.

THE SEASONAL SANTON

In addition to the Magi "from the east," you can find other "strangers" in the Provençal crèche, including a number of Romani, an itinerant people with no homeland of their own. There is a Romani woman—*la bohémienne* (literally: "from Bohemia")—in my manger, tambourine in hand, presumably providing rhythmic accompaniment to the

*La bohémienne
(the Romani woman)*

WEEK 1 ∞ *Pause*

"Now after Jesus was born in Bethlehem of Judea in the days of Herod the king, behold, wise men from the east came to Jerusalem, saying, 'Where is he who has been born king of the Jews? For we saw his star when it rose and have come to worship him.' . . . And going into the house, they saw the child with Mary his mother, and they fell down and worshiped him."
MATTHEW 2:1-2, 11

Christmastide in the twenty-first century is busy: "Only a few more shopping days left!" Who has time to fall down and worship? No falling down on the job!

🍂 Christmas is not just one day. Epiphany, also called "Twelfth Night," is the twelfth day of Christmastide. This reminds us that the birth of Christ is part of a much larger narrative, and that the Magi were not actually at the manger on Christmas Day, for they too were on a pilgrimage before finding the Christ.

songs of the local musicians. Several Provençal tunes have a notable zest about them (a Bohemian flair?), possibly even rhythms from northern Africa or Arabia—places through which the Magi (who knows?) may have traveled as they spread their strange news. This *bohémienne* adds something seemingly foreign to the manger scene, confirming Epiphany's message that Jesus' appearance is for the sake of those from far away, not just this one village in Provence. This little saint intriguingly suggests that there is a place for ethnic and cultural differences with the holy family. Differences need not divide; instead, they enrich the church—one bread with many grains, one coat of many colors.

STRANGERS IN PROVENÇAL CULTURAL TRADITION

The appearance of strangers from other lands is a scene that has been repeated throughout world history, often on a grand scale. War, famine, unemployment, or a simple sense of adventure cause people

> The Magi remind us that Christmas is not for Westerners only. The Bible explicitly says they were "from the east." Christ is made manifest to all peoples, his light shining even to outsiders, even beyond our personal borders. Think of the scope of God's promise to Abraham that "in your offspring shall all the nations of the earth be blessed" (Genesis 22:18). What does this tell you about the scope of God's love? What can we Christians do to manifest Christ to the rest of the world?

> The star, unseen by the locals, was noticed, followed, and shared by outsiders. Might those seen as "outsiders" help me to see the light of Christ in new ways? Do I know any strangers that have helped me see Christ more clearly? Do I know any strangers? Consider reaching out to someone from "away" this season.

to leave their homelands, and sometimes their families, both individually and en masse.

In Provence, when the tradition of the santons was just getting underway, the typical strangers in the land were the Romani. (Today, most immigrants making their new home in Provence come from North Africa.) These outsiders, with their dark skin and foreign ways, were typically kept at bay, confined to their caravans off from the villages, and "encouraged" to move on.[2] They were nomads in Provence, yet in the background, all the same.

Their presence in the crèche is unexpected. What is a seeming outsider doing next to the holy family? Is she there to remind everyday saints that the wise men were only the first people from foreign lands to be beneficiaries of the gospel? Or is she there to remind us that the baby was himself a stranger, and one who also welcomes strangers?

The Romani figure in the pastorales as well. The villagers are invariably leery of them. Who knows? They might put a spell on you, ambush you, rob you, kidnap your children, or all of the above! So go the local stories. Sadly, these ethnic stereotypes remain common—and not only in Provence, and not only in modern times. Even after Joseph had saved Egypt from famine, the Egyptians would not eat with him or his brothers: "The Egyptians could not eat with the Hebrews, for that is an abomination to the Egyptians" (Genesis 43:32).

In Yvan Audouard's version of the Christmas play, at the very moment of Jesus' birth, a Romani steals a turkey from a rich landowner, only to be caught red-handed by a *gendarme* (local policeman). The culprit justifies the act by arguing that everyone should have turkey for their Christmas dinner—to which the *gendarme* responds (perhaps with a wink) that he has never heard of "Christmas" (even though he's a character in a Christmas pageant!). All three—Romani, policeman, and landowner—become unwitting actors in the drama of this Christmas night of miracles. And, like the other pilgrims, they sense a change coming over them. For as they arrive at the manger, the hungry Romani feels obliged to return the turkey. The policeman feels oddly compelled to free the thief (itself a *petit miracle* because, according to the story, he had been chasing the thief for twenty years). Finally, the rich landowner, repenting his lack of hospitality and "feeling himself becoming a better man with every passing second," offers the turkey back to the thief! At the end of the play, the three kneel together at Jesus' feet.

There are noëls specific to the Epiphany season that imagine the entrance of the Magi. (The thirteenth-century Provençal noël "March of the Kings" is particularly noteworthy.) Another, "We Three Kings in the Countryside," mentions the Magi by their traditional names: Gaspard, Balthazar, and Melchior the Moor.[3] In the carol, the latter hesitates on the threshold when he hears the child cry at his approach. Joseph says to Melchior: "Don't be shy, come and meet him, you are not unworthy. It is not because of your dark face that he is crying—*it is because of the sad story of the first sin.*" But maybe the babe is crying because the sinful children of Adam have not welcomed this Black king, who has traveled so far to see him? This Epiphany noël has a mournful tune that accompanies the tragic necessity of having to reassure strangers that they are welcome in Jesus' presence, be they Greek, Jew, Romani, barbarian, Scythian, or Moor (see Colossians 3:11). In this season of Epiphany, a king's halting entry becomes a precious reminder of the coming new order of things in Christ. Seen from Epiphany, the angels' Christmas message, "and on earth peace" (Luke 2:14), takes on added weight—and urgency.

The little saints, we now see, are a multiethnic, cross-generational company. Prompted by the Spirit's stirring, they gather round the child Christ, the one King of all peoples of the earth, who welcomes them. I like to think that these strangers are in the crèche to offer their own special gift. Not the gold, incense, and myrrh of the Magi, but simply the gift of the stranger—the gift of *being* a stranger. To meet those who are not like us, not from around here, is to taste the spice of a fresh perspective—just what the man who has everything needs to help him step outside his comfort zone, and perhaps his conventional conception of Christ. Strangers see the world through different lenses. The Magi's

Spices from around the globe

Eastern origin offers us a new orientation. Andrew Walls, a missiologist, says that each time the gospel is received in a new culture or new language, "It is as though Christ himself actually grows."[4] *This* is the true gift of the Magi and the stranger.

The Bible is full of stories of people going to strange lands, and thus becoming strangers: from Abram who leaves Ur to the Israelites who spend years wandering through the desert before settling in the Promised Land, and then being forced to leave again to go into exile. Being a stranger is part of Israel's very identity: "A wandering Aramean was my father" (Deuteronomy 26:5). This is why the Lord keeps reminding them to welcome the stranger in their land: "Love the sojourner, therefore, for you were sojourners in the land of Egypt" (Deuteronomy 10:19). We can go further—the people of Israel were also to be a blessing *as strangers* in other lands: "But seek the welfare of the city where I have sent you into exile, and pray to the Lord on its behalf, for in its welfare you will find your welfare" (Jeremiah 29:7). The church, God's new people, are exiles too. Peter addresses his epistle "To God's elect, exiles scattered throughout the provinces" (1 Peter 1:1 NIV). The company of everyday saints who now follow Christ are "from away," even as they are called to welcome the strangers in their midst.

The season of Epiphany reminds us to spread *our* own "exotic" nature as Christians, not a foreign spice but salt, not of the earth but the kingdom of God. It takes an *epiphany* to realize the extent of God's hospitality, the largesse of this God whose sky is large enough for all the stars, whose house is large enough for many rooms (John 14:2).

MY OWN PILGRIMAGE

My own pilgrimage started in earnest when I was still following random stars in my native hills, sometimes in conversation with my brother, who was undertaking a similar search for—something. We took long walks together and talked about the possibility of God's existence, not realizing that we had inadvertently begun our own Advent walk toward an epiphany. He urged me to visit some people he had recently met who apparently had some answers. They were strangers sent to my land from other places in Europe and North America, expressly to bring to it the blessing of the Christmas story.[5] I knocked at their door and, as improbable as it seems—Who opens doors to strangers late at night?—the strangers in my own land opened it and welcomed *me* in. They came from various lands and had different accents (from my perspective, they were from "away"), but also had one important thing in common: their Lord Jesus Christ. They listened patiently to my questions, then spread a table with food that was new to me: peanut butter, Bircher muesli, and Kenyan coffee. Their food refreshed my body, but their answers fed my soul, where the hunger was greater. Their table held both forms of nourishment, for next to the peanut butter lay an open book, which offered

WEEK 2 ❧ *Ponder*

"Love the sojourner, therefore, for you were sojourners in the land of Egypt." DEUTERONOMY 10:19

❧ Jesus says that doing something for those with the lowest status is like doing something for him (Matthew 25:40). Does this apply to welcoming strangers, foreigners who lack status, connections, maybe citizenship? Think about your neighborhood. Do you know any strangers living in your locale who may need welcome? Are there any strangers in your church that you have not yet met? Can you pass them the peace of Christ rather than simply passing them by as if you don't see them?

❧ Am I the rich landlord who won't share my Christmas turkey? How can I be a gift to the stranger, or appreciate the gift the stranger is to me?

❧ Have you ever thought about hospitality as one way of making Christ "appear" in the world, an epiphany in its own right? Think about how you could make Christ appear to a stranger, or to anyone else, this week, by welcoming them in Christ's name.

an even more substantial meal: the Bread of Life himself. Was it by virtue of their strangeness that I had an epiphany, and met the Stranger who came into a world that did not recognize its Maker? What I know is that I ate of the Bread, and have not hungered in the same way since.

These strangers to the land of my birth were in that season my hosts as I entered what Karl Barth called "the strange new land of the Bible."[6] Were they echoes, centuries later, of that earlier blessing of the Magi? As one who married into a different culture and has subsequently journeyed and lived in other lands, the blessings of strangers have been a recurring theme, leading me to wonder: What gifts do I have for strangers who visit me?

The season of Epiphany is an apt time to recall those strangers, wise men and women who opened their door to me, and became "little epiphanies" themselves, making Christ known to one more inhabitant of the world by showing me his hospitality. I sit at my desk and write New Year's greetings to distant friends and relations in the quiet of this season, as is the custom in Provence. I send them my good wishes, and my prayers, pondering the blessing even a simple note might be. And I wonder: Are there strangers in my neighborhood, those who may be standing and knocking at a door they don't know exists? How can I pay hospitality forward and welcome others into the same Great Story into which I was welcomed by open-armed strangers on my miraculous night?

THE ART OF EATING IN SEASON

Epiphany is the season, early in the new year, when food, especially fruit, becomes scarcer in the land of the santons. Everyday saints try to eat locally, yet when next to nothing grows, they make allowances, and occasionally turn to foods, menus, and spices from far away. Stores stock vast varieties of citrus from sunnier places—tangerines, mandarins, and more—all loaded with timely vitamins. From the tropics come the subtle hint of vanilla, the warmth of cinnamon, the striking appearance and scent of star anise—all reasons to marvel at God's worldwide provision. This is a season to thank the Lord for his vast garden, and for

Wintertime mandarin oranges

strangers in foreign climes who work the distant fields. Perhaps we can
identify with Joseph, who had his own epiphany when he understood
how his captivity in Egypt was the means that God used to bring all
Israel to a place where there was wheat instead of famine.

The culinary highlight of the season for the Provençaux is *le Gâteau*
(or *Galette*) *des Rois*, the Cake of Kings. *Vive les rois*! This frangipane-
filled pastry carries the story of the Magi further into our daily lives and
tables, at the very time when Christmas is fading into memory. In
Provence, this traditional cake is a crown-shaped brioche, glazed and
covered with jewel-like candied fruits. It is displayed in bakeries and
shared in families, neighborhoods, schools, workplaces, and churches
for a few weeks. What makes it special is the little porcelain figure of the
baby Jesus (*la fève*) hidden inside (usually hidden in a slice intended for
the youngest child).[7] The cake is sliced on the twelfth day of Christmas
(January 6), distributed, and eaten communally, for it is cut in as many
pieces as there are guests.

Notably, an extra piece is set aside, *la part à Dieu* (God's serving), a
portion traditionally reserved for a needy outsider. What could be an

excuse to overeat instead becomes a profound object lesson. The *fève* of the child Christ is hidden, yet appears when the company sits and eats together—a powerful symbol for the deep mystery that makes Christian hospitality unique. "Do no neglect to show hospitality to strangers, for thereby some have entertained angels unawares" (Hebrews 13:2; cf. Genesis 18). Beggars and strangers and Jesus himself merge into a single figure—a true epiphany![8]

WHAT'S AN EVERYDAY SAINT TO DO?

Everyday saints, hosts and guests alike, must remember that the Lord has a role in his Great Story not for them only, but also for the stranger. Everyday saints do well to ask: Who is the stranger in my land? How can I exhibit the Christ who revealed himself at Epiphany to others, in every season?

WEEK 3 ∞ *Pray*

"When he was at table with them, he took the bread and blessed and broke it and gave it to them. And their eyes were opened, and they recognized him." LUKE 24:30-31

"Father, help me to see you in my guests. Give me the grace to treat them as I would treat you. Stir my imagination to see that a gesture of hospitality is also a gift I offer to you.

"Assist me to keep welcoming you, not just at Advent, and not just in the abstract, but every day, in concrete ways, especially my words and gestures to neighbors, whatever they look like and wherever they come from!

"Thank you for the foods from afar that grace my table, and for the strangers who work in distant fields to set it. Show me how to care even for faraway strangers in my daily choices of foods."

Tom Tarrants, a "recovered Klansman," urges us: "Pray for God to give you at least one friend of another race and help you build an open, honest relationship with no agenda other than love and the friendship it produces."[9]

Everyday saints can welcome outsiders with foods as simple as a bowl of soup and a cuppa (tea), or as elaborate as a three-course dinner; with gestures as simple as a kind touch and an attentive ear, or with fêtes and feather beds; with a meal delivered to the door or an invitation to Christmas dinner. As those who know themselves to be strangers en route to their heavenly home, everyday saints ought to sense a kinship with strangers in general, particularly the migrants and refugees in our midst. The art of living in the season of Epiphany—or rather, of being "little epiphanies"—has everything to do with our readiness to offer outsiders the hospitality of our mangers.

Let hospitality to the stranger be our gift to the child Christ in the season of Epiphany—and later. It is only fitting. For open hearts and open homes give tangible human shape to the immense hospitality of

WEEK 4 ∽ *Play Your Part*

"Being a blessing as a stranger and practicing hospitality to the stranger are rooted in an overarching narrative central to the biblical message and the Christian life."[10]

The Old French term *oste* or *hoste* meant both "host" and "guest." The double-meaning reflects the remarkable exchange that happens in Christian hospitality. Jesus, our open-handed host, waits for us to knock at his door, yet is also our guest, who waits to be welcomed into our home and heart. Host and guest each have a responsibility to be a blessing to the other, no matter who the "other" is: the gift of the everyday saint in the season of Epiphany is to be a little epiphany, a local manifestation of the Christ who is both host and guest.

One suggestion for an Epiphany project is a King's Day celebration. This used to be a special day in many countries. Can you think of ways to borrow or adapt the tradition of King's Cake for your family, neighborhood, or church?[11] Invite a few people, including a stranger or two. Make the invisible God, the King of the ages. Let us remember how the three kings first welcomed the babe, and were welcomed by him, at the manger. Come to the manger, and invite others in to the place where God has entered into our place in order to invite us into his. Spread to the world the good news that in Christ, "all the families of the earth shall be blessed" (Genesis 12:3).

it an opportunity to start a conversation, perchance to occasion an epiphany. Start with these questions:

- Can you recall a time when you felt warmly welcomed by someone? Can you tell the group about it? Have you tried to do this for someone else?
- Have you ever felt unwelcome and unseen in a people's group, a church, a country, a job? How has that affected you? Have you thought of acting more welcoming to others—of "doing unto others as you wish they had done unto you"?
- Can you recall feeling welcome by someone in whose home you never entered? How might welcoming happen outside the home?
- Is there an ethnic minority in your locale to whom you or your church could extend hospitality and a helping hand—and perchance be a little epiphany of Christ to them?

Chapter 4

CANDLEMAS

THE ART OF REMAINING ALIGHT

How long, O LORD? Will you hide yourself forever?

PSALM 89:46

In the bleak midwinter, frosty wind made moan,
Earth stood hard as iron, water like a stone;
Snow had fallen, snow on snow, snow on snow,
In the bleak midwinter, long ago.

CHRISTINA ROSSETTI, "IN THE BLEAK MIDWINTER"

WHERE CHURCH CALENDAR AND NATURE MEET

Candlemas, "the mass of Candles," celebrates the presentation of the baby Jesus in the temple (Luke 2:22-24). It is an ancient observance that still figures in the calendar of my ancestors, where it is known as *la Chandeleur*. It comes forty days after the birth of Christ and conforms to the custom of the Law (see Leviticus 12:3-4). When his parents dutifully brought the child to the temple in Jerusalem, they were met by Simeon who, inspired by the Spirit, cried out, "my eyes have seen your salvation . . . a light for revelation to the Gentiles" (Luke 2:30-32). The traditional church celebration today concludes with a nod to Simeon; when the priest sends forth the parishioners in a candlelit procession, each member carrying his or her candle as a symbol of the light of Christ they are to embody as they leave the service and go out into the world.

Forty days after Christmas brings us to February 2, winter's halfway point, when the earth is at its coldest, and when sunlight is too feeble to warm either body or soul. Although it is the shortest month, February often feels like the longest. My ancestors the Gauls entered February with a festival celebrating the return of light (meanwhile, on February 2, North Americans obsess over Punxsutawney Phil's shadow in the hope of an abbreviated winter and early spring). Clearly, the wanning light weighs heavily on the soul.

Dormant bulbs

Carolers may sing Christina Rossetti's beloved hymn "In the Bleak Midwinter" in December, but it also works as a *middle of winter* lament—both words and tune resonate with bleakness, endless snow, and "earth stood hard as iron." The haunting melody roots the words in an empty landscape, in which even the evergreens that connoted life and joy only weeks before now look like lonely, rugged arboreal individuals. The post-Christmas question, "Now what?" reverberates in the chilled air.

How can the bulbs I put in the ground in good faith last autumn possibly be growing in soil as hard as iron, with no sun to raise them? Yet Jesus' words give hope: "unless a [bulb of hyacinth] falls into the earth . . . " (John 12:24).

A quick calendar note: technically, we are still in the season of Epiphany, during which the light of Christ is revealed to all, even in winter. The Scripture readings during Epiphany are placed between two important bookends: Jesus' baptism and his transfiguration. God declares at both events: "This is my beloved Son, with whom I am well pleased" (Matthew 3:17; 17:5). Epiphany can last as much as nine weeks, depending on the date of Easter in any given year; this means that Candlemas as I am describing it can last anywhere between one to five weeks. Candlemas continues the theme of Christ's publication to the world, focusing on light.

CANDLEMAS COMES TO PROVENCE

In the land of my ancestors, the crèche traditionally stays in its prominent place until Candlemas, at which time the santons leave the village and the whole scene gets boxed up. This quiet ceremony allows crèche keepers a moment to mentally relive the holiday. They linger over memories and wrap the figures gingerly before closing the door on another Christmas past. Jesus now goes *underground*, as it were—into basement or cellar storage. That his figurine remained in our midst, even after the visit of the kings, signaled the mystery of his presence, even amid our workaday mundane occupations—and darkest winters. Throughout Epiphany, everyday saints pass by the child Christ on their daily way to and from work, *he* the extraordinary in their ordinary.

Jesus was born by starlight: "The true light, which gives light to everyone, was coming into the world" (John 1:9). Later, long after his presentation in the temple, the adult Jesus declared: "I am the light of the world" (John 8:12). Jesus' candlepower lights up the winter like shining glitter after the fireworks of Christmas. Now that our visual reminder of Christmas no longer adorns the living room, however, the biting cold and bare landscape take over, even indoors. We are in the thick of the bleak midwinter, and everyday saints have to look harder to see Jesus and let his light warm them. In the village of my youth, the freezing vineyards wait with frosted limbs for the vintners to start their pruning, a lonely chore. The piercing wind whistles incessantly behind their shutters at night and assails them in the fields by day. And yet go out they must, for if they do not, there will be no grapes to bring to

WEEK 1 ✍ *Pause*

"I have come into the world as light, so that whoever believes in me may not remain in darkness." JOHN 12: 44-46

Once the manger is dismantled, we often experience a let down, a sense of disappointment and disorientation: Now what? Turn the page, for the story that began at Christmas continues with a new chapter. The light of Christ is not gone, though we may need to look harder to see it.

- In the traditions of my ancestors, the child Christ remains visually present in the crèche days after Christmas, while the little saints return to their mundane occupations. Why is that important? Do you think it's possible to make a regular workday a holy day? What would that look like in practice? Listen to "In the Bleak Midwinter" as you think about it.[1]

- Try to do that this week: remember him on your way to work and back, marvel again over the miracle of Immanuel—Jesus, light from light who has become the light of the world.

- Read Simeon's story (Luke 2:22-35). Did you know that his prayer has been set to music so many times it has its own name (*Nunc dimittis*—from the first words, "Now dismiss"), also known as the Song of Simeon? Jesus' presentation in the temple was Simeon's Advent moment, and he knew it. Simeon's song has spread the light of Christ over the centuries. What can we do to keep the candle burning in our place and time?

Jesus next Christmas. In the bleak midwinter, the vintner tends his vines, the shepherd keeps his lambs, the wise men do their part. As for the rest of us, what shall we do now? What is our part in the bitter season outside and beyond the manger? How can we stay alight?

A SEASONAL SANTON

Perhaps the humblest figure of all the santons at the manger is "the woman with kindling." She brings to mind the episode of the poor widow whose penny was a mere trifle compared to wealthier donors

La femme au fagot
(the woman with kindling)

(Mark 12:42). As the penny was all the widow had to live by, so the woman with sticks put in all she had to warm herself. I imagine her coming from the village of my ancestors where she had been pruning the vines—a thankless annual task that must be done in the winter, by hand—in a valley where the vineyard is swept by the unrelenting *mistral* (a wind from the north that one of our sayings describes as "strong enough to tear the tail off a donkey"). In all likelihood, the vine she prunes is not hers, let alone the field. No, she scours the local vineyards to gather up the *sarments* (twigs) left by the vintners for gleaners like her—as I sometimes did with my grandmother in her village.

This background helps us appreciate the real cost of this gift. I imagine this little saint leaning into the blustery winds of February, bending down on her old legs, and carrying the kindling she has gathered back to her home—and then, miraculously, presenting it to Jesus and his family. She may find herself in a bare landscape, yet her impressive inner landscape is what matters most. She may only be carrying kindling, but she is on fire!

MIDWINTER IN PROVENÇAL CULTURAL TRADITION

Candlemas is when the wind meets the wick of everyday saints' candle-power. The gifts they carry are getting heavier; they risk losing the motivation to keep going in their midwinter desolation. Even in Provence—known as *le Midi* (noon) because of the abundant sun—there are overcast times that dampen and darken our spirits. There are

WEEK 2 ✆ *Ponder*

"How long, O LORD? Will you hide yourself forever?" PSALM 13:1

- Do you sometimes feel as though winter will never end? I do. Do you sometimes feel overwhelmed with the lack of light outside, and in your life? And did you know that light deprivation can lead to vitamin D deficiency? Perhaps this is why so many people are tempted to fly south for the winter. If you answered yes, your challenge is to see the light of Christ in unexpected places—and perhaps in unexpected people, like the woman with kindling.
- Do you sometimes feel that your job, gifts, and perhaps entire life have no importance? Think again about the woman with kindling and be encouraged: in the big picture, there are no mundane or minute contributions. Remember that "the LORD looks on the heart" (1 Samuel 16:7). What if something as simple as a little bunch of kindling was enough to keep a neighbor warm? Can you think of what "kindling" you may be carrying?
- It is possible that getting up, dressing, taking care of yourself—and being watchful for the neighbor who needs help—might be all the gift that Jesus requires of you today. "For my yoke is easy, and my burden is light" (Matthew 11:30).

also seasons of personal midwinter, of loss and grief, that burden our hearts. At such times even everyday saints are tempted to ask: Why keep going?

There is an age-old name for this age-old temptation: *acedia*. The word has fallen out of fashion but, sadly, the reality to which it refers has not. *Acedia*—from the Latin for "lack of care"—means "listlessness" or "apathy." It can come knocking at the door at any season or time of day or life—although the dead of winter is particularly opportune. If we open the door to it, it slinks in and whispers: "I don't feel like doing anything, I don't see the point," then louder, "I don't care." If untreated, a fog of depression may descend. We lose perspective, and faith; we stay in bed, seeing neither the gift nor the Lord of the day. "How long, O LORD? Will you hide yourself forever?" (Psalm 13:1; see also Psalm 89). The bleak midwinter marks a precarious moment in our pilgrimage, when humble saints are tempted to think (may it never be!) that God himself does not care.

I too know acedia, having experienced it—all the more reason, I have discovered, to keep company with these intrepid santons as they come to Jesus in the manger and then follow him beyond the manger in the seasons ahead. The crèche may be absent, but lo, Jesus is with us always, even in the bleak midwinter, for where two or three little saints are gathered, he promises to be with them, until the end of the world—and beyond.

ANOTHER SEASONAL SANTON

The miller is one of these santons who not only brings gifts to the baby Jesus (in his case, flour), but also comes with a story. You wouldn't know his story, however, simply by looking at the figurine. As it is told in the Yvan Audouard pastorale, we meet the miller after his wife has "run off with a Spaniard." Contrary to the woman with kindling, the miller has fallen prey to acedia. He has abandoned his daily rhythms, given up working, and tied down the blades of his windmill with strong ropes. The wheat is piling up on the floor of the mill, to the delight of the local rats, and all he can say is, "Who cares?" Though the miller's story is set at Christmastime, as are all the pastorales, it also serves as a lesson for midwinter—maybe not the natural season of winter but the midwinter of our existential discontent, those seasons of life that tempt us to give up.

Another play from the same region features, coincidentally, a baker who stops baking after his wife runs away as well. He, too, experiences a personal midwinter: the shop is closed, the oven grows cold.[2] In each case, the supply chain breaks down, and the villagers go hungry, for the miller grinds wheat into flour for the baker, who in turn bakes bread for the people. Bread is the Frenchman's basic sustenance, the one element sure to be found on the table three times a day: "Give us this day our daily bread" (Matthew 6:11) may be the one verse we French take seriously! It's also worth noting that the French term for bread (*pain*) shares a root with "companionship."[3] A companion is a person with whom you share bread.

The miller and baker are thus figures in a Christmastide and Epiphany parable. Their stories underline the importance of remaining faithful in the simple vocations, and grateful for the simple gifts they give us. Not surprisingly, there is also a santon who brings a basket of baguettes to Jesus! He would not be there without the miller and the baker—it takes *companionship*.

The miller's story is not finished. Amid his personal bleak midwinter, after having abandoned his routine, when his light is almost extinguished, he suddenly awakens with a strange urge to return to his daily grind: "I don't know why, but I suddenly feel like working!" It is Christmas, after all, a night of miracles, and Jesus, the light of the world, has entered the scene. Everything has changed, for Jesus is "the true light, which gives light to everyone" (John 1:9). Instead of sinking further into his bed, the miller resumes his work, only now with renewed purpose, and meaning—he has not grist but Christ for his mill! Eugene Peterson describes such faith: "Faith is not a leap out of the everyday but a plunge into its depths."[4] The miller begins grinding wheat at great speed, and immediately runs to the crèche in exaltation with three bags of flour, "one under each arm, and the other one on my head. I shall walk until I find him, this divine child, even if my neck collapses into my shoulders."[5]

The miller's cameo appearance in the pastorale explains why he is now a fixture in the traditional crèches. Not so the woman with kindling. Her character is absent from any official pastorale story. Yet, here she stands, a member of the company of those following Jesus after her own humble fashion. This is why I think she belongs to the ongoing story of discipleship. She is a small figure, but she carries a big stick, or rather, a whole pack of sticks, which together witness to the way she *cares* about doing it as unto the Lord, *and for her neighbor as herself* (Mark 12:30-31).

In times of bleak midwinter, the woman with kindling reminds me that she cares enough to attend to her daily responsibilities. It is by faithfully embracing her vocation, humble though it be, that she finds meaning in this season. Being faithful in small things is the way she stays alight and keeps her neighbors so (literally) as well. This, I like to

WEEK 3 ᴥ *Play Your Part*

"Faith is such a necessary virtue: unless you teach your moods 'where they get off,' you can never be either a sound Christian or even a sound atheist, but just a creature dithering to and fro, with its beliefs really dependent on the weather and the state of its digestion."[6]

The Farmer's Almanac does not predict bleak midwinters (that is, existential crises). The storms that test faith can be both sudden and terrible. Is there anything an everyday saint can do to get ready, or to deal with the crisis once it arrives?

First, identify it: Is this just a normal mood change in response to seasonal changes (i.e., the winter blues) or something deeper? If the former, can I treat it with the usual distractions (a shopping trip, a Facebook trip, an overseas trip, or a refrigerator trip) or should I look for something more than a quick fix?

imagine, is why she too, though far from being an angel in the realm of glory, is part of the manger scene.

Even King David, who did so well at the start of his own pilgrimage, rousing Saul from his royal funk with his lyre music, had his own struggles with acedia. One day, while everyone was busy in fields and battlefields, this man after God's own heart *remained at Jerusalem* instead of going to battle, as kings should in the spring (2 Samuel 11:1). David was out of sync with his seasons. He must have been idling, for we're told that "late one afternoon, [he] arose from his couch" (2 Samuel 11:2). One suspects that, like the miller, David had stopped caring about his state responsibilities, his people and, ultimately, his God. This is a far cry from how he cared for his flock as a shepherd. William Shakespeare might have asked: "Why, what's the matter, That you have such a February face, So full of frost, of storm and cloudiness?"[7]

David's idleness had grave consequences. He soon commits the worst mistake of his life, in which he breaks, in record time, three of the

> ∽ When Dorothy Sayers was tempted by sloth, she reportedly chose to believe in more reality, not less. This is the purpose of Christian doctrine: it's not just for the ivory tower, or the pulpit. It's a way of understanding the biblical story on a deeper level, and thus a grace—a way of believing in more reality, not less. What if this quiet time of the year were an opportune moment to learn more about God? What if this knowledge (doctrine) helped enlighten, sustain, and mature your faith?
>
> ∽ Ask your pastor to direct you to some books that might help you learn doctrine with the aim of becoming a better reader of the Bible. Organize a reading group with other pilgrims who crave the light of understanding on their path of faith, and encourage one another when doubts assail you to believe in more reality (more of the word of God), not less.

Ten Commandments: coveting another man's wife, taking her for himself, and killing her husband (2 Samuel 11:17). It was a high price to pay for a spur-of-the-moment decision. One wonders: If David had been alight—awake and alert to God's reality—would he have done what he did when he looked out from the roof of the king's house?

MY OWN PILGRIMAGE

There are different kinds of winters. In my early childhood on the edges of the Mediterranean shore, before my Christian pilgrimage ever started, I memorized the melancholy seasonal words of one of our poets: "In the interminable / ennui of the plain / the snow, uncertain / shimmers

WEEK 4 ⌒ *Pray*

*"Cast me not away from your presence,
and take not your Holy Spirit from me."* PSALM 51:11

David, in God's grace—though at a dear cost—will repent and find his way again. The pilgrimage continues; the Good Shepherd rounds up his straying sheep.

"Lord, thank you for the example of David, a man after your own heart, who nevertheless found himself so low, so far from you. Help me to recognize the temptations to stray, and guide me to stay close to you, even in my lowest times.

"Thank you for forgiving even David. In your mercy, show me where I need to repent. Better yet, help me to see your light and stay on the path, even if my world seems too dark to walk straight at times.

"Help me to stay rooted in your word, the most reliable word there is. Send good teachers my way who will teach me to understand, and give me companions who want to grow me as we pursue our daily pilgrimage."

End your prayer time with this famous Welsh hymn: "Guide me, O thou great Jehovah / Pilgrim through this barren land; / I am weak, but thou art mighty; / Hold me with thy powerful hand."[8]

like sand."[9] The midwinters of my youth all too often involved frigid winds and bitter drizzles that kept us indoors, our noses stuck to the window in hope of a midwinter miracle that would allow us to play outside—especially in the snow we rarely had.

Much later, while living in the land of the Scots, I discovered that there were places where, for three months out of the year, the sun never managed to rouse itself enough to brighten our second-floor flat. I braced myself each new winter against the fearful prospect of another dreary Candlemas, and then celebrated almost like a pagan when our living room burst into color thanks to the sun once again hitting the prism hanging in the window.

Eventually I learned to preempt this midwinter ennui. How? By spending more time in companionship with Christ, and with the Word that was indeed "a light to my path" (Psalm 119:105). Yes, Christ was out of the manger, but not out of my world. Observing Candlemas helped me perceive the light of his presence in winter too. Indeed, observing Candlemas was what first prompted me to think about following the santons out of the manger throughout the year. This was the lesson I learned during those winters when the sun barely rose above the horizon, one that Augustine had learned centuries earlier: "The Christian soul ought to feel itself desolate, and continue in prayer, and learn to fix the eye of faith on the word of the divine sacred Scriptures, as 'on a light shining in a dark place.'"[10]

Since then, I have encountered still other kinds of ennui, like the omnipresent grimy mounds of roadside snow in Midwestern winters, as well as personal seasons of loss, including sudden waves of homesickness and the drawn-out demise of loved ones. If I had avoided these earlier winter wildernesses by flying south—literally or figuratively— with the flocks who did, I might have missed the comfort I receive not from sunlight (or a plug-in Happy Light) but from the Son's life-giving light, even in unscheduled winters or pandemics. Admitting that sunlight pales in comparison with the light of Christ does not come easy for someone from southern France, a place that artists like Paul Cézanne or Vincent van Gogh valued above all for its painter's light! Perhaps

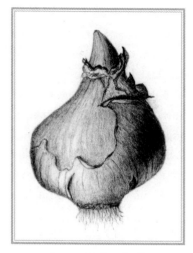

An emerging bulb

those seasonal midwinters are there to train us for coping with the unexpected winters of our lives? To help us learn the discipline of attending to the light of Christ in all seasons? To remind us that, as Augustine says, our hearts will stay dark until they find their light in him?[11]

As for the lifeless-looking bulbs that I planted on my knees last autumn, they did need weeks of cold and darkness, even burial under that thick layer of snow, before showing any sign of life. These days, I instruct my faith by placing a hyacinth bulb over a vase of water at Candlemas. At first, it looks utterly lifeless. In the quiet of midwinter, I watch the miracle of life unfold indoors daily. Outdoors in the cold woods, I look for similar signs, like green shoots pushing upward through the snow. Nature is alight with life. A prayer uttered in the bleak midwinter does not go unheard.

END OF SEASON

The last Sunday of Epiphany season celebrates Jesus' transfiguration, where Jesus not only makes himself known to the world, but does so gloriously: "His face shone like the sun, and his clothes became white as light" (Matthew 17:2). Everyday saints, who walk by faith in winter's darkness, may now see glimmers of transfiguration in winter landscape, a hint of the extraordinary in the ordinary—*des petites épiphanies* all around!

THE ART OF EATING IN SEASON

My ancestors had a distinctive way of setting this season on their tables. They were not immune to bouts of midwinter blues, but they knew that table companionship ("bread together") is a palliative for a number of inner illnesses. Accordingly, Candlemas is *la saison des crêpes*. Crêpes, traditionally eaten on February 2 (Crêpe Day), make for a welcome change at a time when the local soil is still at rest and the seasonal diet of chickpeas, cabbage soups, and root vegetable stews is beginning to taste as monotonous as the gray sky looks. Families gather around the stove to flip crêpes: uncles show off, tossing their supper toward the ceiling while giggly aunts exclaim and parents cheer each time a child's crêpe successfully somersaults.

The spectacular "beauty radish"

According to Provençal lore, the crêpe symbolizes the (round) beam of candlelight, that in turn symbolizes the light of Christ, as well as the light of the sun that we are missing so dearly in midwinter—after all, we Provençaux are light-starved little saints. Crêpe-making is a liturgical seasonal act of its own that reminds everyday saints to give thanks for the light that has come into our world and that shines in the darkness (John 1:5).

But there is more: if one looks hard enough at what God does provide even in the bleak midwinter, an everyday saint might be surprised that even a dreary-looking root vegetable, such as a farmer's winter radish, has an inner beauty waiting to be discovered. The winter radish is also called the "beauty radish," a hidden firework designed by our ever-attentive creator God.

WHAT'S AN EVERYDAY SAINT TO DO?

Everyday saints learn at Candlemas to go toward the light—the light of the world—and to stay alight when dark thoughts beckon us away from him toward lesser lights or perhaps toward the gloom. It is all too easy to feel tempted at times to think that the light has gone out of the world, or that our own light is too dim. Who knows? Perhaps the woman with kindling has come for such a time as this, enabling others to make fire,

WEEK 5 ∞ *Play Your Part*

"Let us hold fast the confession of our hope without wavering, for he who promised is faithful. And let us consider how to stir up one another to love and good works, not neglecting to meet together, as is the habit of some, but encouraging one another, and all the more as you see the Day drawing near." HEBREWS 10:23-25

Some churches have a pancake day to mark Mardi Gras. What if, instead of seeing it as a time to overindulge in food before Lent, you reclaimed Candlemas as a time to see Christ in your bleak midwinter?

- Invite a small group of neighbors to flip crêpes with you. Make crêpe batter beforehand. Let each person flip her own crêpe, spread her own filling. Eat right there in the kitchen. Nothing fancy. Then gather as a group and read aloud the Bible passage that gave us the Candlemas tradition (Luke 2:22-38).
- My tried-and-true crêpes recipe (makes 8):
   1. With a wire whisk, mix 1 cup of flour, 2 eggs, 2 tablespoons of oil, and a pinch of salt. Add 1½ cups of milk and whisk gently.
   2. Heat an 8-inch frying pan over medium-high heat, then pour in batter and rotate the pan to spread batter evenly. When

give light, thereby transfiguring dim places into lit-up places, places of epiphany? Perhaps a crêpe-flipping party around a stove, or a simple collection of electric heaters for neighbors in need (as our church did one Christmas), is the way we can be children of light? "And who knows whether you have not come to the kingdom for such a time as this?" (Esther 4:14).

after one or two minutes the crêpe begins to turn brown, shake the pan or use a spatula to loosen, then flip (it's all in the wrist!) and cook for another minute.

3. Serve with savory fillings, such as the simple French classic of ham and Swiss cheese, or for dessert crêpes, with sweet fillings like my favorite, chestnut cream.

- Ask each person to share a personal bleak midwinter experience that became an epiphany. How did it happen? How does one snap out of the doldrums? Is it through study, companionship, prayer—maybe carrying kindling or flipping crêpes? Faithful practices like these help you dispel your personal shadows and keep others alight.

- Bundle up and take a walk outside to observe what is happening in nature. Were you able to see any signs of life, no matter how small? Can you see them as gifts of God?

- Think of something you could do that might help you remain alight the next time you feel a tinge of acedia. Think of ways that you, a humble santon, can keep alight and be a light shining in someone's bleak midwinter.

Chapter 5

LENT

THE ART OF SELF-PRUNING

Search me, O God, and know my heart!
Try me and know my thoughts!
And see if there be any grievous way in me,
and lead me in the way everlasting!

PSALM 139:23-24

Almighty and most merciful Father; we have erred, and strayed
from thy ways like lost sheep. We have followed too much
the devices and desires of our own hearts. We have offended
against thy holy laws. We have left undone those things which
we ought to have done; and we have done those things which
we ought not to have done; and there is no health in us.

"MORNING PRAYER," BOOK OF COMMON PRAYER

WHERE CHURCH CALENDAR AND NATURE MEET

The forty-day season of Lent corresponds to our Lord's being "led up by the Spirit into the wilderness to be tempted" (Matthew 4:1). There, for forty days and nights he fasted and grew hungry. The season begins with Ash Wednesday (a reminder of our mortality—"ashes to ashes, dust to dust") and ends with Holy Week, where Jesus was tested and taken to the limit again, until such time when, spent, he uttered, "It is finished" (John 19:30). The length of Lent never varies, but the dates do, because we count backward forty days from Easter, itself a movable feast. The forty days exclude Sundays, making Lent last six weeks altogether.

What is Lent? Not all people celebrate or even observe Jesus' forty-day period of testing. For Lent is indeed associated with giving up something, usually some kind of food. What is the point of fasting and abstaining from good things when we know that Christ is risen? Is Lent just an obsolete manmade tradition harking back to olden days, as passé as leading lambs to slaughter as sin offerings? Even those who observe Lent often struggle to decide what to abstain from or give up. Those who practice it routinely ask one another, "So, what are you giving up for Lent?" But the more pressing question is, Why? What does it accomplish? Nature, as well as Scripture, may give us a clue.

Thorny branches

The weather at this time of year is as changeable as the Lenten period. Popular sayings corroborate these uncertainties on both sides of the English Channel. The English say, "When March comes in like a lion, it goes out like a lamb." The French see things differently: "When March enters like a sheep, it goes out like a lion." But either way the temperatures tend to remain cold, keeping much of nature in its dormant state a while longer, making it the best time to prune the shrubbery.

My opening illustration is purposely thorny, and somewhat bare. The hawthorn, one of the few trees with real thorns, often symbolizes the crown of thorns that concludes our Lord's own Lenten season. My dormant branch bears emerging buds, heralding a change of season ahead, something new—*noël*—after dormancy. The thorny black raspberry in my backyard heralds a similar message, anticipating future growth even through the long weeks of Lent.

PRUNING SEASON IN PROVENCE

In the land of the santons, the earth may not be as hard as iron anymore during Lent, but only because it has turned into a muddy mess. The farmers wait, knowing all too well that working the soggy soil would compromise its structure. This is a time to focus on other tasks, such as repairing and cleaning tools in the sheds. When the tools are ready, the farmers turn to pruning, and can often be seen dotting the Lenten landscape. Farmers know that without regular pruning, a vineyard, shrub, or fruit tree will gradually lose its ability to produce fruit—its raison d'être. They know that pruning is a matter of agricultural life or death. They have a saying to remind them that now is the best time for the job: "Early pruning, late pruning, what matters is March pruning."[1]

Le rémouleur
(the knife sharpener)

THE SEASONAL SANTON

The knife sharpener is a well-known santon who represents one of those modest *métiers* that has now largely vanished (not unlike the traditional practice of Lent). In the nineteenth century, the period represented by the santons, a knife sharpener would transport his occupation from village to village while propelling his itinerant "shop": a grindstone on a pushcart. Then when he arrived on the village square, he would call out to remind people that it was time to sharpen their tools, everything from kitchen knives to garden shears. People counted on the *rémouleur* to get their tools ready for the all-important pruning necessary to ensure spring growth.

The farmers understood the importance of well-maintained tools. This is simply pruning 101: lesson number one is to ensure you have the

WEEK 1 ✍ *Pause*

"And you shall remember the whole way that the LORD your God has led you these forty years in the wilderness, that he might humble you, testing you to know what was in your heart, whether you would keep his commandments or not." DEUTERONOMY 8:2

The forty days of Lent correspond not only to Jesus' forty days in the wilderness (Mark 1:13), but also to Israel's forty years of wilderness wandering. The Israelites are our spiritual ancestors; their story is our story, "written down for our instruction" (1 Corinthians 10:11). They had their own thorns to deal with during their pilgrimage.

- Read 1 Corinthians 10:1-13. What were the Israelites' adversities, their temptations? How did they respond to their trials? How did God respond to the Israelites?
- Read Luke 4:1-13. What were Jesus' temptations? How did Jesus respond to his tempter? Do you see any parallels between Israel's temptations and Jesus'?
- Think about your own temptations. Specifically, think about what you might find it hard to give up for a few weeks. Why would it be hard?
- Everyone experiences temptations from time to time, but they don't need to destroy us altogether. As Martin Luther supposedly wrote: "You can't stop birds from flying over your head, but you can stop them from nesting in your hair."

right equipment in good order. Dull knives produce unclean cuts that invite disease.

PRUNING IN PROVENÇAL CULTURAL TRADITION

For everything there is a season—and a time for every tree to be cut back. Flowering shrubs have their own place on the botanical maintenance calendar, and their own pruning needs—every so often, they need to undergo renewal pruning.

Once our tools are ready, we can proceed with this paradoxical activity: cutting off for the sake of future growth. Here is how the master pruners go about it: first, they cut off older stems all the way to ground level, in order to let in essential light. Then, they get rid of the dead and damaged limbs, which are now more visible. Next, they cut every

WEEK 2 ~ *Pray*

"And you shall remember the whole way that the LORD your God has led you these forty years in the wilderness. . . . And he humbled you and let you hunger and fed you with manna, . . . that he might make you know that man does not live by bread alone, but man lives by every word that comes from the mouth of the LORD." DEUTERONOMY 8:2-4, CF. MATTHEW 4:4

Israel's desert hunger was related to God's teaching about a greater hunger, for him and his every word. Jesus' desert hunger, and his answer to the tempter, corroborates that. These lessons are millennia old, but far from obsolete. The desert we always have with us.

> When you feel a deep hunger that nothing seems to satisfy, what is your gut reaction? Do you rely first and foremost on God's word for solace, as Jesus did (and Israel didn't)? Could your temptations simply be a season that allows God's invitation to a higher dialogue by meeting him in his word? O Lord, like a deer pants after water, I thirst for you! (See Psalm 42.) Please, come and quench my thirst, and give me streams in the desert!

branch that crosses and rubs over another: iron may sharpen iron, but wood against wood just creates open wounds. The next step is to eliminate all the watersprouts—growth shoots that spurt from the trunk or older established limbs, subverting the integrity of the plant. Finally, they consider the overall appearance of the shrub, then clip the remaining branches here and there in a way that preserves its intrinsic shape. Ask yourself: What kind of character should this shrub display? Should it droop like a bridal veil, spread out like a French lilac, or grow low like fragrant sumac? Pruning is not insensitive to aesthetics!

An attentive everyday saint may notice a striking resemblance between pruning and the Lenten season in which she finds herself—and not only because the two happen to coincide on the calendar. The task of pruning in the quiet and tranquility of late winter fields and gardens invites us to

- Practice the ancient discipline of immersing yourself into God's word this week with lectio divina, a discipline of slow, deliberate, and repeated reading of Scripture. Choose a Scripture passage (try Deuteronomy 8:1-7).

    1. *Read* the passage aloud slowly, listening for a word or phrase that jumps out at you in a personal way.
    2. Read the same passage again but this time *Reflect* for a minute or two in silence after reading.
    3. Read the same passage again and this time let your heart speak out a spontaneous *Response* to God for a few minutes.
    4. Read the same passage again and *Rest* in it quietly, listening for God's still, small voice (1 Kings 19:12-13) speaking to you.

- Think of the above practice as one way to inspect your life tools. Lent is the season to sharpen them! After all, the word of God is "sharper than any two-edged sword" (Hebrews 4:12). Meditating on Scripture is one of the best ways to prepare for pruning the dead branches in your own life.

wonder at what is involved in renewing a shrub: "Every branch in me that does bear fruit he prunes, that it may bear more fruit" (John 15:2).

The knife grinder in the Maurel pastorale is a key character with an important role and his own name: Pimpara. He is a jovial fellow who makes people laugh, particularly when his good humor is fortified by good drink. Wine, he says, "makes me joyful . . . helps me sleep like a log at night . . . and eases my daily labor." We should not begrudge the knife sharpener his Christmas cheer: there is nothing wrong with a glass of wine to make the heart glad, or caffeine to boost energy for daily labor, or chamomile tea to induce sleep. Each is a gift from God's good garden. However, when these blessings become the predominant desire of our hearts, or "your only comfort in life,"[2] it's time to cut back.

Alas, Pimpara speaks of drink in every other sentence, so much so that on his pilgrimage to the manger, he readily admits, "This God who holds my life in his hands will soon heal me and *remove this desire* to take pleasure in drink."[3] Behind his merry façade lies a sober understanding of what needs to be cut off: not the wine itself, but the *desire* that occupies his thoughts and captures his heart and imagination. His desires need reordering. Knife grinder, grind thyself! Pimpara is a pilgrim in need of self-pruning.

The apostle Paul is a master pruner of disordered human desire. He asks the Ephesians "to put off your old self . . . corrupt through deceitful desires . . . and to put on the new self" (Ephesians 4:22-24). And to the Corinthians, who are likewise governed by their unruly desires, he says, "I die every day!" (1 Corinthians 15:31). Isn't dying daily the paradigmatic form of self-denial, a means of self-pruning whereby we cut ourselves back to our existential roots, so that all that is left is life in Christ?

MY OWN PILGRIMAGE

I first discovered the wonders of renewal pruning—the botanical counterpart of regeneration?—from the master gardeners at the Chicago Botanic Garden. I took a class that included field work, clipping this or that branch to bring some coherence to overgrown shrubbery. It was then, snipping away in the freezing rain, that the question of personal pruning first occurred to me.

The agricultural metaphor yields spiritual fruit. I was struck by the similarities between an unkempt viburnum and the deadwood in my own life. Was I carrying unnecessary baggage that weighed me down, inhibiting my growth? Was my schedule an impenetrable thicket of activities? Did I think I would be a better Christian by being busier? Was there something in my life that needed pruning?

I then began to wonder: What was the state of my tools? The master gardeners at the Chicago Botanic Garden demonstrated how to sharpen our shears—and I became a knife grinder! What if, during Lent, I became a life-grinder? What if I decided to sharpen my spiritual life by carving out time to read the Word, and pray several times a day (as Jesus did,

WEEK 3 ~ *Pray*

"O merciful Father, who dost look down upon the weaknesses of Thy human children more in pity than in anger, and more in love than in pity, let me now in thy holy presence inquire into the secrets of my heart."[4]

Did you know that Jesus advocated self-pruning too? He may have used hyperbole, but his intent is unmistakable: "And if your right hand causes you to sin, cut it off and throw it away" (Matthew 5:30; cf.18:8). It's therefore best to enter this season of self-pruning prayerfully.

> "Lord, is there something that has taken a disproportionate place in my heart, something that occupies my mind and my days that crowds out my desire to let the life of Christ grow in me? Is there something in my life that I rely on for my daily joy more than life in Christ? Show me where to cut back!
>
> "If dying daily is a way of pruning out my disordered desires, activities, and thoughts, a form of taking up my cross daily, then help me to self-prune. Give me faith, knowing that in dying to self, I live to you, for 'you satisfy the desire of every living thing' (Psalm 145:16)."

according to the Jewish practice of praying three times a day).[5] What if I stopped to reconsider my growth trajectory, step back and observe the desires in my heart, conversing all the while with the Master Pruner, bravely cutting off what needed to go in order to make room for what was really meant to grow? What if I paused to remember what kind of tree I am meant to be, what fruit I am meant to produce? Am I an apple tree fruitlessly striving to be an oak? What if? The answer is in Psalm 1. The self-pruning person "is like a tree / planted by streams of water / that yields its fruit in its season, / and its leaf does not wither" (Psalm 1:3).

I also noticed another remarkable feature of my botanic exercise: we had been sent into the gardens two by two. One person held the shears, the other stood back to evaluate where and how much cutting was needed. I saw that a companion pruner is often necessary in our personal pruning exercises as well. "What do you think? Should I prune a little more here?"—to which our companion, with a different perspective, might answer, "no, I like that branch; it fits," or "definitely get rid of that one."

WEEK 4 ⮞ *Ponder*

"Speaking the truth in love, we are to grow up in every way into him who is the head, into Christ, from whom the whole body, joined and held together by every joint with which it is equipped, when each part is working properly, makes the body grow so that it builds itself up in love." EPHESIANS 4:15-16

🍃 Take some time to consider what self-pruning practices you might adopt this Lenten season. If you don't have the time to do that, consider pruning your schedule! Remember that self-pruning is not a one-time event but a perennial activity that we all need.

🍃 How do I react when a companion pilgrim—whether friend, family member, or passing acquaintance—approaches me with

This is how my little knife-grinder santon at his grindstone showed and continues to remind me that, sometimes, the pilgrimage is not about walking, but about standing still while evaluating my life and sharpening my spiritual tools.

THE ART OF EATING IN SEASON

The one thing people know about Lent is that it's the time to give up eating something sweet, rich, or meaty. What, if anything, might fasting have to do with the art of eating in season? Well, as it happens, March is the one month of the year in the northern hemisphere when local food growth is at its skimpiest and root cellar shelves are increasingly bare. Hardy vegetables—like winter spinach, cabbage, kale—become the staples *du jour*. These plants actually thrive in fickle temperatures, even the occasional late frost (thank God!). Still, late winter/early spring is the time when those who try to eat mostly in season begin to feel, if not real hunger, then at least occasional hunger pangs, particular for foods they have not had in a while: fresh strawberries, or tomatoes warmly ripened in the sun . . . *mmmm*!

concerns about one of my branches? Do I listen? Do I get upset? Do I laugh it off? Am I self-aware and humble enough to admit they might be right? Consider seeking out one or two "companion pruners" with whom you could agree to look out in love for each other.

- Am I a good companion knife grinder? Can I help others to self-prune, and do it in a loving and edifying way without wanting to shape others according to my own likes and dislikes? Do I listen to others with an intention to be a blessing to them? Do I pray for wisdom before I speak the truth in love to a companion who needs help with self-pruning?
- Might local churches be healthier if we all became intentional pruners—of our own branches, and of each other's?

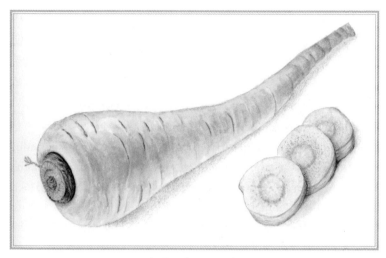

A simple parsnip

These seasonal pangs—the stomach's watchful waiting, as it were—keep people of faith dependent on the Giver of all that grows. The natural rhythms of fast and feast are there to train disciples for everyday spiritual realities. From this perspective, fasting comes to resemble another sort of pruning, of cutting off those "extras" we take for granted, and on which we perhaps rely too heavily. Fasting prunes our appetites—a kitchen lesson in spiritual discipline.

It is normal for everyday saints to sometimes worry about missing their favorite foods: "Second breakfasts? Elevenses? Luncheons? Afternoon teas? Dinners? Suppers? Does he know about those?"[6] Yes, Pippin—thankfully, our Lord knows! This is why he provides weekly as well as seasonal rhythms: "On the seventh day you shall rest" (Exodus 34:21). Early Christians viewed those Sabbaths as "little Easters," times to rest from work, and also from fasting.[7] Throughout the year, saints gather at his table in worship each Sunday. Sunday is also the day when friends and family gather around dinner and tea tables to share the best from their root cellars. Cooks work kitchen miracles of transformation, reviving long-stored parsnips by roasting them with thyme, giving wrinkled apples face lifts as they become glazed apple pies. On the seventh day, everyday saints stop pruning, and instead celebrate previews of the coming chapter ahead: the Great Easter.

END OF SEASON: HOLY WEEK

According to the liturgical calendar, Palm Sunday is the last Sunday in the season of Lent. In the land of my ancestors, churchgoers enter once

WEEK 5 ⁓ *Play Your Part*

"And when you fast, do not look gloomy like the hypocrites, for they disfigure their faces that their fasting may be seen by others. . . . But when you fast, anoint your head and wash your face, that your fasting may not be seen by others but by your Father who is in secret." MATTHEW 6:16-18

"What are you giving up for Lent?" is the wrong question, according to Jesus. How much we fast, and what we're fasting from, are not things we should broadcast to the world. Fasting more than others is not the point of the exercise. It's a spiritual exercise. We don't use physical exercise simply to show off our muscles (well, most of us don't), but in order to get our core into shape so that we can use our bodies as God intended: to glorify him and build up the church. The goal is not to become a spiritual super-athlete, but to be fit in Christ so that we can finish the course.

- So, what are you giving up for Lent? Don't tell me. Just think about what kind of self-pruning could be of benefit. Try to complete this sentence: "When I feel overly tired, blue, fed up, or [fill in the blank], I sometimes turn to cake, a glass of wine, a shopping spree, a post on social media, or [fill in the blank]."
- There is nothing wrong with cake, shopping, films, or sports in and of themselves. Pruning these things from your life makes sense only if such things have become substitutes for the Vine in whom we must abide in order to bear true fruit (John 15:4-5). Lent is a time for pruning what inhibits our growth in Christ. Could it be that abstaining from one item, in secret, is simply a daily private reminder of who comes first?

Budding magnolia

again into Jesus' story, this time toward the end of the story, but still in their own context and place. For they celebrate his triumphal entry into Jerusalem by waving the branches they have brought to church, not from Jerusalem palms, but from the native olive and bay branches pruned from their own fields or a neighbor's garden. In this way, they become life-sized santons who enter into Jesus' story, not on their own terms but on their own terroir.

GOOD FRIDAY

Lest the everyday saint is tempted to think that one can make things right with God simply by his or her self-pruning efforts, the season of Lent concludes with a radically severe "pruning." What did Jesus give up for Lent? Well, to begin with: equality with God! He shows us the full extent of his love by making himself absolutely nothing, even to death on a cross (Philippians 2:5-11). This is not seasonal but extreme pruning. By his pruning, we are renewed. Jesus on the cross has cut off the old man with its disordered desires in order to make room for new growth—and a new heart. Indeed, in the last act of Maurel's pastorale, we find the knife grinder on his knees, speaking to the infant Jesus for himself and his companions: "While we were busy making a racket outside, in your goodness you came and redeemed us."

In my garden, Lenten buds swell with life, ready to burst open on the magnolia tree—the result of proper pruning. My illustration pictures the magnolia when faint leaves appear behind the bud, a distant memory of past summers, and the promise of new green life ahead.

WHAT'S AN EVERYDAY SAINT TO DO?

In this season of pruning and self-pruning, the everyday saint does well to slow down and contemplate, in conversation with God, the trajectory of her growth: "Are there things in my life that come before you, choking your presence and activity? Are there personal gratifications or worldly satisfactions in which I take daily pleasure more than you? What, finally, needs to be pruned? Is it chocolate, or my daily Frappuccino, or might there be something altogether more serious (and inedible) that I need to eliminate?" The everyday saint discovers that self-pruning is a part of being "transformed by the renewal of [her] mind" (Romans 12:2). As she cuts back old growth to make way for the new, an everyday saint reorders her desires and finds her vocation coming back into focus. With the overgrown shrub that has obscured her path tamed, she once again sees her way to taking up her part in the Great Story of redemption. For the Lenten season is a grace period, an opportunity for everyday saints to suffer the loss of all extraneous things, counting them "as rubbish, in order that [they] may gain Christ and be found in him" (Philippians 3:8-9).

WEEK 6 ∾ *Play Your Part*

"The discipline required to relinquish food or entertainment or anything else can often be the opening that admits God more fully into our lives."[8]

- To die daily is to prune the thorns, material or immaterial, that choke the seeds of the word of God (Matthew 13:7). Think of all the things that can choke the life of Christ in us: inordinate desires for fame, drink, rich foods, fancy homes, social status, or whatever "treasure" people pay to keep in storage units.
- What are the pictures, and desires, that hold me captive? If I can identify a disordered desire (whether for something edible or not), then I know where I need to begin pruning. Lent is a good time to start!
- Have you identified through your Lenten reflections which things need to die so that the life of Christ in you can be renewed and grow? Have you done your pruning?
- Everyday saints must do more than give up. The gift Christ wants from us in this Lenten season, as in every season, is the gift of faithful heart. Practice self-pruning, then watch and wait for new growth. This is Advent in Lent!

Chapter 6

EASTER

THE ART OF REJOICING

Behold, I am doing a new thing;
now it springs forth, do you not perceive it?

ISAIAH 43:19

Our Lord has written the promise of resurrection, not
in books alone, but in every leaf in springtime.

ATTRIBUTED TO MARTIN LUTHER

WHERE CHURCH CALENDAR AND NATURE MEET

*E*aster comes at the height of spring, usually in April, in a grand explosion of new life. It propels us into a bright new season after the somber passage of Holy Week when Christ died and was buried. Between Good Friday and Easter, Holy Saturday is the hinge that allows the door to new life to open. Everyday saints find themselves on the other side of the Easter door, the stone that was rolled away. Trumpet flowers open up in woods and gardens, proclaiming botanical alleluias, in step with church bells and brass ensembles that ring out the good news on Easter morning. The tomb is open. What was buried (remember those bulbs?) sprouts new life, ferns unfurl, seeds and hatchlings alike crack open their shells.

All this freshness communicates a sense of freedom, the desire to dance and sing alleluias for new possibilities. In Emily Dickinson's words:

A little Madness in the Spring
Is wholesome even for the King . . .
Who ponders this tremendous scene—
This whole Experiment of Green.[1]

WEEK 1 ✏ *Pause*

❧ Am I sufficiently in touch with the seasons of nature in my locale to have noticed the explosion of life that accompanies spring, the "whole Experiment of Green," a tacit promise (first cousin to the rainbow, perhaps?) of the resurrection in God's creation?

❧ Go outside this week. Observe what is happening in nature. Pay attention to leaves unfurling on branches, new shoots sprouting out, fern fiddleheads uncurling, daffodils trumpeting, muscari's blue bells ting-a-linging. Do you sense, and can you breathe in, the freshness in the air? The novelist Willa Cather expresses it like this:

> There was only spring itself; the throb of it, the light restlessness, the vital essence of it everywhere; in the sky, in the swift clouds, in the pale sunshine, and in the warm high wind. . . . If I had been tossed down blindfold on that red prairie, I should have known that it was spring.[2]

> Think about it: If you were blindfolded in your own place and terroir and went outside, would you know that it was spring? This too is one of God's wonderful works!

❧ Conduct this "whole Experiment of Green" yourself in order to help you rejoice in this parable of the coming kingdom of God— for that is what spring is. Praise God for renewing life, in nature and human nature alike!

Like King David who danced before the Ark of the Covenant, we too are caught up in this primeval jig and, again like King David, we don't care if onlookers call us fools.

The ancient church baptized new Christians on Easter morning to demonstrate the great renewal that happens when believers are united with Christ. The story that started in our Christmas crèches blossoms and comes into its own in Easter. Bethlehem, the beachhead of Christmas newness, gains new ground. The babe who was born in the manger is God born again in us, making us new. For "if anyone is in Christ, he is a new creation. The old has passed away; behold, the new has come" (2 Corinthians 5:17). Easter signals winter's end, yet it is only the first-fruit of the end.

Muscari, known as "bell flowers" or grape hyacinth

EASTER COMES TO PROVENCE

The end of winter is the traditional time for Provençaux to give a thorough scrub to one's home, a baptism by soap and water or, as it is commonly known, a spring cleaning. We throw open doors and windows, beat winter dust out of rugs, hang fresh laundry in open air, mop floors, and whitewash kitchen walls—religiously. Everything gets turned inside out.

Although we celebrate Christ's birth at Christmas, earlier generations thought that spring was a more suitable time than December or January to celebrate the new year. In medieval times the date for the new year was movable, a flash point for an important debate that touched on issues pertaining to both theology and nature: Should the calendar year start at the time of Jesus' circumcision (January 1), near winter solstice, or at Easter, during nature's annual renewal and when Christ rose from the dead? Both seasons herald good news, making each a potentially fit new year's start.

The French, who had long favored April 1 as New Year's Day, finally gave way, with the rest of Christendom, to celebrating January 1 when they adopted the Gregorian calendar in 1582. Still, no one can deny the sense of newness that accompanies springtime.

Spring is not Christmas; the crèche, carols, and pastorales are now only fading memories. Yet as this book shows, many of the characters and stories in the Christmas plays and the Provençal santons pertain not only to Christmas, but to other seasons as well, including Easter. Consider, for example, a carol from Nicolas Saboly, "Adam and his Helpmate."[3] This story takes us all the way back to the Garden of Eden! Six stanzas recall the temptation of Adam and Eve and their sorrow after the fall. Their pain is ours: we identify with them in this melancholy

WEEK 2 ∽ *Ponder*

"The LORD said to Moses and Aaron in the land of Egypt, 'This month shall be for you the beginning of months. It shall be the first month of the year for you.'" EXODUS 12:1-2

Before the institution of the Passover meal as a reminder of God's rescue operation, God told Moses where the great beginning of the year was to be placed in Israel's calendar. The Lord even instituted something like spring cleaning. The people were to clean diligently every crumb of leavened bread from their house, as many still do: "On the first day you shall remove leaven out of your houses" (Exodus 12:15).

Spring cleaning literally creates a "new order of things." Out with the old (man), in with the new! But, do we truly appreciate chant. However, the last stanza of this carol announces that "Jesus, at his birth, came to free us." This noël, like many others, reminds us that Christmas is much more than a na-tivity story. As we have seen, in southern France it has grown into a story about the human condition, and about what it takes to put it right. The crèche anticipates the cross. And Easter, on the *other* side of the cross, is our door back into—nay, *beyond*—that lost Eden of joy and delight, the spring garden that springs to life in Christ.

THE SEASONAL SANTON

The *ravi* is a beloved santon in the Pro-vençal manger scene. The craftsmen depict him with arms raised in excla-mation. He has stood transfixed in this

Le ravi (the overjoyed)

the kind of "cleaning" God has done in us, temples of his holy presence? Give thanks for the cleansing waters of baptism, our own "little Easter."

🕊 Many people worldwide make New Year's resolutions. We long for renewal, and for a while (usually a few weeks) we feel it may lie within our reach. Which season seems to you most appropri-ate for a brand-new start? Remember your baptism, and think about making a resolution, not to change yourself, but to let the Christ who lives in you live out his life in you (Galatians 2:20). "We were buried therefore with him by baptism into death, in order that, just as Christ was raised from the dead . . . we too might walk in newness of life" (Romans 6:4).

Daffodils, or "trumpet flowers"

position of awe and wonder for decades, since the early crèches, even before he appeared in a noël. The ravi made its official debut in 1960, when Yvan Audouard finally gave this little saint a role in his pastorale (throughout the play, he keeps exclaiming about the beauty of the baby, the goodness of God, and the wonders of everything around him).

Older popular tradition often cast the ravi as a simpleton—sadly, "the village idiot" (i.e., someone with mental disabilities)—but Audouard's pastorale casts him instead as a radical and jubilant convert: a fool for Christ (1 Corinthians 4:10). He is an innocent, not yet jaded or cynical, who still experiences exhilaration of new things, who feels free to praise without self-consciousness. The ravi, with his raised arms, looks something like a daffodil, facing upward and outward, to all corners of the earth, overjoyed to have blossomed into life. The daffodil's nickname, "trumpet flower" of Easter, is apt for it is one of the first spring flowers to bloom and is a symbol of resurrection.

In the Provençal nativity story, the ravi is so delighted to hear about the birth of the miracle child that he dashes around with his nightcap still on, shouting excitedly along the way. Disbelieving neighbors say he is raving mad—but what does he care? He does not have to be convinced by the shepherds—though he has not seen, yet he believes. The other characters find his incessant exclamations and joyful praises bothersome: "You are starting to annoy us!" they tell him. Then they find fault: "You haven't even brought a gift!" Mary, speaking for her infant son, tells the ravi not to mind what they say: "You were placed on earth in order to marvel, and you have fulfilled your mission. The world will be wonderful as long as there are people like you, capable of marveling."[4] Being a fool for Christ is the ravi's special gift!

SPRING CLEANING IN PROVENÇAL CULTURE

My mother used to recall the days when, in early spring, the village women would do the first great laundry of the year, outdoors in ancient stone basins (*lavoirs*) in the middle of the village square.[5] This was the season when women would finally emerge from their homes to tackle the dirty clothes that had been accumulating for months, neglected during the cold winters because there was no running water. Year after year, through seasons of weddings and new births, celebrations and losses, women gathered around that basin, talking, laughing, singing, and speaking in lower voices of burdens and tragedies, buried griefs, pains, and resentments. At times it was hard to say whether it was the fresh spring water or their tears doing the washing.

The cleansing around that basin transcended mere laundry. The lavoir was a place to "air things out"—as the ancient plane trees overhead (and overhearing) might well testify. Once again, the seasons coincide. Like spring itself, Eastertide calls to mind the aftermath of a deep-cleaning ritual, a celebratory time to chase out the old and welcome in the new—linens, yes, but ultimately hearts, made white as

WEEK 3 ⨯ *Praise*

"Then Jesus answered, 'Were not ten cleansed?
Where are the nine? Was no one found to return and give
praise to God, except this [Samaritan]?'" LUKE 17:17-18

Whether or not the ravi was, like the Samaritan leper, a social outcast, it's clear that he is more aware of what's going on, and how best to respond to it, than his companions. He rejoices—not just once, but again and again during the entire play. What about us grown-up, mature Christians? Is there anything that can still give us a thrill? Is there not a sense in which we should be imitators not only of the apostle Paul (see 1 Corinthians 4:16), but also of the ravi? Are we the kind of people who, like the ravi, can praise without ceasing?

It's noteworthy that the ravi gave thanks and praise in faith, before he ever arrived at the crib. What about you? Are you thankful only when "good things" happen? Can we get excited, and keep rejoicing along our pilgrimage because of the one big thing we know? "Rejoice in the Lord always; again I will say, rejoice" (Philippians 4:4).

snow (Isaiah 1:18). Kathleen Norris agrees, saying that one "might characterize [laundry] as approaching the moral realm; there are days when it seems a miracle to be able to make dirty things clean."[6]

That the washing basin stood in the middle of the village as a gathering place for people to, ahem, wash their dirty laundry in public, communicated a powerful image. Historians sometimes describe the lavoir as the place for of a ceremonial ritual of public cleansing, where people exchange and rinse out their differences and grievances. They come as individuals; they leave as neighbors.

It is fitting that the pastorales culminate with miracles of both repentance and reconciliation—twin aspects of a deep inner cleansing—thereby already anticipating the Easter chapter of the story that begins at Christmas. The concluding scenes of these Christmas plays include a hungry robber who returns a stolen turkey and an injured party who forgives and then returns the pilfered bird to the thief, acknowledging that *he too* needs forgiveness for his greed; a wealthy landowner who at long last accepts his poor son-in-law, thus reconciling the family and preventing a tragic ending; a miraculous reunion that takes place when a blind man finds not just his sight, but also his long-lost son, right there in the manger. That such restorations take place in the environs of Jesus is the substance of Easter hope for renewal, of broken hearts and relationships alike.

MY OWN PILGRIMAGE

The first time I celebrated Easter as a new Christian, I found myself playing the role of the ravi. After what felt like a hopeless search during my own "long night," I finally arrived, not at the manger, but at the meaning of that infant-God-made-flesh-for-me, the one who had been searching for me before I had even begun searching for him!

I was seeking the meaning of life in various existential philosophies and utopian systems, but in God's grace I discovered I needed a change more radical than anything the philosophies of the day had to offer. I now saw that the problem was not with outer circumstances, society, or other people, but with me alone. I had finally found the God to whom the beauty in nature pointed, but he was so holy that I could not see how I could ever come near him (Isaiah 6:5). So near and yet so far! I needed a spring cleaning of my inner being that only a spring of living water could provide.

The Thessalonians were right: the gospel that proclaimed renewal was a message that could turn worlds "upside down" (Acts 17:6) as it did to mine. "I believed, and so I spoke" (2 Corinthians 4:13)—and sounded

WEEK 4 ∽ *Pray*

"Forgive us our sins, as we forgive those who sin against us."
MATTHEW 6:12 NIRV

Do I catch myself, at times, thinking of reconciliation in Christ only as an individual transaction, between me and God, in my own private chamber? Do I realize that what happened on Easter morning reconciles me not just to God (alleluia!), but also to my brothers and sisters in Christ?

Pray this week:

"Lord, thank you for the gift of reconciliation in Christ, and for my brothers and sisters who are also reconciled to you—even those with whom I do not always agree. Thank you for helping us come together to your 'basin,' in whose waters we learn to forgive one another as you have forgiven us. Help all of us who make up your church to make peace with one another, despite our differences and our grudges.

"Show me how I can be part of your 'ministry of reconciliation' (2 Corinthians 5:18), and where I might need to initiate an act of reconciliation with brothers and sisters: 'Behold, how good and pleasant it is / when brothers dwell in unity!' (Psalm 133:1)."

The cleaning basins have become obsolete and disappeared from the old villages—but not so with the cleansing that God offers. We were cleansed once for all in the lavoir of baptism, yet we continue to sin. But we know that "If we confess our sins, he is faithful and just to forgive us our sins and to cleanse us from all unrighteousness" (1 John 1:9).

raving mad to those who knew me, family and friends alike. I was becoming a real, live, and life-size ravi! My teenage friends—would-be philosophers, social radicals, mystics, and political visionaries—tried to reason with me. (My heart had its reasons that their reason could not know.) When reasoning did not work, some mocked, others called me a babbler, but everyone eventually forsook me. I was an embarrassment.

What did I care? The Gospels told me of the disciples who were both confused and overjoyed, like the ravi, when Jesus appeared to them on Easter. And some of their friends did not trust their reports either, just like my friends and the ravi's neighbors. It is hard not to be suspicious of a "raving" witness: "some doubted" (Matthew 28:17), others thought their testimony "an idle tale" (Luke 24:11), and Paul himself was called a "babbler" (Acts 17:18). So I was happy—no, ecstatic—to join the ranks along with the apostles. How could I not become a ravi? Not an April fool, but an Easter fool for Christ, giddy for the grace of God!

This is why the ravi santon continues to present a standing challenge (at two inches tall), a mad mentor who reminds me, in Audouard's words, that "the world will be wonderful as long as there are people like you capable of marveling."[7]

THE ART OF EATING IN SEASON

When everyday saints celebrate the Easter feast, the Lenten fast recedes into memory, a distant hunger pang. Emily Dickinson's "Experiment of Green," having exploded in nature, now moves into the kitchen. Jesus himself ate with his disciples after his resurrection, including breakfast on the beach (John 21:12-15)—a vivid reminder of his presence with us, for as one biblical commentary reminds us, "In that culture to eat with a person was tantamount to saying, 'I am your friend.'"[8]

Pâques, the French word for Easter comes from the Latin term *pascha* for "passover." It therefore refers to two events in the history of salvation—each a story of good *news*: God's deliverance of Israel from Egypt and his deliverance of Jesus from the grave. The Passover meal enacts the first event (Exodus 12:14); the Lord's Supper recalls the

Colorful asparagus

second (1 Corinthians 11:23-32). Both anticipate the future marriage supper of the Lamb (Revelation 19:9). The Great Story in which we find ourselves is told through the table, and lamb is indeed on the menu in the land of my ancestors, a reminder of God's provision of sacrificial lambs with which to make atonement for sin. The roasted lamb that was raised by shepherds in the nearby hills comes garnished with green salads—crunchy radishes and spring peas sprinkled with local olive oil and the salt from the sea—not

WEEK 5 ❧ *Praise*

"Could I write a list of a thousand things I love? . . . One thousand blessings—one thousand gifts . . . I begin the list. Not of gifts I want but of gifts I already have."[9]

Ann Voskamp learned the simple discipline of counting the blessings, based on the term *eucharistō* (Gk. "I give thanks"). Grace awakens gratitude. Accordingly, she kept track of the blessings she received over the next few months. Here are just a few: "1. Morning shadows across the old floors, 2. Jam piled high on the toast, 3. Cry of blue jay from high in the spruce," "18. Wind flying cold wild in hair," "245. Bare toes in early light" . . . and hundreds more.[10]

In this discipline of gratitude there is joy: she is transformed into a ravi. Instead of the haunting recollections of childhood trauma, she is cheered by new awareness of daily present blessings.

forgetting the asparagus that has begun to shoot up in spring's verdant explosion.

According to nutritionists, "Greens are always the first things to come out of the ground because our bodies need them. Greens help us detoxify after the accumulation from a long winter indoors. Bitter leafy greens, asparagus, and other spring-time early veggies and herbs clear our bodies of taxing viruses."[11] *Voilà!* Yes, Jesus could have been raised from the dead at any time of the year, yet it is fitting that we celebrate Easter in the spring. How can an everyday saint who is attentive to his place, his season, and the liturgical calendar not be overjoyed, like the ravi, to see the dead raised green from the ground?

END OF SEASON

The Easter season begins with an open tomb and ends with our Lord ascending to heaven forty days later. To ordinary saints, both the resurrection and the ascension are extraordinary events. It is therefore only

- What about you? Could you make such a list, a thousand items long? Start with the grace of new life, the focus of the season of Easter; then, Christ's body broken, raised, and given for you. And so on.
- Can you make your list more concrete and personal, not just a litany of what Jesus has done according to the Scripture, but what he is doing now in your daily life? Try counting your blessings every day this week. All this discipline of gratitude requires is Adventish attention: a watching and waiting for God's presence and activity in your life—from the smell of morning coffee to answered prayers and the people he places in your path. Can you keep counting your blessings for a month? For the months ahead? Can you sense the inner joy growing? Are you beginning to see that this too is a way of carrying your devotion to Christ throughout the day?

appropriate that we take up the posture of the ravi once again, at the end
of the season as we did at its beginning. At end of Easter season, we
stand with our arms raised, lost in wonder, love, and praise, gazing into
heaven like the apostles on Ascension Day, now waiting for a second
Advent of the Lord, for he has promised to return the same way as he
went (Acts 1:9-11). Everyday saints therefore join the company of disciples who "worshiped him and returned to Jerusalem with great joy"
(Luke 24:52).

Christ has died.
Christ is risen.
Christ will come again.
Alleluia!

WEEK 6 ∽ *Play Your Part*

*"And he took bread, and when he had given thanks, he broke it and gave it
to them, saying, 'This is my body, which is given for you. Do this in
remembrance of me.'"* LUKE 22:19

Tables are good places to pass on stories. This is how Jews retained their
identity during their diaspora. One chronicler, Elizabeth Ehrlich, wrote
of the stories "that the grandmothers had once dished out with their
soup. . . . The connection to something larger than everyday life."[12]

- Jesus directed his disciples to go ahead into Jerusalem and
  prepare the Passover meal (Matthew 26:18-19). He shared a
  family story at that meal—Israel's history. The Passover table
  commemorated the great saving event of the Old Testament: the
  exodus, God bringing his chosen people out of Egypt to a new
  land. How much thought do you give to preparing your Easter
  dinner, and what stories to tell?
- With bread and wine, the simplest of staples, Jesus introduced his
  disciples to a new story, centering on a new exodus: the "departure"

WHAT'S AN EVERYDAY SAINT TO DO?

Everyday saints have risen with Christ, been clothed with Christ, been made new in Christ. As the poet Gerard Manley Hopkins puts it, "Let him easter in us."[13] And, we might add, let us practice not only resurrection, but rejoicing.

This is why I find it striking that the santon-makers included the ravi in the crèche. Perhaps people will think *them* fools for placing a simpleton close to the holy family. Unlike the other santons, the ravi's vocation is unsalaried—and odd. Yet, as we've seen, he is a cherished figure with a vital role to play: he is *lost* in wonder, love, and praise. Able-bodied and right-minded everyday saints would do well to go and do likewise, being willing, like the apostle Paul, on occasion to act like "fools for Christ's sake" (1 Corinthians 4:10).

(Gk. *exodos*) that he would make from Jerusalem (Luke 9:31). That Last Supper is a scene that churches all over the world reenact in remembrance of him, and to remember who they are. Next time your church celebrates Communion, think of how you are part of and passing on a millennia-old tradition. Thank God for placing you in his ongoing Great Story.

❧ Do you have stories connected with some dish you could tell your children and share with your guests that might make your Easter feast a way of expressing your family identity? Easter table traditions provide an opportunity to remember who you are: a people made new in Christ, a family who has been led by Christ to this place. You might have a recipe, a family platter you use, or a symbolic table ornament. There's no one right answer: what matters is its story. You can even ask friends over for a "little Easter" dinner (i.e., on any Sunday), and ask them to bring one dish and a family story to accompany it.

The ravi is no Candide, Voltaire's comic figure, the eternal optimist who thinks that everything is for the best in the best of all possible worlds. To be sure, eternal optimists are in rather short supply just now: in our present world truth, goodness, and beauty are continually at risk, casualties of cultural, spiritual, and celestial war (Revelation 12:7). Nevertheless, everyday saints have every reason to rejoice, for they are caught up in the Great Story where they help the Hero restore the brokenness, Adventishly anticipating the not-yet, when they will be whole and there will be no more tears. This is more than sufficient reason to rejoice! Alleluia!

WEEK 7 ∝ *Ponder*

"I have learned in whatever situation I am to be content. I know how to be brought low, and I know how to abound." PHILIPPIANS 4:11-12

What does it look like, on the ground, to "rejoice always"? Does it mean I have to wear a happy face and raise my hands in worship, like the ravi, or perhaps exclaim "Alleluia" every hour when the clock strikes? Is there an art of rejoicing that is less loud exclamation than deep-seated joy? Introverts of the world, rejoice!

Might rejoicing resemble Paul's contentment? Might our joy stem from a constant awareness that the promise of resurrection was written not just in every leaf in springtime, but in every little saint's heart—in my heart?

Can I be joyful, however, when there is still healing to be done, when it becomes clear that many pilgrims make up a company of the walking wounded? We're not there yet. Nevertheless, what brings us joy is knowing that, even though there are still open wounds, we can participate in the healing process. As Sam Gamgee would say: "There's some good in this world, Mr. Frodo, and it's worth fighting for."[14] And this is what we shall get to do as we progress in our ordinary pilgrimage ahead. Alleluia!

Chapter 7

PENTECOST

THE ART OF POURING OUT ESSENTIAL OILS

*This Jesus God raised up . . . having received from the
Father the promise of the Holy Spirit, he has poured out
this that you yourselves are seeing and hearing.*

ACTS 2:32-33

*It may not have been only the common ails of humanity with which
she tried to cope; it seemed sometimes as if love and hate and jealousy
and adverse winds at sea might also find their proper remedies
amongst the curious wild-looking plants in Mrs. Todd's garden.*

SARAH ORNE JEWETT, *THE COUNTRY OF THE POINTED FIRS*

WHERE CHURCH CALENDAR AND NATURE MEET

*P*entecost, fifty days after Easter, celebrates another new thing—
the next milestone in God's saving work and in our pilgrimage.
The disciples, praying in the upper room, were doing their best not to
let their hearts be troubled for the Lord had assured them, "I will pray
the Father, and he shall give you another Comforter" (John 14:16 KJV).
Jesus' promise was fulfilled at Pentecost when a mighty rushing wind
filled the room where the disciples had gathered, bringing not only

comfort but also a whole new world. Indeed, the strange new world that had first entered Bethlehem at Christmas now landed in an upper room in Jerusalem, ushering in the beginning of the Christian era, which is marked with the baptism (outpouring) of the Holy Spirit that unites believers to the risen Christ (Acts 1:5).

We might call Pentecost "Dominus D-day," the day on which the Spirit of Christ invades the world. Pentecost marks the spot where C. S. Lewis's liberator "in disguise" has finally landed: from the cradle to the cross to the church.[1]

As Pentecost brings comfort to troubled hearts ("The Spirit himself bears witness with our spirit that we are children of God," wrote Paul in Romans 8:16), so late spring weather is a harbinger of physical refreshment. This is a change from the capriciousness of early spring when despite the new sprigs of life, one could not always rely on the weather to deliver by evening what it promised in the morning. The suspicious French have a saying for this seasonal uncertainty: "In April, keep your sweater, in May, it will get better!"[2] During my eight-year sojourn in Edinburgh, I discovered the Scots had their version of the saying: "Don't cast your clout [coat] till *May* [not April] is out." In any case, around Pentecost Sunday the air finally becomes delicious and stays that way. It is time to start planting fragile seedlings and trust they will bear fruit in their season—just as we trust the seedlings the Sower has rooted in our hearts will also bear the fruit of the Spirit.

On the calendar, Pentecost is but a one-day celebration at the end of May or beginning of June: the last of the movable feasts. In this book it serves as an extended entryway into Ordinary Time which, as we shall see, is a way of speaking about ordinary life empowered by the Holy Spirit. (If you're reading in season, please note that the reflections in this chapter should be read in one week, not four, until the start of Ordinary Time.)

PENTECOST COMES TO PROVENCE

In the land of my ancestors, the season of Pentecost roughly coincides with the blooming season of lavender. Throughout the month of June, lavender dominates the *plâteaux* of *Haute Provence*. Row after row of lavender-blue mounds adorn the hills like ribbons until, at the top, they mingle with the azure-blue of the skies. Lower down in the valley and closer to the coast, with its own cerulean sea-blues, bright bows of stand-alone lavender plants reach out to buzzing bees overhead. Many fragrant buds will end up on kitchen counters and dining-room tables. Still others will become even more intimately integrated into the household, infiltrating the pillows on which we lay down our heads to rest at night. The scent of lavender is ever-present, permeating every nook and cranny of town and country life. Lavender wafts through the air even when the plant itself is not visible, like the wind that is known only by its effect, or like "the wind that blows where it wishes" (John 3:8).

THE SEASONAL SANTON

The lavender woman santon is a ubiquitous character in the family crèche, even though we do not find her in any play, song, or story related to Christmas. What, then, is she doing there? Lavender is an integral part of the land and its culture, so there she must be, story or not. She is a fixture in her place, much like the shepherds in the hills. We can go further: she is the *essence* of Provence, like the herb she carries.

La femme à la lavande (the lavender woman)

Lavandula angustifolia is an ancient plant that has inhabited the Mediterranean basin from earliest times, long before other varieties were successfully developed and harvested in far-flung places such as England and, more recently, California. As we saw in Advent, lavender, like thyme, is one of the traditional "manger herbs." According to legend, lavender was originally a plain

A sprig of lavender

shrub and became the beauty it is today only when the baby Jesus laid down his head on it, at which moment it produced its singular blue flowers with their distinctive fragrance.

The lavender woman understands the relation between people and plants. She is, for this reason, what we will call an ethnobotanist *par excellence.* She understood the many beneficial uses of this native Mediterranean that is lavender, long before the term *aromatherapy* became fashionable. The name *lavender* comes from the ancient Romans who settled in (well, conquered) the land of my ancestors; the root is from *lavare* (Lat. "to wash"), a nod to its therapeutic properties in bathing, cleaning, disinfecting, and even to ward off unwanted insects. From antiquity, then, people have prized lavender for the penetrating scent of its essential oil that remarkably lasts for years after it is picked, a fragrant reminder of summer and the land. The essential oil of lavender is the essence of Provence.

ETHNOBOTANY AND ESSENTIAL OILS IN PROVENÇAL CULTURE

Ethnobotany—the study of how humans have used and interacted with plants—has been the raison d'être of botanic gardens everywhere since the Renaissance, when they were attached to universities as outdoor science laboratories.[3] (One of the earliest, dating from 1593, is in the southern

French city of Montpelier.) Their precursors, the medieval monastic gardens, were already ethnobotanic hotbeds: places devoted to human flourishing. Monks were ethnobotanists, familiar with their terroir and its people, and well versed in local herbs and trees, particularly in those trees whose "fruit will be for food, and their leaves for healing" (Ezekiel 47:12).

In earlier centuries, those in religious orders spent time studying and growing plants to use as medicinal remedies and therapeutic cures. They kept detailed records of these plants, along with early collections of botanical illustrations called "herbals." Their carefully planned gardens, with quiet alleyways of flagstones and box hedges, were typically places of peace and comfort, refreshing both body and soul. Some gardens included strategically positioned benches that served as retreat places. The penetrating scents of herbs such as rosemary, lavender, and thyme lent themselves to peaceful contemplation and served as aromatic reminders of the way in which the fragrance of the knowledge of Christ is to spread through the people of God to others (2 Corinthians 2:14).

Pause

"Aromatic herbs play an essential role in our existence. They procure not only medical benefits, but also add color and savor to our dishes, and scents to our homes. All is good in these plants."[4]

I can't pass by cultivated herbs, in a garden or a pot, without immediately rubbing them between my fingers. I sniff my hands and am both revived by the scent and awed by how long the perfume lingers. Try it! If you have essential oils at home, or if you cultivate herbs or know where to find some, rub them between your fingers or dab a drop of oil on a scarf, towel, or tissue (careful: oil will stain!). Do you notice how it lingers? If you have lavender oil, place the tissue under your pillow tonight. I wonder which essential oils the author of Song of Songs was thinking about when he penned this line: "How much better is your love than wine, / and the fragrance of your oils than any spice!" (Song of Songs 4:10).

Could this be the lesson of the little lavender saint? Recall that she plays a minor role in the Christmas story. Her gift is not costly or impressive, but nonetheless welcome. Her lotion and herbal infusions may be soothing contributions to Mary during post-delivery; her lavender oil tempers the pungent barn smells. What she has to offer is not as tangible as food or warmth. It is subtler, to be sure, yet it lingers long past Christmas. And this is as it should be because the little saints are

on the verge of exiting the special seasons and of entering Ordinary Time, where they will return to their everyday jobs. And yet . . . the Holy Spirit lingers, diffusing the essential oil—the essence—of being in Christ into every part of their being and through them into the world.

The application of essential oils may not be the first thing one thinks of in relation to the Bible. However, being anointed with oil is a theme that permeates the Old Testament, where it is a sign of the special presence of the Spirit. Before David could become king of Israel, for example, "Samuel took the horn of oil and anointed him in the midst of his brothers. And the Spirit of the LORD

A sprig of rosemary

rushed upon David *from that day forward*" (1 Samuel 16:13 emphasis added). We have the recipe for this holy oil, for God gave it to Moses: liquid myrrh, sweet-smelling cinnamon, aromatic cane, cassia, and olive oil (Exodus 30:23-25). When poured over David, or Aaron and his sons in the temple, the scent would have lingered in their hair, clothes, and furnishings—an aromatic sign of the Spirit's empowering presence with those he was setting apart and equipping for service to God.

We find the practice of anointing throughout the New Testament as well, and often it is explicitly the Holy Spirit, not oil, that is said to be poured out. All four Gospels record Jesus' baptism, when "God anointed Jesus of Nazareth with the Holy Spirit and with power" (Acts 10:38). Later at Pentecost, Peter explains that God has fulfilled the prophecy from Joel 2, pouring out his Spirit on Jesus' disciples, empowering them for witness. Still later, "the gift of the Holy Spirit was poured out even on the Gentiles" (Acts 10:45). All these "anointed" people were thus set apart (i.e., sanctified, made holy) not as prophets, priests, or kings but rather as "saints"—everyday saints, charged with living for the Lord, himself the anointed one of Israel (namely, Messiah, the "Christ") in every area of life.

Our santons represent these everyday saints. To be sure, their pilgrimage began in Advent, long before Pentecost. Yet the Spirit was there already, the prompt in the santons' hearts, drawing them, gifts and

Ponder

Have you ever noticed the importance of essential oils in relation to the outpouring of the Spirit throughout the Bible? Did you know that God had given a "recipe" to Moses? If you did the experiment mentioned above and rubbed some lavender or thyme between your fingers, does it help you better understand how the essential oil of the Holy Spirit, the fragrance of the knowledge of Christ, can spread through us throughout the world? The lavender woman refreshes people and places through her botanic gift. She might be an aromatherapist, or a nurse, a midwife, a pharmacist, a doctor, or a mother. These are all service-oriented jobs, opportunities for the Spirit to refresh while caring for the body. How might you minister the essential oil of the Holy Spirit?

all, to the Christ child. This suggests, once again, that the pastorales are much more than a Christmas story. These villagers are aptly called little saints, even with their foibles. Neither they nor we everyday saints are perfect, and though they may not have been in an upper room, the Spirit nevertheless descends on them too. Who else but the Spirit moves us to undertake this great pilgrimage? We see now that the Holy Spirit was the joy of the musicians' dance, the conscience who convicted the rich man to welcome the stranger, the medicine that healed the heartsick knife grinder, and the wind who blew the fragrance of the knowledge of Christ, enthusing the whole company of santons.

MY OWN PILGRIMAGE

I became an ethnobotanist very early in life, though I didn't come across the term until much later. I learned it from my parents who, unbeknownst to them, passed down in equal amounts their respective passions. Papa loved his terroir: it was obvious, both in the way he worked his little plot of land—a walled garden just outside the village brimming with produce—and when he quietly contemplated it by night, gazing at it in contentment. *Maman* lived and breathed the customs, songs, stories, and recipes that were familiar to her, as they were to the generations before her, simply from inhabiting the same terroir. It was only in retrospect, however, when I realized that my own passion was to bring these two loves, or should I say two cultures—the botanic and the domestic[5]—together that I understood how much of themselves they had poured into me.

In my pre-Christian teenage years, I spent all my free time in the hills, where I felt somehow closer to heaven—if such a thing existed. I came home from long jaunts in those hills with armfuls of herbs that I used to dye wool, mix with soaps, fill sachets, infuse in tisanes, and add to casseroles. There was always the essence of lavender lingering over my youth. Every time I opened a drawer, leafed through a book, or took out a scarf, the essential oils of my land poured over and overpowered me, a poignant echo from the hills and the God I sought who made them that hovered in the air I breathed.

When I eventually came to faith in Christ, I experienced Christ's essence poured into me through his Spirit. At first, I was tempted to separate myself, emotionally and practically, from my ethnobotanical pursuits. My old terroir—part of the world that is passing away (1 John 2:17)—now seemed insignificant in comparison to the new heaven and earth ahead. Must not dying to myself mean rinsing off the scent of lavender in the waters of baptism? Thankfully, this phase was short-lived.

The little lavender woman soon taught me—yes, the oils are an essential object lesson—that following Christ need not mean becoming disconnected from my physical world. On the contrary: I saw that discipleship invites one not to escape from but rather to inhabit the world more fully, to the glory of God. That after all is part of our vocation as humans, put on the earth to work and keep the garden (Genesis 2:15). As Dorothy Sayers puts it: "Every maker and worker is called to serve God in his profession or trade—not outside it."[6] If essence of lavender can penetrate our comings and goings, our activities and rest, how

Pray

"The Spirit's mission is to put us in Christ—to unite us to Him, and to let His life flow into us."[7]

Do you sometimes feel that the job you love or the passion you pursue is not worthy of Christ? Do you feel you should instead do something that others would more readily identify as spiritual? If so, remember that the essential oil of the Spirit, the faith that lays hold of Christ, seeps into every pore of your existence. Commit yourself to becoming a fragrance of the gospel in all that you do, and not the spiritual things only.

> "Lord, help me to see how the Spirit of Christ in me may be poured into my everyday places! Anoint me with the 'oil of gladness' (Psalm 45:7). Pour your Spirit over me and show me how to be a lavender women or man for you!"

much more can the essence of Christ—the essential oil of the outpoured Spirit—do so? The Spirit of Christ permeates my every day, "whatever [I] do, in word or deed" (Colossians 3:17).

How far can this outpouring extend? As a baptized and adopted child of Christ, could I be part of the process by which the essential oil of Christ spreads even further? Could my humble ethnobotanical gifts—not least my paintings of lavender!—be a healing and refreshing presence? If the essential oil of lavender is the essence of Provence, should not the essence of Jesus in me similarly infuse the place where I dwell, or just pass through? Could I be a lavender woman for God, his essential oil wafting around me, transforming the very atmosphere in common places, including those places where two or three are gathered in his name?

THE ART OF EATING IN SEASON

Pentecost Sunday anticipates a season when doors are thrown open and dining is taken *en plein air,* where the atmosphere is saturated with native herbs on the grill that transform what would be otherwise ordinary dishes into something extraordinary.

Herbes de Provence collectively names the herbs of the culinary palette that grace the foods in my little corner of the Mediterranean basin. The scents from the hills spill over into the meandering streets and kitchens, giving the Provençal cuisine its distinctive aroma. My ancestors knew long ago where to find the essential ingredients—thyme, rosemary, savory, and marjoram—for their local cuisine. These herbs grow wild in local soil, along country paths, and even out of drystone walls. People also use them for herbal infusions, or *tisanes*: thyme for cough, rosemary for memory, savory for circulation, marjoram for digestion, and so on.

The Bible mentions many herbs as well, several of which are native to Provence, given the common Mediterranean climate. I happily acknowledge that our creator God has planted an even greater herbal diversity in other gardens and terroirs of his good earth, each yielding its own distinct palette (palate?) of flavors, from the varieties of Indian curries, to Ivorian fufu, Peking duck, Argentinian asado and, yes, Provençal ratatouille. As food writer Elizabeth Lambert Ortiz says: "The great dishes of the world's cuisines . . . have developed in individual regions to give us the foodstuffs determined by climate, soil and local culture."[8]

At Pentecost, the Spirit of God broke barriers and enabled anointed peoples from all corners of the world to understand each other: "each one was hearing them speak in his own language" (Acts 2:6). Could it be that the diversity of herbs that garnish the farm table is the botanic counterpart of the miracle of the first Pentecost, and since then every Sunday at the Lord's Table, thanks to the out-pouring of the Spirit? One Spirit, poured out in many places, to form

A sprig of marjoram

one people. One Supper, served to people gathered in fellowship around one table, composed of many flavors. There is communion at the Lord's Table, yet both saints and spices retain their distinct characters.

END OF SEASON

As the special seasons of the church draw to a close, the wooden Christmas manger gives way to a Pentecost scene: the new dwelling place of God, the body of Christ, through whose open windows the

Spirit wafts in and out, a pleasing aroma and harbinger of heaven. Meanwhile, we serve Jesus where we are in our own locales with what we have, our respective gifts, empowered by the knowledge that "the anointing that you received from him abides in you" (1 John 2:27).

What began with the baby Jesus has come to a climax in the body of Christ; the mission of the newborn babe was always to be the cornerstone of a newborn temple (see Acts 4:11; Ephesians 2:20; 1 Peter 2:6-7). Pentecost begins a new act in the drama of redemption. As the Father sent the Son, and as the Son sent the Spirit, so the Spirit equips the new body of Christ to be sent into the world with a mission: "But you will receive power when the Holy Spirit has come upon you, and you will be my witnesses . . . to the end of the earth" (Acts 1:8). So the pilgrimage continues, as does Pentecost, for ultimately what the Spirit does is equip everyday saints for everyday life. With the end of Pentecost, the "special seasons" are complete.

WHAT'S AN EVERYDAY SAINT TO DO?

Everyday saints might ask, What do I do with my lavender—the love or vocation that occupies my life, the giftedness I cannot explain, the existential herbs that give the unique flavoring to my own person, place, and season of life? As the chapters on Ordinary Time will show, what we do to follow Christ may look different for everyone. Yet we all bring our own gifts to lay at Christ's feet.

We, like the little santons, have been set apart, consecrated to God. We too have our foibles. We too are being renewed in the image of Christ through the work of the Spirit, who sanctifies us as together we follow the way, truth, and life of Jesus Christ (see Acts 9:2; 24:14). Through the Spirit with whom we have been anointed, Jesus makes *us* his dwelling place, a temple made of living stones (1 Corinthians 6:19; 1 Peter 2:5). The Spirit is the essential oil of Christ, the one who infiltrates every part of our body and soul and every place and season through which he calls us to journey. Theologian Julie Canlis reminds us that "the Spirit's playing field has always been with real people in a real world."[9]

In the ordinary season to come, Jesus meets his everyday saints not only on the special feast days when they wear their Sunday best or when they are on their knees in their upper chambers. Rather, Jesus meets them in their daily tasks when they go about their quotidian business, sleeves rolled up: in fields, barns, herbal laboratories, or wherever they are called to serve. The lavender lady turns out to be a woman for all seasons. Indeed, each everyday saint, woman or man, can diffuse the aroma of Christ to God always, everywhere, and to everyone. "Thanks be to God, who in Christ . . . through us spreads the fragrance of the knowledge of him everywhere" (2 Corinthians 2:14-15).

Play Your Part

"All of life is spiritual. Work. Bearing children. Hobbies. Friendships. Repairing gutters. Commuting. This is our worship —the offering of our everyday stuff to God."[10]

Once transformed, we seek to transform others. To respond to Jesus' Great Commission, it helps to have both words and a stage in which to bear witness to the life of Christ in us.

Here are a few ideas to celebrate this outpouring of the Spirit of the living God in and around us this season:

- Host an international potluck where everyone brings a dish and a story from a different country. Talk about the activities of the Spirit in the church in these faraway places and pray for their needs (and why not organize a donation!). Use your church's human resources: different nationalities or ethnic groups, former missionaries, etc.

- Bake or cook using some specific herb (I'm partial to lavender madeleines!), then share the results as well as the story of the little saint with lavender. Ask each person to share an example of how they spread the fragrance of the knowledge of Christ in their everyday places. Think how you can be a "lavender santon," the fragrance of the knowledge of Christ, in your place this season.

EVERYDAY SAINTS _in_ ORDINARY TIME

With what shall I come before the LORD?

MICAH 6:6

The strength of a man's virtue must not be measured
by his efforts, but by his ordinary life.

BLAISE PASCAL, _PENSÉES_ 352

WHAT HAPPENED DURING the special seasons changes Ordinary
Time forever.

What the church calendar calls "Ordinary Time" starts with Trinity
Sunday (a week after Pentecost) and ends with Christ the King Sunday,
just before Advent (in other words, from June to the end of November).
The main reason it is "ordinary" is that the church calendar counts each
Sunday in this season as an "ordinal" number (e.g., "first Sunday after
Pentecost").[1] Even so, it is worth noting that during this long season,
the church celebrates no significant events in the life of Christ; hence it
may be "ordinary" in the ordinary sense as well!

Ordinary Time presents us with an empty stage and open calendar, a long season with no holy days to punctuate it. Yet there is a *newness* to this particular period too. Ordinary Time is a time for everything—"a time for every matter under heaven" (Ecclesiastes 3:1). The challenge for everyday saints is to walk across that stage and, with Christ in them, transform their ordinary into scenes of holiness. This is the adventure—or dare I say, the *Adventishness*—of living in a period of watchful waiting, seeking opportunities to live out the life of Christ in *ordinary* ways.

Jesus' entrance (Christmas) and exit (Ascension) mark the beginning and end of the special seasons that trace his story. Pentecost marks the special season where the Spirit of Christ came to dwell in the ordinary time of everyday saints in order to continue his story. This is what we now *ordinarily* have to do: follow Jesus by faith in the power of the Holy Spirit. The question for every Christian is not, "To be or not to be?" but rather, "How can I be in Christ, here and now?" How should everyday Christian saints practice the art of living in season *outside* the special seasons of the church?

This is where the santons come into their own. For in Ordinary Time, we follow the example of these little saints who experience the petits miracles of the everyday, the ordinary graces by which God sustains the cycle of the seasons, day and night, the movement of clouds and stars, and the activities of fauna and flora (Psalm 104). The little saints remind us to offer up our everyday activities as gifts of gratitude to our gracious Savior. Jesus redeems sinners and helps forgiven sinners to redeem the time (Ephesians 5:16; Colossians 4:5), that is, make the most of every opportunity by doing God's will on earth as it is in heaven.

Everyday saints therefore make time to pay attention to the time, the season in which we live to God. The created order matters, and the wonders of God's handiwork in nature will mature and come to fruition over the seasons in local gardens, public parks, and backyards, not to mention the fertile soil of the fields and farmlands that grow the food they eat. These are the petits miracles that take place in the theater of the natural world in which God invites us to participate and which serve as our stage of operations.

Participating can be as simple as engaging in the rhythms of daily meals, neighborly gatherings, or the harvest festivals that our ancestors observed over the centuries. All these help pass on to our children and our children's children a sense of gratitude for gifts that ought not be taken for granted. These rhythms help us to see the gift and thank the Giver. In practicing the art of living in season, everyday saints help those around them to perceive the goodness of the created order and, in so doing, become liturgists of the everyday.

Ordinary time is a time for work, as it has been since God put Adam and Eve in charge of a garden. The little saints that we have followed out of the manger remind everyday saints that they can do extraordinary things in ordinary time and ordinary situations. The indwelling Spirit within them equips them to play whatever part God has given them in ways that may turn the world upside down (Acts 17:6). Christians are not everyday people trying hard to become saints; rather, they *are* saints—re-created in Christ—trying to live out the life of Christ in the everyday. They do this by pursuing their particular vocations in their respective places through the seasons to the glory of God.

Yet again, the seasons offer teaching: ordinary time befits the summer and autumn seasons of growth and fruition. After all, the sowing—both the literal planting of seeds and the sown seed of Jesus' death that anticipates the fruit of the Spirit—happened during the special seasons. Ordinary Time is for cultivation and harvest.

We will continue to accompany the little saints on their pilgrimage. The santons we will meet in the chapters ahead are not heroes in the traditional sense. They slay no dragons, find no treasure, rescue no fair maidens. Why, then, are we following in their footsteps? A cynic might well ask of them, as Nathanael had asked of Jesus, "Can anything good come out of an insignificant Mediterranean village, be it in the Holy Land or Provence?" (I am riffing on John 1:46.) It's true that Jesus was born to an ordinary family in a nondescript Mediterranean village, and that for most of his life he was, in the eyes of the world, a nondescript hero—a carpenter by trade. And, judging from the stories he told, he was acquainted not only with grief but also with the same quotidian realities so familiar to other commoners. He knew hunger and thirst, and homelessness (Matthew 8:20). Yet he also knew how to display godliness in his humdrum reality. What did he do it for? Julie Canlis answers this way: "Jesus is fully human in order that I might become, in Him, fully human once again. Jesus took on my humanity in order that I might, like Adam, live in communion with God in my ordinary life."[2]

We began our journey in a special season, setting out with the santons in the supernaturally charged atmosphere of the Advent hills, with a sense that their land had been touched by the divine. The conviction that Jesus has entered our ordinary time and place sustains everyday saints as they continue their pilgrimage, following the Way in their own diverse ways. *Then*, they walked with Jesus in his special seasons. *Now,* they ask him to accompany them in their ordinary time and places—fields, workshops, markets, homes, neighborhoods—so that their places can become his. "What can I give him?" is the question, but it is not for Christmas only. "I give him my heart" is still the right answer—but how does it apply outside the manger?

"So, here's what I want you to do, God helping you: Take your everyday, ordinary life—your sleeping, eating, going-to-work, and walking-around life—and place it before God as an offering" (Romans 12:1, *The Message*).

Chapter 8

ON THE LAND

THE ART OF GROWING IN PLACE

The LORD God took the man and put him in the
garden of Eden to work it and keep it.

GENESIS 2:15

You look every day at the blue mountains, they're not invented things,
they're old mountains, rooted deep in the past; but they are your
companions. There you are, living together with heaven and earth, at
one with them, at one with the wide horizon and the rootedness . . . you
walk through life barehanded and bareheaded in the midst of a great
kindliness. . . . Man and nature do not bombard each other, they are
agreed; they do not compete or run a race for something, they go together.

KNUT HAMSUN, *GROWTH OF THE SOIL*

WHAT HAS LAND TO DO WITH OUR
EVERYDAY PILGRIMAGE?

*I*n the beginning, "the LORD God planted a garden in Eden, in the
east, and there he put the man whom he had formed" (Genesis 2:8).
He eventually gave him a companion, a woman to aid and abet him, and
told them to be fruitful and multiply. It is only fitting then that we too,

at the beginning of *our* ordinary time, begin with the world's oldest vocation: the charge to work and keep the land, to put down roots in a particular place and flourish.

And yet, we must ask: Why should cultivating the land and growing in place matter to twenty-first century Christians who can have food delivered to their doorstep? Why should those in Christ, who have been born again and are bound for heaven—and yes, a new earth—be concerned with this cursed earth with its thorns and thistles, mud and slime, slugs and grubs? How is land, which is by definition *earthy*, possibly relevant to spiritual pilgrims? Why should non-farmers care about farmland, particularly in an age far removed from the agrarian world of Jesus' first-century Palestine?

A KEY TERM FOR EVERYDAY SAINTS: *PATRIMOINE*

At Advent, we introduced the French term *terroir*. It refers to the particular soil that grounds a place (so to speak), and from which a particular kind of vegetation grows. But this is not the whole story, for a terroir cultivates not only plants but also people together with a way of life: culture. For instance, deserts tend to cultivate cacti and nomadic cultures. A terroir therefore yields two kinds of produce: natural and cultural. The French name for the latter is *patrimoine*.

To understand the land of the santons, we must understand patrimoine. The term refers most literally to the family estate one inherits.[1] Over the centuries, however, it has come to mean something much less tangible than property—a cultural rather than a monetary or material inheritance, as the French tradition of *les journées du Patrimoine*[2] (Cultural Heritage Days) attests. These festival days are opportunities for each region to celebrate its own local heritage—its terroir and the culture that has developed there.

Patrimoine has come to refer to what a local community cultivates and passes down from one generation to the next, a kind of cultural DNA whose transmission creates deep social bonds and communal identity. In this broader sense, patrimoine includes everything that grows out of a terroir, not only material things (e.g., grapes, red clay roof tiles [*tuiles Romaines*], *herbes de Provence*) but also what makes up the "spirit" of the place, its immaterial cultural aspects (e.g., characteristic idioms, folk songs, *pétanque* games under *platanes* trees).

In the little Rhône village of my ancestors, strains of traditional tunes from *chansons de métier*—songs that celebrate typical jobs (like harvesting grapes)—to ancient noëls waft through the streets during the festival. Local artisans set up stands that display regional crafts: oven-fired ceramics, block-printed tablecloths, and of course santons! Vendors sell olive oil soap (*savons de Marseille*), fig jams, and lavender honey. Craftsmen demonstrate ancient skills like braiding garlic or making *soupe du jour*. Local story tellers recount old tales with colorful Provençal colloquialisms. Local vintners offer rides around their vineyards in horse-drawn carriages. What is marvelous is that everything that is displayed, heard, smelled, and tasted in these streets originates from the local terroir. Its products, architecture, history, and stories of our well-loved authors grew out of this place. Nowhere else on earth do just these elements—this light of the sun, this soil, this air, these plants, this Mediterranean Sea—come together to add up to the spirit of Provence.

At the root of any patrimoine is its particular place on earth. Yet what gets passed on from one generation to the next, not just in my village but in places all over the world, is not merely soil but the *soul* that has grown there: the spirit of a place. The most important inheritance is not the physical property but the patrimoine, the distinctive character of a place, how a people have learned to inhabit, cherish, work, and enrich it over time. This is an inheritance—or better, a heritage—to remember, embody, and protect at all costs. It is the *je-ne-sais-quoi*, that indescribable something, with which tourists fall in love.

These annual patrimoine festivals are a corporate testimony to the intimate and powerful bond between a people and their terroir. For, in the final analysis, plants are not the only living things that have roots. The land of our ancestors is a balm against the modern scourges of displacement: the uprootedness common to refugees, exiles, and immigrants. The uprooted suffer all too often from disorientation, homesickness, and, at the limit, alienation. For terroir feeds body and soul. It is an interconnected ecosystem that grows a particular way of life in a particular place that we call home, for there is "no home like place."[3]

AN EVERYDAY VOCATION

The traditional crèche scene includes a farmer santon carrying produce from his field. He is but one of several little saints who come to Jesus bearing their respective gifts from the land: eggs, fruits, vegetables, and so on. One of my favorites is the little saint who brings a bunch of root vegetables in one hand and a shovel in the other, a symbol of his particular vocation: working the earth. His gift involves honest labor. The French word for farmer is *agriculteur*, from the Greek terms for "land cultivation." A farmer santon works the land in service to his landlord: "Man

L'agriculteur (the farmer)

goes out to his work / and to his labor until the evening" (Psalm 104:23).

A farmer planting roots is a good beginning for a reflection on ordinary time, for roots perform an essential life-giving function: they anchor a plant (or a person?) in place for its entire life. Plants absorb water and minerals from the soil to feed the plant through main and fine lateral roots; they store the sun's energy (through photosynthesis, as in the leaves of a root vegetable). No roots, no place, no energy, no life! A deeply rooted radish is not going anywhere.

The environmental journalist George Monbiot writes: "The soil might be the most complex of all living system, yet we treat it like dirt."[4] Not so the agriculteur saint! His shovel is a potent symbol of his awareness that what he has under his feet is not simply dirt, to dispose

A radish with its roots

of as he wishes. It is rather the *dust from the ground* and *soil* that he cultivates from which all life springs. The earth is precious: an inheritance! The term *earth* is the *mot juste* for the everyday saint to speak of soil because what farmers have under their feet is a gift: not just soil, but planet *Earth*, the particular *place* in the vastness of space that God not only created but declared very good, then entrusted to human

WEEK 1 ∽ *Pause*

"The earth is the LORD's and the fullness thereof." PSALM 24:1

❧ At the beginning of time, God put man in a garden. At the beginning of the Christian year, God came to be with us in our terroir. At Pentecost, the Spirit of God descended onto the disciples so that they could extend Christ's body to the ends of the earth. Are you able to see how the good news of new life in Christ continues to spread, and that wherever God's people happen to be is now that place where the Lord cultivates his own produce, his own culture?

❧ How might we express our discipleship to Christ, the one who spoke the world and everything in it into being, by the way we relate to our land? Adam means "earthy," but have you ever considered how your own humanity is intimately connected to the earth, to your locale, and to its land? Do you believe that God's redemptive presence and activity extends to the land, as the essence of lavender permeates all of life?

❧ If you were to write about your locale as I have mine, do you know what you would include? What plants, ethnobotanical observations, or other cultural aspects would you want to feature? Have any authors written stories about your place? Do you know your local history? If you were to offer a welcome basket to a newcomer with products of your land, what would you put in the basket? How might it help them plant new roots?

farmers. For our farmer-saint, working the earth is not primarily a money-making endeavor, but a God-given vocation—not an "agri-business" but an "agri-culture."[5]

By cultivating the land, an everyday saint *roots* himself and others in the local terroir. Farmers provide the necessary conditions for a community to live in place. They prepare the ground for others to contribute something meaningful: a gift that, together with all the other neighbors' gifts, grows into their common patrimoine. As those on an Advent walk root the baby Jesus in the land by gathering native herbs to decorate the crèche, so the agriculteur, in ordinary time, roots the Lord Jesus Christ in his land by working the soil to his glory.

Before there can be a crèche, or a village, there must be a terroir. Terroir, from *terre*, the French word for "earth," reminds us that at the very beginning God formed humanity out of the earth, the *adamah* (Heb. for "earth" and the name given Adam). God both takes us from the earth and then roots us back into it, forging an integral (and reciprocal) bond between Adam and *adamah*, between the humans that work the land and the land that supports them. It is fitting (and perhaps poetic) that the farmer santon himself (like santon-kind in general) comes from the earth of his terroir: the red clay of Provence. Everyday saints are no different. I agree with Alan Sell when he says, "One cannot be a 'Christian in general': Christians are earthed saints."[6] Each one of us has a native biome; a place to keep, cultivate, enrich, and pass down to the next generation; a place that organisms, including humans, call home.

LAND CULTIVATION IN PROVENÇAL CULTURE

In his novel *Regain*, Provençal author Jean Giono tells the story of a village abandoned by a people in search of better opportunities elsewhere. After the people leave, their former home suffers a slow death: the untended fields become weeds, the houses begin to fall apart. One inhabitant alone remains behind, steadfast to his roots. He scavenges for food and struggles to make sense of what is happening, eventually concluding that in order to make a fresh start he needs (like Adam before him) a companion and helper—in short, a wife—so that, together, they might reclaim the land and make a meaningful life. Eventually, his new Eve appears. The farmer then has another vision: he sees "a loaf of bread, large and solid, bread from the fields, bread from flour crushed on a marble mortar . . . the bread *they* will make with their own hands, the three of them: him, [his wife] Arsule, *and the earth*."[7]

The farmer, now reenergized by this sign, chooses a well-situated plot of land and starts the long and arduous cultivation. After a year's labor, he harvests wheat the likes of which people in nearby markets have never seen. News of the newly revived field soon spreads, and outsiders "regain" faith in the formerly deserted place.[8] A family shows up and moves into an empty skeletal house. They open doors and un-latch shutters, reawakening the forsaken structure. The title, *Regain*, leaves the reader to understand that more will come. For where there is wheat a baker will soon follow, and where there is a baker, there is again the possibility of a village and all that comes with village life: villagers haggling with shopkeepers, women singing at the *lavoir*, children playing in the streets . . . and who knows, a church tower with its bells tolling the hours? Place lost, place regained: a born-again patrimoine that started with one man's good and honest work on a patch of earth. In the end, the roots that an agriculteur plants transcend the crops he grows. As the American essayist Charles Dudley Warner said: "It is not simply potatoes and beets and corn and cucumbers that one raises in his well-hoed garden; it is the average of human life."[9]

The striking poetry of the opening chapter of Genesis depicts God creating order, not out of a deserted village, but out of the empty and formless (Genesis 1:2). He created water, earth, and sky and brought forth vegetation, seed-bearing plants, and fruit trees bearing fruit (each according to its kind). And then God created day and night and, even-tually, *seasons*. The music of creation has rhythm too. *And God saw that it was good.* God created humanity, male and female, taken from the good soil, after which he saw that it was *very* good. God gives them the land to keep and work. And then a final gift: God walks and talks with them in the garden in the cool of the day (Genesis 3:8). The earth is the staging area where land, humanity, and God meet and interact. It is a place for patrimoine. Indeed, God charges these creatures in his image to be fruitful and multiply, to cultivate, and so develop a culture out of Eden, a place to steward, and rule, in God's place.

Sadly, the first garden with its provisions and delights was soon lost—tragically abandoned. Fateful human choices transformed what had been a divine symphony into a miserable cacophony. Adam and Eve disobeyed the composer, broke the harmony of fellowship, distorted the melody of creation, and lost the rhythm of the seasons. Their descendants inherited not the Edenic patrimoine that was their birthright but, rather, a creation in disorder. Indeed, the *repeated* loss of the land in which they were to fellowship with God becomes a leitmotif throughout Scripture, with

WEEK 2 ∞ *Ponder*

"Stewardship of creation begins by seeing our place in the order of things as helpers so that God can keep saying, 'It is very good.'"[10]

- Many people in the modern world experience a sense of displacement. Might this feeling be due to our collective forgetfulness of the intimate link God created between people and place? If so, might caring for our places as though they were God's garden repair the missing link and give us new roots?

- Doctors and nurses heal our broken or ailing earthed bodies. What about the places in which we live? Should everyday saints be nurses of God's earth?

- Do you think that God's charge to Adam and Eve to work and keep the earth applies to farmers only? Might it be that everyday saints, no matter how green their thumbs, are called to be cultivators of their place, using regenerative practices of cultivation for all the places they inhabit? Could place-making affect not only the land but the people who inhabit it?

each loss of land—Eden, Israel (the northern kingdom), Judah (the southern kingdom)—signaling estrangement from God. This is why at the end of the Old Testament, there is no patrimoine to celebrate.

God's promise of land to be an "everlasting possession" (Genesis 17:8), a *heritage* that would last forever, was nevertheless not forgotten. Rather, like a seed, it was biding its time: waiting for the right season. For Jesus was that seed of Abraham and David, a seed that God planted in Mary: "There shall come forth a shoot from the stump of Jesse, / and a branch from his *roots* shall bear fruit" (Isaiah 11:1 emphasis added). Jesus came to the Holy Land. But the land in Ordinary Time is a holy place too, for the Spirit of God continues to hover and blow the energy of a creation new in Christ through his everyday saints.

MY OWN PILGRIMAGE

My own roots run deep. I am French on both sides with a lineage stretching all the way back to the Celts, including traces of Huguenot blood for good measure. No wonder I so easily identified with Abraham the first time that I, like him, responded to God's call ("Go from your country" [Genesis 12:1]) and left my beloved Provence. And whenever I return for visits, I realize I no longer truly belong. The land has moved on, so to speak. Though I was not forced to uproot, as many today are, I am nonetheless a displaced person. Homesickness is the common fare of my bleak midwinters. I am a transplant.

One does not have to be a French expat to notice ways that contemporary culture seems to be out of rhythm, existentially off-beat, a result of technology's triumph over natural seasons as evidenced by the year-round abundance of produce at the supermarket. In pondering my own feelings of displacement, I realized that our modern age has lost meaningful connection with the changing seasons (time), making it hard to make any natural connection to my particular location (place). Resident alien, indeed: displaced, disoriented, and disturbed. As I pondered these things over the years, I have come to see that the world, like music, has rhythms of nature, the church year, and life itself. Fair enough. But how could I, a transplant, establish roots in a new Midwestern terroir?

"Speak to the earth, and it will teach you" (Job 12:8 NIV). I did, and it has. I agree with Rachel Peden: "It has taught me a great deal, has given me more questions than answers, and I have learned to listen as well as to speak to it."[11] I, too, decided to dig in and get my hands dirty in order to find the roots of my new place, perchance to grow food in season. What the earth spoke to me was that I inhabit a woodland with its own ecosystem, not a Mediterranean vegetable plot, and there's no use pretending otherwise. It was a major life lesson: accept the terroir in which you are planted—and if need be, keep moving your pot of tomatoes several times each day to catch the sun's rays filtering through the broad canopy of ancient oaks and hickories.

My search for roots finally led me to farmland through a CSA (Community Supported Agriculture) farmer up the road.[12] Aptly named Radical Root, its mission statement is: "Our small family farm adheres to practices that have the health of our land and our neighbors in mind. The respectful approach to farming that's practiced means that our land and environment will be safe for many generations to come."[13] Yes! Here were local agriculteurs who understood and valued their terroir. Here were the beginnings of the patrimoine for which I had been longing, right in my backyard. Sign me up!

Collection day quickly became the high point of my week, but the excitement extends further than the booty of fruits, eggs, and vegetables I set out on the kitchen counter. Collecting my weekly box of produce connects me to a real plot of land, a local community, my CSA farmer, and other regulars at the farm. And at the weekly farmers' market I sample honey, sniff goat-milk soaps, and ogle local products like basil focaccia. Stand-keepers and shoppers come to recognize one another and know each other's names. We start to exchange pleasantries, recipes, stories, and homemade goods. Together, we're growing a local ethnobotanical culture that has revived a world I could only faintly remember when, as a child, we would wait for local fruit trees to come to fruition at the ripe time, in line with the gentle rhythm of the passing seasons. Blessed are the place makers!

I now belong here. I have a place and a role to play in growing my local community. And if this is true of my village, how much more is it true of my local church, which is also a place where something is grown and cultivated, and where seasons are closely observed, anticipated, and celebrated, turning what might otherwise be a nondescript suburban space into a place for people to grow crops and communities alike, to the glory of God.

God moved me from the place I knew so well, but the land he settled me in has unexpected splendors. Isak Dinesen, another transplant, opens her book *Out of Africa* with a famously beautiful recollection of her adopted home, beginning simply, "I had a farm in Africa." I playfully paraphrase her words to speak of my own new home:

> I have a farmer in America, at the edge of a great lake and the threshold of the vast prairies of the Midwest. The geographical position, and the flatlands with their silty clay loam, combine to create a terroir that has not its like in all the world. This land, and its farms, yield roots in bleak midwinter, cleansing veggies in springtime, apricots and peaches that taste like my childhood summers, squashes that reflect the copper brilliance of an autumn skyline . . . and I wake in the morning amongst ancient white oaks and shagbark hickories, and I think: Here I am, where I ought to be.[14]

We have a steppingstone in our woodland garden with etched-on words: "You are here." Indeed. I have established new roots in a new place to which God has called me and, most importantly, where God is present. "*You are here.*" For Christians, there is a deeper meaning in this stone. It reminds me that my deepest roots, the roots of my real existence, are in Christ, and these roots grow in him even as they grow him in this place. For every square inch is part of his domain. My place—house, woodlands, farmland, market, and local church—has become a stage for everyday discipleship, lived out in ordinary time, an easel on which to practice the art of living in season, a way of making ordinary time a "little Advent."

THE ART OF EATING IN SEASON

A farmer-saint is a living almanac, a seasonal liturgist of sorts, a phenologist or student of seasonal appearances whose life beats to the rhythm of the equinoxes in a place entrusted by God. To observe the farmer-saint is to remember there is a time to work the fields and a time to let them rest, a time to glean for food pantries and a time to gather at the table. Culinary offerings vary with the seasons, keeping pace with the changing hues that unfold outside kitchen windows, a sign that we are rooted, through our food, in the fields and seasons of the good earth where God emplots us.

The roots of the land extend even to the indoor table. Roots are the source of all the edible bits of the plants in the kitchen garden, from stems (celery), to leaves (lettuce), to buds (Brussels sprouts), to flowers (cauliflower), and finally fruit (seed-bearing parts). Many roots are vegetables themselves. The marvelous thing is that the supply is always available, as foods in this group are naturally protected underground and able to survive for months in root cellars. They are the only reliable *all-season* source of fresh nourishment, which makes

WEEK 3 ∾ *Pray*

"Creator God, teach me how to understand my place within this cycle of life that I am so privileged to be part of. Teach me to walk slower in the hopes of knowing and caring more deeply for this piece of your good earth that has been entrusted to me.[15]

"Thank you for having created a place of mutual flourishing for plants, people, and the Prince of Peace—a patrimoine complete with all the rights and privileges appertaining to its citizens: rhythms, customs, and celebrations (Leviticus 23:2), a terroir in which shalom would put down roots.

"Show me how to root you here, right where you have planted me and want me to grow and grow you in the center of a holy patrimoine. Help me to remember that my vocation is not to save the earth, but to bear witness to its root in you and your creative word."

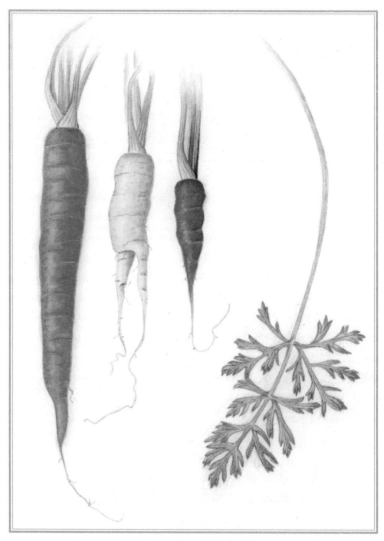

Humble, faithful carrots

them a precious provision of nutrients, essential for all human life, right under our feet![16]

Root vegetables do not always get the respect they deserve. As Barbara Kingsolver explains: "Every crop yields a significant proportion of perfectly edible but small or oddly shaped vegetables that are 'trash' by market standards."[17] The roots' humble origins—everyday soil—and unremarkable appearance (see my carrot illustration) rightly remind us of everyday saints who, like root vegetables, may not be picture-perfect but nevertheless have something valuable to offer.

Everyday saints are taproots, planted deep in the special seasons of the life-giving Christ, branches abiding in the Vine (John 15:4) who do marvelous things through him who strengthens them (Philippians 4:13).

WHAT'S AN EVERYDAY SAINT TO DO?

In the village of my ancestors during our annual cultural heritage festival, people dress up in traditional clothes, sewn for the occasion, from the very same period as the santons, becoming for all intents and purposes large-as-life santons for the day (though *sans* crèche): everyday saints, for real!

The farmer santon is a poignant reminder that each of us belongs to some place. Whether we are just passing through or have had roots for generations, everything we are and do, with shovels or anything else, ultimately depends on the land whence we were created and where we now live and move and have our bodily being. Wendell Berry helps us appreciate that all land is under God: "I saw how beautiful the field was, how beautiful our work was. And it came to me all in a feeling how everything fitted together, the place and ourselves and the animals and the tools, and how the sky held us."[18]

The Bible is all about growth: growth of fields and crops, but also growth in the knowledge of God. The privilege and responsibility of the disciple is to be a blessed placemaker—and to help others grow in their place to be placemakers too. Wherever and whatever my habitat may be, it is part of the Lord's earth and the fullness thereof. A *terroir*, then, is ultimately not just an inheritance, but a vocation—a heritage, to take up and pass on, enriched, to the next generation.

How is a pilgrim to grow in place? Those who follow Jesus through ordinary time are both rooted and in motion. Christ, their Root, travels with them throughout their ordinary time, just as the Rock (who was also Christ) accompanied Israel on her pilgrimage (1 Corinthians 10:4). There is no contradiction between planting roots and being pilgrims. Everyday saints are "sojourners and exiles" (1 Peter 2:11) who grow eternal roots in their *terroir* even as they continue on to a better unseen land ahead. In the meantime, everyday saints remain earthed, growing where they have been planted, or transplanted, and in turn planting gardens, eating their produce, always seeking the welfare of the city, not least by caring for its land (see also Jeremiah 29:5-7).

WEEK 4 ∾ *Play Your Part*

The Reformers believed in the two books by which we can see God: the book of Scripture and the book of nature. We have steeped ourselves in the former during our special seasons. Now, as we start our journey in Ordinary Time, we explore our intricate connection to the second book: creation, with special attention to the good earth. How can we attend to this book too, even as we continue to follow Scripture?

Here are a few ideas to ponder, discuss, and perhaps embody—ways to grow in place.

- Those who know how to cultivate responsibly can do so in their own gardens or reclaim empty city lots to display the goodness and beauty of the Lord's creation. Some churches have started hobby gardens. What a wonderful way to reenact biblical stories and parables, to contribute to the church's calling to root Christ in our land!

- Find simple ways of displaying a healthy relationship to the land by avoiding pollution. What daily habits could you adopt in order to be part of the solution rather than the problem of unnecessary

land waste (and wasteland)? Can your church find alternatives to
Styrofoam for church fellowship times? If you do, the land will
rise up and call you blessed! (Research the creation care organi-
zation A Rocha, https://arocha.org, for more ideas).

- Do you know your church's unique history, its characteristics,
  and how it is linked to its terroir, the earth and the people group
  in your locale? Are you aware that local churches have patri-
  moines too, a particular identity that makes it a place to call
  home? Might such local knowledge help your local church to
  better grow in place?

- In World War II, Americans and their allies grew victory gardens
  on private property and in public parks to help with the war
  effort when food became scarce. They fed millions of people all
  over the world. Might the agriculteur little saint, with his shovel,
  inspire everyday saints to grow healthy roots and fill the land
  with victory gardens for the Lord? The earth is the Lord's, a
  canvas for the art of living in season and growing in place.

Chapter 9

AT THE TABLE

THE ART OF *RESTAURATION*

Why do you spend your money for that which is not bread,
and your labor for that which does not satisfy?
Listen diligently to me, and eat what is good,
and delight yourselves in rich food.

ISAIAH 55:2

Inspired by Jesus Christ, and empowered by the Holy Spirit,
we have the opportunity to turn our homes into places of
hospitality and ourselves into nurture for others.

NORMAN WIRZBA, *FOOD AND FAITH*

WHAT DOES THE TABLE HAVE TO DO
WITH OUR EVERYDAY PILGRIMAGE?

A number of the santons around the manger come to Jesus with offerings of food. Some bring fresh produce from their land, others present foods from their terroir that have been cooked (e.g., *soupe du jour*), baked (e.g., *fougasse*), or processed (e.g., *saucisson*). Farmers and gardeners work together with chefs, all of them supported by the land that makes common life possible. We do not live in just any place, we are here. Each place is a providential arrangement, for God made "plants for man to cultivate," millers who grind corn and wheat into flour, and bakers who use flour for "bread to strengthen man's heart" (Psalm 104:14-15). The expression *farm to table* well captures Wendell Berry's adage: "eating is an agricultural act."[1] So are cooking and baking.

Many today live disconnected from both farming and food processing, with eating as a non-agricultural act. Consumers often do not know where their food comes from, an ignorance that creates a missing link between table and terroir—*not* from farm to table but from-who-knows-where-to-supermarket-to-table. Those who want to eat whatever they want whenever they want choose displacement, uproot themselves from the land, content themselves with out-of-season displaced produce, and inadvertently alienate themselves from their local place—a phenomenon we might call *harm-to-table*, both because it fails to support local agriculture and because it leaves a much larger carbon footprint.[2]

If sin involves not only disobeying God but also failing to respect his created order, is it wrong to eat apricots from Chile in January? Might the sin of gluttony involve not just overeating but other disordered—unreasonable and unseasonable—demands on the table, such as insisting that every food be available all the time? Add to that other distortions of the created order, such as toxins in food that scientists suspect may contribute to infertility.[3] If our table harms us, how are we to be fruitful and multiply? How are we to be *restaured*?

A KEY TERM FOR EVERYDAY SAINTS:
LA RESTAURATION

In the land of my ancestors, the term *restauration* can refer either to the restaurant business or to a process of restoration and renewal (the English word *restoration* comes from this same Latin root, passed through French).[4]

Legend has it that the origin of the restaurant dates to pre-revolutionary days in France when the people relieved their hunger due to the scarcity of food by buying broth from street peddlers. These vendors cried out about their wares, *Un bouillon qui restaure* (a broth that restores). Broth was able to sustain them, even when there was precious little to go with it, hence the idiom *long comme un jour sans pain* (as long as a day without bread), still used today when the French are faced with a discouraging wait. This was the context of Marie Antoinette's infamously tone-deaf supposed suggestion: "If they lack bread, let them eat cake."

Broth is indeed sustaining. Standard soup-making ingredients—everything from simple leftovers bones to withered vegetables, herbs, and seasonings—become a sort of magic potion when simmered together for several hours (chicken broth is still a go-to medicine for

WEEK 1 ☞ *Pause*

We see the beginning of the relationship between land and table early in the creation narrative.

"Out of the ground the LORD God made to spring up every tree that is pleasant to the sight and good for food" (Genesis 2:9).

🌿 What does "good for food" mean? Food is, of course, good for us. It is especially good when it comes out of the local ground to provide nutrition for bodies, themselves created from the earth.

🌿 Think about your grocery shopping trips. What are your priorities? Price? Calories? Freshness? The latest food trend? Country of origin? What does this say about your view of what is good for food? Pay attention each time you serve or eat food this week. How often in this process do you pause and consider what is good for food? What is restaurative?

🌿 Think about the connection between culture and agriculture. How does the way we treat the relationship between land and table, between our place and our eating habits, give rise to certain culture-forming values and practices? Are you able to see it as a restaurative practice, and thus a way of loving your neighbor as yourself?

colds), a brew that few supplemental pills can equal. According to French lore, streets broths became so popular that some enterprising individuals opened establishments where one could sip a bowl of broth while sitting down. These modest facilities were soon called *maisons de santé* (health houses). The trend caught on. Today, we know them as *restaurants*: a place to be restored.

Despite its humility, soup remains a daily staple for my compatriots. It is eaten at *le souper* (suppertime), traditionally the culinary finale of the day for a French wife and mother, who afterward can relax with satisfaction knowing that her brood has now absorbed its daily dose of vitamins. In fact, "*Mange ta soupe!*" ("Eat your soup!") is equivalent to "eat your greens" in other Western cultures, and fittingly so, for the *soupe* is often puréed seasonal vegetables. Feeding one's family is traditionally an important household duty: to *restaure* the family at the table. The *soupe du jour* (soup of the day) is a restoring potion—call it *restaurative*—taken in season from the land. This is the art of living in season, at a table, boiled down to a bowl of soup!

AN EVERYDAY VOCATION

Our santon representing restauration at table is the woman with soup who brings restorative broth to the holy family, presumably after a long day at the stove. She would have started with readily available ingredients, peeling, chopping, stirring, and finally puréeing—a time-consuming operation. Yet this was a quotidian practice so she was ready for the unexpected midnight guest.

I like to think that *la femme à la soupe* brings the quintessential

*La femme à la soupe
(the woman with soup)*

Parsley and thyme

summer soup of Provence, *la soupe au pistou,* itself part and parcel of her patrimoine. This soup calls for a wide selection of chopped summer vegetables, and basil—all things that God has appointed to grow in the local soil. What she gives is not just soup but all that she has available to give. For even in ordinary time, the burning question for everyday saints remains: "What can I give him?" In the case of *la femme à la soupe,* what she gives with her soup is her land and her heart.

As local farmers know, one of the benefits of eating seasonally, in sync with harvest time, is that your body gets what it needs during each season. Eating produce that is local, and therefore fresh, also provides optimal nutrients and vitamins, far more than food shipped from further fields.[5] This simply confirms what the food-bearing santon already knows: that the land in which God plants us is normally sufficient for our daily needs if we pay attention to the effect of the seasons on our place. Restauration begins with this intimate relationship between God, land, and kitchen—a localized health regimen orchestrated by our Creator. The humble task of making soup ends up being a crucial ingredient in an extraordinary economy.

La soupe au pistou is a summer dish, but there are more seasonal tricks in our cooks' kettles. The go-to soup for a Christmas night (and indeed all season) is without a doubt the *soupe de légumes* (vegetable soup). It's made up of onions and leeks (sadly much neglected these days), carrots and potatoes, a branch of celery, and the ever-present *bouquet garni* consisting of a sprig of thyme from the hills, parsley from the garden, and bay leaf from a neighbor's tree—disparate plants making a happy culinary marriage together. This is a simple, sure-fire recipe because it uses only vegetables that are always available in that corner of the world. A Provençal cook in touch with the land of her ancestors knows to add whatever happens to be growing in her garden in any season—*un peu de tout* (a bit of everything). To add whatever happens to be available makes for menus that are both the same and different, varying naturally in taste and hue according to the seasons. The *soupe de légumes* is an ever-changing exhibit of the art of living in season.

RESTAURATION IN PROVENÇAL CULTURE

The farmer in Jean Giono's novel *Regain* partners well with our seasonal santon, for farm and table are inseparable. In the story, a visitor has walked the field with the farmer and examined the soil, crumbling it between his fingers and smelling it. The farmer then invites the visitor to share his lunch table of bread and soup. The guest takes a spoonful of soup with its vegetables and herbs from the land, and the narrator tells us: "It seemed to him as if his tongue were kneading the very hills with all their flowers . . . the man was intoxicated on the inside with good soup, and just as intoxicated by the beautiful landscape outdoors."[6] At the table, the guest sees that the land is very good. He returns the next day with his wife and an armload of children.

The land with its wheat allied with the table and its soup set in motion a local restauration. It takes a village, yes—but it takes a soup tureen, well-cultivated land, and neighbors sitting at a table to *make* a village. The farmer restored the land, but it was his wife who restored the farmer and the home by working the table as her husband worked the land. The marriage of land and table, and the hospitality that accompanies it, is at the heart of a healthy patrimoine. Hospitality is, in

WEEK 2 ∞ *Ponder*

"Arise and eat, for the journey is too great for you." 1 KINGS 19:7

There are many stories about restauration in Scripture. For example, when the prophet Elijah hid in the desert scared, exhausted, and discouraged from being relentlessly hunted down by Jezebel, he fell asleep under a broom tree where "he asked that he might die." Instead, an angel of the Lord woke him, presented him with a freshly baked cake to eat and water to drink, and said these important words: "Arise and eat, for the journey is too great for you" (1 Kings 19:4, 7).

- Did you notice God's use of food to restore Elijah's spirits? What if through your ministry of food you could help restore the spirits of everyday saints on their way? The Lord "prepares a table" and "restores our souls" (Psalm 23:3, 5); we can too.

- Food is a theme that figures prominently in the Bible from the abundant Garden of Eden, through a land of milk and honey and the fellowship of bread and wine, to the marriage supper of the Lamb. Surely this means that God cares about the needs of our physical bodies. What if in the same way we are stewards of the land we are also meant to be stewards of our bodies?

fact, at the very core of restauration. The root of the word is the same as that of *hospice* and *hospital*: a place for taking care and making whole. Giono has painted a small picture of a restaurative economy with his novel. As one commentator puts it, the restauration Giono writes about is "not only an economic activity with profit in mind . . . it's a work that fits in a greater plan, that of inscribing human activity in the order of the universe."[7]

MY OWN PILGRIMAGE

I was raised on a Mediterranean diet before it became fashionable, with a tacit dare-to-be-a-Martha expectation thrust upon me by the example of a mother who began thinking (usually out loud) about her menu for the next meal of the day as soon as the previous one was over. Childhood summers meant going barefoot in the garden, with Maman harvesting runner beans, eggplants, peppers, and tomatoes while I spied late-blushing strawberries emerging from behind their leaves—a pre-breakfast appetizer. There was a happy marriage of kitchen and garden thanks to the wide-open doors of those summer months. Garden produce invaded Maman's kitchen as scents from the cuisine wafted back out into Papa's garden: a two-way communication characteristic of all good relationships.

With her pots and pans, Maman performed what looked like one miracle after another, transforming raw vegetables and herbs into simple but sumptuous meals. The table communion we experienced through her culinary ministry restored us deeply. I learned from experience that the Mediterranean diet is less about eating foods from that blessed basin than it is about living in harmony with the rhythm of the land and its seasons.

When I moved away from home, I lost sight for a time of this reciprocity between land and table. I experienced culture shock in America for the first time at the beginning of the school year when I learned that my husband would leave the house in the morning with a sandwich and would not return until the evening. What?! No sitting down together at

A summer runner bean

home for a two-hour lunch? If we did not take our time to converse with fellow pilgrims over an intentionally prepared balanced meal, how were we to be restaured?

Apparently, we were to eat on the go in order to save time. In an effort to fit in with my new land, I tried it and it worked: I had more time, yes, but for what? To engage in more activities that kept me so busy that I now had no time to cook or eat, at least not properly? Nevertheless, I duly exchanged

Martha's apron for Mary's bookshelf for a few years and worked on the art of packing a sack lunch (a task for which I remain genetically indisposed)—until I had children, at which time, wanting to feed them restauratively, I remembered my roots, my santons, and the woman with soup.

I also discovered an ancient noël about what some villagers do after hearing the good news of the Christ child.[8] They confer, wonder what to do, conclude that God is telling them to find the baby Jesus and then prepare for their pilgrimage. They fill their bags with victuals for the journey that lay ahead. This noël planted the seed for the present chapter inasmuch as it painted a striking picture of little saints preparing to leave the manger as pilgrims to follow Christ, and to restaure themselves on their Christian way. I still sing this noël even now as I peel my farmer's beets and wash his radishes, as I paint a tomato plant.

Our kitchen is once again a place not to escape from as quickly as possible but a place to contribute to restauration for our pilgrimage.

WEEK 3 ~ *Pray*

"O God, who calls those who will to follow along with you, show us our duty today, and give us bread for our journey. Through Jesus Christ. Amen."[9]

"Lord, I may be neither professional chef nor nutritionist, yet I would like to do my part in your restauration project.

"Help me to have eyes to see all those to whom I might exercise the ministry of restauration at the table whether they are part of my household or guests passing through. Help me to have eyes to see those who lack access to a restauration table and enable me to do unto these others as I would certainly want to do unto you. I pray that churches worldwide would consider expanding their own ministries of restauration, even to the point of opening soup kitchens for the homeless.

"Show me other ways as well that I can serve you through the daily work of restauration with food or otherwise."

The family table meanwhile is the perfect place to come and find sabbath rest. It remains the center of the house, the gathering place of restauration, conversation, and prayer. Is this what the woman with the soup is doing in the crèche? If so, let me be that santon!

THE ART OF EATING IN SEASON

If the farmer-saint is a seasonal liturgist, the little saint with her soup kettle is a liturgist of the everyday. She sets a rhythm of rest and restauration to which her household marches, a time to eat and a time not to eat. French author Mireille Guiliano writes of these liturgies: "There are . . . rituals of everyday life by which a civilization defines itself, like *le pain quotidien*, our daily bread. . . . These rituals are a frame of reference as well as a source of comfort and reassurance . . . key to our well-being, part of our cultural programming about what is right and good."[10]

Each restaurative meal combines agriculture and human culture—farm and table—in a symbiotic relationship, bringing together botanic and domestic cultures in a perfect marriage (ethnobotany) that results in blessing—restoration—from the land for the people that work it in all seasons. What happens at such tables helps guests recognize the goodness of God in his seasonal provisions. It is therefore fitting to say grace for these table graces.

The fittingness of land and table is on display in ordinary time in more extraordinary ways still. Apparently, some plants that complement one another in our plates at the table also do better when planted together in the land.[11] Consider the odd couple of tomato and basil: interspersing basil amid your rows of tomatoes mysteriously renders both stronger and healthier. And when the two are freshly picked and mixed in your summer cuisine—sliced tomatoes, chopped basil leaves, sprinkled with vinaigrette, with or without crumbled cheese—the result is a full-blown restauration experience! This is but one example of an amazing correspondence of what is good for agriculture being good for human culture too. It is as if the whole farm to table process is a parable on the wonders of terroir and patrimoine.

Cherry tomatoes and fresh basil

Sitting down for a good meal is a blessing in more ways still. After all the dishes appear and guests finally sit, there is a moment to look around, smell and see, and give thanks—something that does not happen when we eat on the run. "Companionship" (breaking bread together) is another blessing. The table is a place not simply to fuel up but to fellowship: to see one other, to share gifts, to trade stories, and in general to build one another up through conversation, egged on by the food that itself builds us up, restoring body and spirit. In Norman Wirzba's words:

> Eating together should be an occasion in which people learn to become more attentive and present to the world and each other. Because eating is something we regularly do, it can be the training ground where people . . . can practice the skills of conversation, reflection, and gratitude that contribute to a more completely human life.[12]

And it all started with an everyday saint's soup tureen!

WHAT'S AN EVERYDAY SAINT TO DO?

Everyday saints are called to participate in restauring their world not by bread alone but by every word that comes out of the mouth that is a

WEEK 4 ⌇ *Play Your Part*

"In certain primitive cultures, the doctor and the priest are one and the same person."[13]

Taking a page from Provençal culture, we might be inclined to say the little saint with her soup is this same person.

Here are some opportunities to practice being an everyday saint during table times.

- Anthropologists say that culture begins with the transition from eating food raw to cooking it. Ask yourself: What kind of culture are we passing on to our children? Do they know what foods are restaurative and why? Do our everyday eating practices communicate how we relate to the land God separated from water and declared good? If not, are you able to suggest or make changes, even minor ones, in your place?

- Practice hospitality at home with your own family. Dining rooms have traditionally been places of physical and social restauration, minister of Christ, who abides in them and in whom they abide. The Lord is our chef; we shall not want. Whether human sous chefs grow produce or sell prepared food, whether they cook or eat, whether they serve a cup of soup or tea, they do it all for the glory of Christ their Lord. What they do at their tables witnesses to what local churches do at *their* tables, breaking bread in remembrance of the one in whom they live and grow and have their well-being. Everyday saints find meaning in everyday life by participating in these ways in the church's witness to the restoration of all things in Christ (1 Peter 5:10).

All Christians are in the restauration business wherever two or three are gathered in Christ's name. Consider again the celebrated union of basil and tomato that like Jews and Gentiles came from different places and once had nothing to do with one another. But Christ, at his table, creates "one new man in place of the two, so making peace" (Ephesians

but the pressures of modern life make carving out time for a family meal quite challenging. Try to make time nevertheless if not daily, then perhaps every other day. Restauring at table may well be the most important countercultural Christian thing you do on a regular basis.

- Organize a potluck meal. Ask each person to bring a contribution made from local ingredients. Ask your guests to share a story of being restaured through food and table fellowship (I have many). Ask what it was that made it restaurative, and whether this kind of table service should be a regular part of the Christian art of restauration.
- Is your church in a position to restaure the needy through food? If so, can you help?

As the French say at suppertime, *"À table!"* ("To the table!") As we can now say, "To the health house, to be restaured!"

2:15). This is the radical restauration in which everyday saints are privileged to take part.

Whenever possible, an everyday cook should be intentional about what goes into her soup. But should we be making efforts to be more like Martha or Mary? Should we take time to prepare something from scratch, fresh from the fields, or buy something ready-made from the store? Is it more important to save time for some other activity, or could growing and preparing our own food still be a responsible use of time? There is probably no one right answer for everyone, everywhere, in every season, although I like to think that Martha could have invited Jesus into her kitchen to converse with him while she cooked, as Brother Lawrence did. The table is more than a piece of furniture. It is the center of the kitchen, traditionally the center of the house, its hearth and heart. It is a place to taste and see that food is good, a stage for culinary performances, a place to glorify God through cuisine.[14] The kitchens of everyday saints should be restaurants—health houses—for pilgrims on the way.

Chapter 10

ROUND THE GARDEN

THE ART OF BEAUTIFYING

And the LORD God planted a garden in Eden.

GENESIS 2:8

*The flowers appear on the earth, / the time of singing has
come, / and the voice of the turtledove / is heard in our land.*

SONG OF SONGS 2:12

*Wherever you cast your eyes, there is no spot in the universe
wherein you cannot discern at least some sparks of God's glory.*

JOHN CALVIN, *INSTITUTES OF THE CHRISTIAN RELIGION*

*The ripening field, motionless in sunlight, seems the very symbol
of peace . . . underlined by a surge of joy, a reverence in which the
whole conviction of creation for a purpose is indelibly coded.*

RACHEL PEDEN, *SPEAK TO THE EARTH*

WHAT HAVE FLOWER GARDENS TO DO
WITH OUR EVERYDAY PILGRIMAGE?

*I*n the beginning, God made to spring up every tree that is *"pleasant to
the sight* and good for food" (Genesis 2:9 emphasis mine). Gardens
give us more than salad and fruit for lunch or dinner. A garden is a place

of delight with trees pleasant to the sight and flowers that appeal to all the senses. Without blossoms, trees could not produce fruit. Yet many non-fruit bearing trees, like the magnolia, blossom for no apparent reason other than to become a passion for avid gardeners, or muses for poets who roam the countryside in search of aesthetic inspiration, or stimulation to artists who bring the botanical world to life on canvases that adorn the walls of homes. The question persists: Why are there flowers rather than nothing? Why do flowers matter if we do not need them in order to exist? And why is there a santon whose gift to Jesus is a spray of flowers?

A KEY TERM FOR EVERYDAY SAINTS:
JOINDRE L'UTILE À L'AGRÉABLE

"To join the useful to the agreeable" is a well-known idiom in the land of my ancestors. France is known for its artists, many of whom have gained world renown, yet the proverbial *art de vivre* (art of living) is an everyday affair practiced by everyday people. It describes a certain

WEEK 1 ⌦ *Pause*

"And lilies did not seem to me overdressed, but it was easy for me to believe that Solomon in all his glory was not arrayed like a great yellow marigold, or even the dear little single ones that were yellow and brown, and bloomed until the snow came."[1]

- Can you think of flowers you find particularly beautiful? Have a daily walk around your garden, neighborhood, or public park. Stop and examine one flower attentively. Take note of each blossom's particular shape, count its petals, look at the shape of its leaves, find its name, and—why not?—try to sketch it. Can you do this once a day this week? Thank God who created flowers not as distractions but as balms to your soul.
- Can you re-write the sentence above ("And lilies did not seem . . .") for yourself? Can you see a flower as part of the

flair that beautifies the everyday and is arguably as vital as breathing. It all starts with taking time and paying attention, with savoring the *je-ne-sais-quoi* flavor of the present moment.

While our painters adorn the indoor walls of our homes with outdoor beauty, artisans are artists in their own rights, embellishing every corner of our dwelling places, beautifying everyday objects with botanical themes and motifs that they carve on musical instruments, etch on glasses, print on material, delicately embroider on napkins and dish towels—even on handkerchiefs used for the meanest of purposes (*à tes souhaits, Gesundheit!*). This too is ethnobotany.

The artist-journalist Bérengère Desmettre was so moved as a child by the description of an embroidered handkerchief in *The Three Musketeers* that she has been collecting antique handkerchiefs ever since, part of a lifelong quest to satisfy her great thirst for the poetry of everyday *objets d'art*. In her words: "Artisans exist to create these useful objects in such a way that they might elevate one's very soul by their rare and

fabric of God's glory? Do you ever thank God for the beauty of the violet, the nasturtium, the poppy, the [fill the blank]?[2]

- Try to recall Bible passages, poems, or folk songs that speak of botanical beauty or mention a flower by name. Have you ever noticed how many wise sayings or lines from songs feature something botanical? Can you recall and sing any hymns or choruses that feature flowers (e.g., "All things bright and beautiful")?

- Find practical objects around your house that have botanical motifs or ornaments on them, joining the useful to the beautiful. Check your linens and furniture, dishes and picture frames, pantry and cosmetics. Did you buy a particular product because you were attracted to its botanical ornamentation or maybe its floral label? Why join the beautiful to the useful? What does this say about you and me? At least this: the art of living involves art!

A monarda flower

moving beauty."[3] The monks who drew intricate floral patterns and interlacing vines in the illuminated manuscripts of the Bible would surely agree. They joined the beautiful not only to the useful but also to the proper object of Christian enjoyment: God and his word, the sacred page.

AN EVERYDAY VOCATION

Our santon for the season, *la bouquetière*, is a "maker of bouquets." Bouquetières traveled by cart to open-air markets where they would make floral arrangements to beautify special occasions: a marriage proposal, a dinner party, a funeral, perhaps a Sunday dinner table, or in the case of our santon, to celebrate a newborn babe. The bouquetières doubled as hat makers too because ladies' hats were often decked with flowers—and still are for special events like Easter and weddings.

The traditional little crèche figure of la bouquetière holds a pair of scissors, an essential tool for gathering bouquets. Her scissors have more than one purpose. If she owns a patch of land and grows her own flowers, she uses them to make clean cuts as she goes about her daily task of deadheading (cutting off dead flowers), a necessary part of horticulture. Deadheading allows most flowering plants to continue blooming throughout the growing season.

The plant is hardwired to produce fruit; this is its botanical mission. The dead flower begins its development first in the form of a seed or seed pod. The plant then spends its energy on growing the emerging fruit. Failure to deadhead results in flowers like roses, pansies, and campanulas producing fewer and fewer blossoms. Such untended plants look limp and unkempt—not fit for a flower market! Whereas the plant's purpose is to produce fruit, la bouquetière's purpose is to pick and preserve flowers; her special offering to Christ is the gift of adornment.

For the flower gardener, daily watchfulness is the watchword. In the quiet of her garden bed, while deadheading among her roses and daylilies, our bouquetière stays vigilant, looking out for various invaders and intruders such as weeds, aphids, beetles, and slugs. Left unchecked, these intruders will drive her cultivated flowers out of their garden paradise. Everyday horticulturalists know that the best way to deal with invasive species is to get down on one's knees to keep watch over one's floral flocks—not by night but preferably first thing in the morning—and, when necessary, beat back the invaders, again and again, for as long as it takes.[4]

la bouquetière
(the flower peddler)

The discipline of pinching—removing deadheads to make room for new growth—takes place in ordinary time starting around mid-June, just as everything is coming into bloom. This light pruning brings to mind the spiritual discipline of self-pruning that everyday saints practice at Lent. However, Lent involves intense cutting back, while deadheading calls for a different kind of discipline. This is not a seasonal but an everyday ordinary task, one that can be practiced throughout the day among one's flower beds.

While engaging in this task, the everyday saint cannot help but think of the deadheads and intruder dandelions in her own life, which similarly choke and prevent her from blossoming. She engages in inner conversations with the Master Gardener, Lord of her flower patch. She guards the garden of her own life by recalling the Scriptures that light and water her soul, enabling her to flourish. Spiritual growth is, in the end, merely an extension of the disciplines she has learned through gardening.

WEEK 2 ~ *Ponder*

"This place [home] has wonderful powers. . . . It kills what is dreadful and makes what is beautiful live."[5]

- Do you ever associate beauty with simple everyday moments, or does it belong only to museums and cathedrals?

- Think about your inner garden and what you might need to do to identify the deadheads and dandelions in your life that need eliminating to promote spiritual growth. Might this be what Peter was thinking about too when he says, "but let your adorning be the hidden person of the heart with the imperishable beauty of a gentle and quiet spirit, which in God's sight is very precious" (1 Peter 3:4)?

- What if, since we are earthed beings, our inner renewal were to spill out in beautiful ways into all we do, with or without flowers, whether or not we are trained artists, poets, or song writers? Do you identify as a maker of beauty?

- What if the beautiful were simply a vision of God's beauty? Do you think the God who made trees pleasant to the sight, and whose Son compared the beauty of the lilies to Solomon in all his glory, takes pleasure in earthly beauty? If so, might beautifying our place be a way of pleasing and glorifying God? Can you plant a thing of beauty and care for it this season?

Life stages of a rose

For the everyday gardener-saint, the key is to keep watch over both garden and one's own life on a daily basis throughout the growing season—which is to say the entirety of life. The result: her place, whatever its size, turns into a thing of beauty, for her well-tended plants bear profusions of blooms. Neighbors ask for advice and covet her green thumb. If you ask her, her knees are greener than her thumb—all that kneeling to weed and pray. Her greenness, whether of thumbs or knees, represents her vocation; her garden, the place in which she plays her part for the child Christ: "Surely, if you are privileged to own a plot of earth, it is your duty, both to God and to man, to make it beautiful."[6]

FLOWERS IN PROVENÇAL CULTURE

Flowers are an inescapable part of southern French life. They are everywhere in both wild and domestic settings: market squares, châteaux parks, rural gardens, and the countryside. Local festivals have for centuries featured *les charrettes de fêtes*, horse-drawn carriages heavily decorated with local produce and flowers. Provence is also home to the

WEEK 3 ⚒ *Pray*

"His temple is . . . the earth. Ordinary life on earth is temple life, worshipful. Everywhere a place of communion with God."[7]

Perhaps the medieval monks who illustrated Bibles were inspired by the example of King Solomon's temple. He commissioned artists to decorate the pillars of the inner sanctuary that housed the Holy of Holies (and the book of the covenant) with ornate botanical motifs. Every object in the temple had a useful purpose but was also made beautiful. First Kings 6-7 lists specific handcrafted artwork representing gourds, open flowers, palm trees, and pomegranates that adorned various parts of the inner sanctuary. Who knew that two chapters in the Bible were dedicated to the art of interior decorating (of the house of the Lord)? Some suggest that Genesis depicts creation itself as God's temple in which women and men serve as place-making, care-taking priests.

Take ten minutes each day this week to practice *lézardage* ("lizarding," see below), as though you were in contemplative prayer in God's temple:

🍃 Find an inviting place with a nice view, flower scents, bird songs, and crickets chirps. It must be free from distractions and have some natural beauty. In winter, find a room and a seat with a view.

world's top perfumers thanks to the abundance of scents at hand, including the essences of jasmine, rose, and lavender.[8]

Flowers have been part of the rhythms of mundane and church life for centuries. They figure in children's simple rhymes that sing of "lilacs in my father's garden"[9] or "loves me—loves me not." Christmas roses[10] and Easter daffodils grace churches in which pilgrims gather during special seasons, and throughout ordinary time as well, when local bouquetières use seasonal colors and scents in their altar arrangements. As Peter Leithart says, "Creation exists to offer praise to the Creator, and in her worship, the Church participates in that cosmic liturgy—humanly articulating the sounds, sights and aromas that already ascend to heaven."[11]

> ☙ Sit there without a book, phone, or electronic device. Refrain from thinking of lists, or what else you have to do that day, in order to pay attention to what is present before you. Wait quietly until you spot movement: a fluttering butterfly, a squirrel frantically digging for nuts, or a goldfinch swinging on purple coneflower.
>
> ☙ Don't try to capture the moment for a later Facebook triumph: just attend to and enjoy the moment, letting it sink in deeply. Then thank God for reminding you why he placed man in the garden in the first place. Thank him for the deep sense of vocational renewal, then return to your activities, reoriented, rerooted, and in conversation with him.
>
>> "Creator God, show me how to magnify the beauty of your temple, the earth, and all that is in it.
>>
>> "Show me how to participate and cultivate your own art de vivre in your creation and my life by beautifying my place, my church, and in everything I do.
>>
>> "Show me how to practice ethnobotany in my worship. Better: how to make ethnobotany worship!"

The Provençaux express their *art de vivre*, that living harmony between people and terroir, in a practice described by one of my favorite
French words: *lézardage*. This word literally means "lizarding"— from
the French cognate *lézard*—and can be conjugated as a verb (*je lézarde,
tu lézardes, il lézarde*, etc.). What does this image mean? It refers to the
way lizards find a place to sun themselves, usually on a rock or stone
wall, in order to bask in the warmth! This art of lézardage has been
practiced and perfected in Provence for centuries.

My ancestors have substituted garden benches for rocks, joining the
useful (a place to "lizard") with the beautiful (a flower garden), inviting
a moment of repose and reverie. This garden lézardage brings to mind
Emily Dickinson's verses:

> To make a prairie it takes a clover and one bee,
> One clover, and a bee.
> And revery.
> The revery alone will do,
> If bees are few.[12]

For the everyday saint, lézardage is not simply an occasion to soak
up the sun or daydream. It has nothing to do with laziness. It is rather
a crucial moment in the cultivation of the discipline of letting go, seizing
small moments of joy that beckon us to stop, trusting that the world is
in good hands even when it is out of ours. Lézardage can even be part
of one's ongoing devotion and soul restoration—a midday sabbath
moment, a time to bask in the company of the grand Artist and his
horticultural handiwork, a moment of grace that can turn into a habit of
gratitude. At its best, when practiced by its most accomplished artists,
lézardage is the art of seeing a gift and thanking the Giver for small
beauties than which nothing greater can be perceived.

MY OWN PILGRIMAGE

My lifelong quest to come to terms with the place God put me eventually
led me to an unexpected discovery: a course in plant science and
Midwest gardening at the Chicago Botanic Garden and eventually to

classes and certificates in botanic art.[13] The courses transported me back to early school days when we would return to class after our walks with armfuls of flowers from the fields. Violets, daisies, and buttercups provided our teacher with impromptu opportunities to teach us about our place. I remember fondly sitting at my school desk with colored pencils, drawing and labeling the parts of the plants that belonged to my land and my story as my elders, born naturalists, had done before me.

I had not expected my courses in botanical art would become the curriculum in what amounted to a spiritual discipline: learning to look until I could really see, to pay attention to the intricate details of flora whether in the wild or destined for vases. Why do I call it a spiritual discipline? Because attending—being stretched out of oneself toward something else—takes time and practice. The French verb "to wait" is *attendre*, which also comes from the Latin *ad* + *tendere*, meaning "to stretch toward." Paying attention, I came to learn, involves a stretching of the soul.

My first art lesson at the Chicago Botanic Garden came with an unexpected twist. Our instructor said, "If you don't love it, you can't draw it." I quickly came to understand that the discipline of making daily sketches involves much more than drawing. It begins, before even taking up your pencil, with a thorough inspection of what you will be drawing. Find a connection with it, examine it from all sides; magnify it, feel it, trace it with your hands and, in some cases, dissect it, until you truly appreciate it for what it is and can say: I see you! Now—and only now—you are ready to start drawing and with practice to turn a scientific illustration into a thing of beauty: botanic art.

I can't honestly say it was love at first sight with the calla lily my teacher brought to class as an assignment. I felt zero personal connection with it, having no previous encounters with callas: these flowers were nowhere in my patrimoine! (Why couldn't it have been a sprig of lavender?) I nevertheless buckled down, coming back to the drawing board again and again throughout that summer, even after the class was over. Then one day I was struck dumb with its elegance and saw, as if

A calla lily in full bloom

for the first time, the graceful movement of its gently twirling leaves, the way the light and shadow played in its deep conical flower, and the intricate secret parts inside it. By wintertime, I had at last established a personal connection with the calla lily. I came, I saw, I colored. I was reminded of a line from Antoine Saint-Exupéry's beloved story

Le petit prince: "It's the time you spent on your rose that makes your rose so important. . . . People have forgotten this truth. . . . But you mustn't forget it. You become responsible forever for what you've tamed. You're responsible for your rose."[14] I wondered: Am I responsible, forever, for my own garden, whether I cultivate flowers, or paint them, or whatever else God calls me to do to beautify my place?

I now regard my daily sketching as a botanical contemplation. This discipline leads me to peel off layers of previously acquired knowledge of an object and learning to resee it as it really is. G. K. Chesterton was right: "Our perennial spiritual and psychological task is to look at things familiar until they become unfamiliar again."[15] I watch my hand try to draw the sepals of a rose, nice and regular, until I realize that my hand is following my mind and not my eye: I have forgotten again to see the particularities. As I correct my lines, I unlearn old habits of perceiving and train my eye and mind to look and see, then look again. And I wonder: How many things (or people!) in the world does my mind inadvertently "correct" to conform to my expectation? O Lord, help me not to make up your world into my own image!

In the end, my art is on a pilgrimage, as am I. Making art reminds me that I am always reforming (and often redrawing—a kind of deadheading). The works of art on the pages of this book depict one everyday saint's attempt at the art of making beautiful while living in season. Because botanical art came to me in a new (ahem, somewhat late) season of life, it might not measure up to the work of more seasoned artists. Not to worry—that is precisely what makes it right for this project, a sketchbook as it were for what life might look like as we undertake the Christian pilgrimage with other everyday saints through the year. Like the bouquetière santon, I am in company with other imperfect pilgrims, traveling the way of holiness in the ordinary. What makes us saints is the way we attend to the ordinary: we see it as God's handiwork, an invitation to use whatever gift we have to adorn ordinary (crèche) scenes into things of beauty!

THE ART OF EATING IN SEASON

Our flower lady, like all who cultivate beauty, might not be fully aware that her art is also useful. The beauty she cultivates is indeed useful, for were it not for her flower garden that attracts the bees that zip from the black-eyed-Susan to the zucchini blossom, she might not have the vegetables to make ratatouille on a summer day. No flowers, no pollinators. No pollinators, no fruit. In the grand scheme of God's creation, the beautiful often serves a practical purpose. Each flower has a raison d'être, beyond beauty, even if it is simply to attract one honeybee—with or without Dickinson's "revery"! In the beginning, God beautified the useful.

Flowers grace the table not only to beautify vases but also to season dishes. In early spring, an everyday saint bouquetière might add a few leaves of the bitter dandelions she pulled out of her patch of earth to her salad. Later in the season she may scatter pansies over her greens to add

WEEK 4 ∽ *Play Your Part*

Jesus mentions the beauty of the lilies. Could he have been thinking of ethnobotany as worship?

When a woman bathed his feet with expensive perfume, Jesus said to his shocked disciples: "Why do you trouble the woman? For she has done a beautiful thing to me" (Matthew 26:10).

- If you are in the business of making beauty as an artist, poet, horticulturist, landscape designer, or the like, can you use the little bouquetière saint as a role model? When you begin a new work, whether in the studio or the garden, can you offer it up to Christ? Can you remember that you are simply adding a dab of color or spot of beauty on a canvas that has already been created good?

- Almost every church has someone who arranges flowers, but are there other ways to beautify God's house? Tom Wright laments that the church has too often dropped the ball when it comes to beauty, a sin of omission insofar as "the church should reawaken its hunger for beauty at every level. This is essential and a soupçon of sweetness. Then in summertime, the pièces de résistance for her Sunday teas are the nasturtiums that add a bright paint stroke to the icing on the cake. She might also harvest rose petals to make rose jelly for her winter repasts to recall the deliciousness of summer days. In short, she embodies the art of living in all seasons. Meanwhile, everyday saints all over the world, florists or not, scatter fresh sprigs of parsley, one of the most common herbs, as garnish on any number dishes for a final touch. Voilà! And bon appétit!

WHAT'S AN EVERYDAY SAINT TO DO?

The role assigned to the crèche figure of this season's everyday saint, la bouquetière, is to place flowers at the feet of the child Christ. In reality, of course, there are no fresh roses in Provence during the Christmas season. It is a timely reminder that as we now follow Jesus outside the

urgent."[16] What part might you play in your local church? Are you an artisan who beautifies the everyday through the domestic arts of weaving, knitting, culinary arts, or anything else? Are you a landscape artist who might involve youth in cultivating flowers outside your church? Is there a place for thinking about the art of worshiping in season?

Perhaps you feel out of your depth here: you do not grow flowers, you do not have a green thumb, and you have never felt particularly artistic. If so, remember that art de vivre is not always about creating art but, as artist Ted Orland says, "trying to do something you care about really well. . . . Ordinary people make art when they make extraordinary concerns a part of their daily life."[17] What might this look like for you? Perhaps you are an everyday saint of whom Christ might say: "Why do you trouble my little saint? She has done a beautiful thing for me."

manger, our own callings may not result in a concrete gift we can lay at Jesus' feet at the end of the workday. Yet we also learn that whatever we do to beautify our place—whether deadheading, sketching, or presenting a restaurative meal with a few sprigs of parsley—can be an offering too if done as unto him. When it is, it will surely produce fruit in season—when the time, if not the tree, is ripe.

The flower lady's gift is to see the peculiar beauty of God's handiwork in her place and to help her neighbors to see it. What she has to offer is less a matter of artistic talent than of daily devotion: paying attention to her environs while working and keeping her garden. It is a gift for all seasons. It starts in winter, when she seeds indoors the promise (later to be transplanted) of her summer flowerbeds, beautifying her cold and bleak midwinter landscape with a dab of color and hope. Even a very small garden, as Celia Thaxter discovered and wrote about, "extends upwards, and what it lacks in area is more than compensated by the large joy that grows out of it."[18] Like la bouquetière, everyday saints would do well to ask: How can what I say, do, or make participate in God's beauty, truth, and goodness in my place and time? How can what I do where I am reflect the glory of the God who is always and everywhere? Can I do other beautiful things that similarly adorn his temple? Could my garden, a small color patch of land, itself be a brushstroke, a dash of color, on the Lord's cosmic canvas?

Chapter 11

IN THE MARKETPLACE

THE ART OF MAKING A LIVING

*Whatever you do, work heartily, as for the Lord and not
for men, knowing that from the Lord you will receive the
inheritance as your reward. You are serving the Lord Christ.*

Colossians 3:23-24

*Remember for whom you work: whether you work for a private company,
the government, a large corporation, or yourself, the true disciple
understands that he or she ultimately is working for God in that place.*

Norman Shawchuck, *A Guide to Prayer for All
Who Walk with God*

WHAT HAS THE MARKETPLACE TO DO
WITH OUR EVERYDAY PILGRIMAGE?

The landscape of Provence embraces several regions from the vineyards and olive groves of the Rhône Valley and villages like Gordes that cling to the rugged hills of the back country among rustling pines and the incessant calls of cicadas to the looming mount Sainte-Victoire and the threshold of the Basses-Alpes. Any of these sites can serve as the backdrop of the crèche scene, but the "authorized version" sets the little clay saints in one Provençal terrain: the Mediterranean coast with its fishing villages and vast horizons, as well as the large city of Marseille, a major trading port since pre-Roman times, which is where the santons first appeared in the nineteenth century.[1]

Elaborate manger scenes feature not just the stable for the baby Jesus but also an extensive village that surrounds it, including shops, cafés, streets, market squares, and small harbors. Not all santons in these panoramic scenes can bring gifts from the land to the child Christ. Instead, they make or trade things, offering the kinds of goods and services that are the warp and woof of the town life that grew out of their terroir. Some crèche scenes therefore feature, rather anachronistically, a policeman, a notary, and even a mayor strutting around with his official tricolor sash. These extrabiblical figures remind us that everyone is part of the company of everyday saints who follow Jesus, including the educated classes, captains of industry, and leaders of society. They also remind us that like the produce from the land, a vocation in the marketplace can also be offered to Jesus.

Of course, to many, the marketplace, never a paragon of virtue, seems far removed from anything spiritual. What does the stock exchange have to do with the "wondrous exchange" in which Jesus becomes like us so that we can become like him? These seemingly secular santons prompt the question: Why are there merchants in the manger? We can generalize: What does the marketplace of Marseille have to do with Jerusalem?

KEY TERM FOR EVERYDAY SAINTS: *SANTONNIER* (ONE WHO MAKES SANTONS)

Artist Jean-Louis Lagnel, a *santonnier* before the term ever existed, inched Marseille closer to Jerusalem when he first came up with the idea two centuries ago of crafting santons to populate the crèche. Through his creative appropriation of the story of Jesus' birth, he reintroduced the traditional Christmas mangers at a time when the Reign of Terror during the French Revolution prohibited such public displays.

We cannot say for certain whether Lagnel was reacting to this prohibition or simply trying to preserve endangered local crafts. However, I like to imagine him deliberating: "Since we cannot have public displays, let us make smaller, private ones. Let us sculpt the holy family in miniature, small enough to put in people's homes, and let us situate them in Provence, in our own time and place, among the various merchants at their daily trades and occupations and our neighbors with whom we daily interact on the streets of Marseille. And let them bring presents representing their respective trades to the child Christ." And it was so.

Lagnel did more with his santons than keep the Christmas story alive in a time of repression. He creatively juxtaposed the Christmas story and the simple, ordinary working women and men of his time and place. One small figure of a man; one giant leap for French-kind. For through his art, he effectively inserted the world of the nineteenth-century Provençal village into the biblical text. Lagnel worked a wondrous exchange, representing Marseille as the place to which the baby Jesus had come—call it everyday contextual theology. Secular and sacred trade places in these manger scenes too. Blue-collar workers now rub shoulders with the holy family, showing in a tangible albeit miniature way that everyday work is not separate from but rather intricately related to our faith. This is true even of work that at first glance seems unspiritual (perhaps especially there). As we saw in a previous chapter, the Holy Spirit, poured out like the lavender from the hills, infuses the very streets of a merchant town and its harbor. Every home that has a Provençal crèche therefore houses a central Christian truth: Jesus came not to abolish but to sanctify everyday life. This is why these simple workers who come to adore the baby Jesus and, as I imagine, follow him out of the manger, are aptly called santons: little saints.

The santonnier himself is a craftsman who plies his goods just like any other worker. He too aspires to display the prestigious award of *Meilleur Ouvrier de France* (or MOF, Best Craftsman of France) on his shopfront, as do the other winners.[2] Receiving this award means that workers have attained a level of excellence through attention to their craft, diligence, and years of apprenticeship. Interestingly, all the vocations represented by the santons are also potential candidates for this accolade.

A leading monthly periodical waxes eloquent in its description of the award: "Those who hold the award are considered custodians of their craft. They are charged with upholding its standards and passing on their knowledge to those who come after them."[3] This vision resonates deeply with one of our central themes: patrimoine. For what is expected from these standard-bearers is not merely excellence in workmanship and technical precision but also a dedication to their respective crafts, as well as a respect for local culture and its traditions, and thus indirectly for the terroir from which they developed. In the final analysis, the prize is less about business than roots: the chief aim is not to sell what one has made but to preserve the ways of making it. These ways are the stuff of patrimoine, a cultural heritage to be passed on to future generations.

AN EVERYDAY VOCATION

This chapter's featured santon, representing the marketplace, is the fishmonger: *la poissonnière*. She also represents the santons' birthplace of

WEEK 1   *Pause*

"The Bible and saints who have gone before us give ample evidence of God's consistent call to each of us. . . . No one is left out, exempted or overlooked. All are of equal worth and all are called. While we may think of certain vocations as callings, God appears to consider all of life as our calling, and that includes every honorable vocation."[4]

In the Gospels, the disciples themselves serve as examples of how to follow Christ even as they go about their earthly—or rather, maritime—jobs. Jesus first meets a number of his disciples while they are at work as fishermen casting their nets. He tells them, "Follow me, and I will make you fishers of men" (Matthew 4:18-20). And they do. Yet they did not renounce their day jobs altogether: we find them fishing again later (John 21:3). Indeed, Jesus cared enough about their occupations that, after his resurrection, he helped them catch a record number of fish

Marseille, home to Provence's leading fishery. The fishmonger is a regular fixture in the crèche, typically holding a basket of fish in one hand and a hanging scale for weighing them in the other. Fish figure prominently both in *le Vieux-Port* (the Old Port) of Marseille and in several of the Gospel stories; the fishmonger therefore represents a tangible connection between biblical Jerusalem and village life on France's Mediterranean coast. Like the farmer, the fishmonger is an important link between her place and her product—not farm but sea to table—for example, the tuna in a *salade niçoise*. Like all the other crèche

La poissonnière (the fishmonger)

(John 21:4-14). Even those who had left everything to follow Jesus were nevertheless able to pursue their everyday vocations, precisely what the worker-santon represents.

Do you tend to think in categories of jobs that are more spiritual than (and therefore superior to) others? Or do you think that jobs and spirituality have no real connection whatsoever, so that this question does not even enter your mind? Do you sometimes feel as though you have less to offer to neighbors and to God because you are just a [fill in the blank], which is not an official kind of Christian ministry?

Reflect on your vocation in light of the quote above and the example of the disciples. Try to view your work through the lens of the crèche and all the occupations that figure in it. How could each one of these jobs, including yours, become not just a job but a vocation, a calling to live out for Christ under his lordship?

A strawberry plant

figures, la poissonnière is the santonnier's workmanship, predestined to come to the manger with her gift of fresh fish for the child Christ.

The scales she carries make her a fitting representative of the shopping district. The scales are there to weigh her fish yet they also stand for fair measure: the scales of justice. We assume that she conducts her affairs virtuously (Proverbs 31), that she aspires to be faithful in small things and in large. Like vines that symbolize steadfastness, clinging to their support in all seasons, everyday saints show up at their post every ordinary morning, clinging to Christ in order to abide in the Vine (John 15:4).

Abiding is particularly important in ordinary time. This long season of our Christian pilgrimage is rife with opportunities to grumble about our work, role, and place. Indeed, we may even be tempted to give up, for staying the course requires endurance even at walking speed. Yet an everyday saint perseveres and produces fruit, as do the ripening vines and strawberry runners.

Three centuries before Lagnel, Martin Luther was already saying that all vocations, "whether in the field, in the garden, in the city, in the home, in struggle, or in government . . . are the masks of our Lord God, behind which He wants to be hidden and to do all things."[5] The Reformation brought a new dynamism to society and ordinary time by insisting that workers were to practice their everyday trades as unto the Lord. As Jesus proclaimed all foods clean (Mark 7:19), so the Reformers affirmed all forms of work as holy. All vocations are instruments through which Christians in their respective places and lots in life can demonstrate their love for God and neighbor. When they do, everyday saints become the means through which Jesus again enters the world—not in a manger but in each person's workplace.

Still, even well-intentioned pilgrims fall into the trap of thinking that sainthood is reserved for a select few, that our mundane occupations are not as pleasing to God as "professional" Christian ministries, and that consequently our daily business on earth does not matter to heaven. The fishmonger santon presents a standing challenge to these faulty conceptions: the santonniers were right to include the marketplace in the manger scene.

THE ART OF MAKING A LIVING
IN PROVENÇAL CULTURE

If the crèche stands at the heart of the patrimoine of Provence, then the santonnier, a revered craftsman, may well be its standard-bearer. It is he who infuses his little clay creatures with the essential characteristics of their local places and professions. The santons remind us that Christ has come to Provence (as it were)—or rather, that Provence has been caught up into the story of Christmas. Either way, the story of Jesus has become an integral if indirect feature of the terroir of Provence itself. As to the santons themselves, I see them as a petite but potent symbol of the Christian life, a visual aid to remind us that although we have left the crèche behind, we are still on a pilgrimage with other everyday saints following the Lord where he leads.

WEEK 2 ❧ *Ponder*

Everyday saints should not need official awards, like *Meilleur Ouvrier de France* (MOF), to want to do their best. Those who serve Jerusalem want only to hear these words from their Lord: "Well done, good and faithful servant. . . . Enter into the joy of your master" (Matthew 25:21). Clearly, nothing can top that. Yet it is good to keep in mind that the heavenly reward is for earthly work.

We live in a culture that thrives on awards and rewards for personal glory. Can we turn off that switch in our head, in the assurance that God is pleased with our work because we are offering it to him?

The original santonniers effectively inserted the world of the nineteenth-century Provençal village into the biblical text. If you could build a crèche for your own place and time, what would it look like? What kinds of work and workplaces would you want to represent? Remember, every square inch of the earth, including the marketplace, is the Lord's!

The MOF winners are custodians of their craft. Do you ever think of yourself as being a custodian of your craft or line of work? And, going further: Do you ever think of yourself as being a custodian of the gospel? If so, what might that look like in your context? Think about how you as an everyday saint can live out the life of Christ always, before everyone, in places high and low.

The fishmonger woman figures prominently in Yvan Audouard's pastorale.[6] In the story, she wakes up in the wee hours of Christmas morning, tossing and turning on account of a troubled conscience: "I have nightmares . . . the fish I am going to sell tomorrow is more than eight days old." Her husband, now awake, teases her that her fish haven't been fresh for the past twenty years yet this had never bothered her before. Still, suffering from a newly wakened conscience, she checks to see how rotten the fish really are and says to her astonished husband, "If they are not as they should be, I shall throw them away." For this is once again Christmas Eve, a night of wonders, and another petit miracle is now taking place: her *rascasses* (scorpion fish), a staple in the *bouillabaisse*, a local *spécialité* of Marseille, looks and smells as fresh as if it had just been caught. "Look at my *rascasses*! They look alive. . . . One might think they could start speaking," she exclaims.

Her husband admits that it is *un vrai miracle* (a real miracle), and la poissonnière wonders if it has something to do with what the shepherds told her: "So do you think it could be true, that this wee one comes from the Good Lord?" Audouard tells the story so that the audience understands that the real miracle is not the freshening of the fish but the refreshing—or re-fleshing—of the fishmonger's heart. The birth of the baby Jesus has transformed the merchant and, through her, the marketplace itself. Her husband, witnessing her conversion, is convinced: "we must go [to the manger] right away!" And so, with a new perspective on her vocation (and fresh fish), she takes her offering to the child Christ, sanctifying her business and thereby becoming a model for other everyday saints who purvey goods.

The New Testament accounts of the apostles' travels do not take us all the way to Marseille, but we do arrive at similar marketplaces on other Mediterranean shores. The biblical narratives count some everyday saints and their vocations important enough to mention: Dorcas who made beautiful tunics (Acts 9:39), Simon the tanner (Acts 10:6), Tertius the secretary (Romans 16:22), Erastus the city treasurer (Romans 16:23), Priscilla and Aquila who, like Paul, are tentmakers

(Acts 18:2-3). Lydia, the seller of purple cloth for the well-to-do, is particularly noteworthy. Thanks to her industry and economy, she has kept a home and servants that enables her to provide hospitality to the apostle Paul (Acts 16:14-15). Lydia shows that one can be both a disciple and a flourishing businesswoman, an everyday saint whose purple goods become an offering to the child Christ.

Trading purple goods may seem inconsequential. No doubt many trader saints have modest businesses that never meet worldly standards of success, yet they play a key role in their local communities. That God gave humans work in the first garden, before the fall, demonstrates that work is good, part of the created order. Tim Keller says that work is "rearranging the raw material of God's creation in such a way that it helps the world in general, and people in particular, thrive and flourish."[7] Work is one way we contribute to and pass on a patrimoine; work is not the meaning of life, but it is a way of making a meaningful living.

A workplace is more than just a place where work is done. It is a place to practice love for God and neighbor, perhaps even, at the limit, a place of worship. Like every place on earth, the workplace is a setting in which God's will can be done. In Tish Harrison Warren's words: "God can even change the world through shopkeepers who serve tea without sugar."[8] The marketplace is one more locale for everyday saints to do justice, and love kindness, and walk humbly with their God (Micah 6:8).

MY OWN PILGRIMAGE

Maman first sent me shopping to the village *boulangerie* (bakery) when I was in grade school. I had a list, a few *centimes* that I had learned to add and subtract, and her reminder to consider well before I handed over my little fistful of coins. Later, I learned how to do more complicated, even "philosophical" math, especially when Papa got involved: was it advantageous—not just to me, but to the whole community, not to mention the baker—to buy a more expensive single croissant from a master artisan baker or a cheaper, mass-produced one from the newfangled supermarket (*hypermarché*)?

From the time I joined the company of everyday saints, questions about work, money, and what to spend it on have grown only more complicated. I can't seem to make one shopping trip without asking myself: *Were any people, animals, or land hurt in the process of making this food or object?* or *If I buy organic for myself, should I not offer the same quality to food pantries?* or *How can I most glorify God with my shopping cart?* I hear the same voices when I am the seller: *What is a fair price—for my art, my French lessons, my lemon madeleines?*

You don't have to be a Christian to pose questions about fairness and market prices. What the fishmonger santon taught me goes deeper than the scales of justice she holds in her hands. Because—let's be serious—the baby Jesus is too young to eat fish! What, then, is it that the fishmonger and her companions are offering to Jesus? On a surface level, they're presenting gift baskets, which, when given to the poor, are a way of giving unto Jesus. On a deeper level, however, they're offering their time and energy, the sweat of their brow, consecrating—setting apart—their everyday labor for Christ and his kingdom, just as they, little saints, are also set apart. And, as they present their daily work as a kind of worship offering, Jesus sanctifies their shops, tools, fields, and kitchens, acknowledging their respective lines of work as worthy, even saintly, vocations.

The company of little saints may no longer be in the manger, but this does not mean they abandon their spiritual vocation. Yes, they go back to work, but now with Jesus in their midst! Like them, so we, everyday saints, keep on working after encountering Jesus. Like them, we earn a living, but hopefully in a way that glorifies him who sanctifies us. Like Lydia, after coming to Christ, we return to our business with Christ at the center of all that we do, including earning our daily bread.

Everything I am, and have, and do can be an offering—a year-round Christmas present!—to Christ. The story of my life, including the story of my work, is ultimately not about me but about the one who calls me, equips me, and graciously receives my humble offerings for what they are: gifts from the heart. Learning how to make even drudgery meaningful by doing it as unto Christ is an important part of the art of living in season.

The santons help me to remember why I do what I do, and for whom I do it, even when I play the humble tradesperson eking out a living. My little mentors teach me that in bringing my everyday goods and services to market, as part of my offering to God, I am not only restored but "restoried"—reminded whose story I am living out—and so is my occupation. As James K. A. Smith writes: "Our work and our practices should be foretastes of that coming new city."[9] What might otherwise degenerate

WEEK 3 ~ *Pray*

John Baillie writes the following examen:

"O merciful Father, . . .
> Have I today done anything to fulfill the purpose for which Thou didst cause me to be born? . . .
> Have I been lazy in body or languid in spirit? . . .
> Have I been scrupulously honorable in all my business dealings?
> Have I been transparently sincere in all I have professed to be, to feel, or to do?"[10]

Ask God to show you personally how your work fits into his purpose:

"Merciful Father, open the eyes of my heart so that I can see my workplace as the earthly setting where you have placed me to bear witness to your truth, goodness, beauty, and justice.

"Keep me from the greed that tempts me to ask for a higher price than is fair. Keep me also from the fear of not having enough. Give me the joy of honest labor!

"Keep me from the temptation to overlook, overwork, and underpay my staff. Help me to create a healthy workplace that gives them time for family and for keeping the sabbath holy.

"Show me, when I play the role of consumer, how to make fair decisions. Give me the courage to support the right kinds of producers and patronize the right kinds of commerce! Help me to be a blessing to my local marketplaces."

into meaningless routines or selfish ambition is instead grafted into the newer, bigger, and better story in which God is doing a new thing, a building project made up of living stones. And I am one of them.

THE ART OF EATING IN SEASON

At this confluence of late summer and early fall, the kitchen garden is as full and varied as it was empty in midwinter. On market days, the scents of ripe apricots, peaches, and cantaloupes mix with the buzz of bees around freshly harvested grapes and apples. In the land of my ancestors, many tradespeople live above their shops and do not have their own patch of earth, nor do they have much time for cooking on a normal workday. A fishmonger might broil her own fish, but she is likely to purchase the rest of her dinner at the market on her way home, mixing the traditional *bohémienne* (a colorful mix of stewed tomatoes and sautéed eggplants) with paella or couscous that add a tinge of other lands to the native scents.

When everyday saints thank God for creating the diverse ingredients that make up their daily meals, they remember that the various dishes

A fresh apricot

A ripe summer peach

that comprise their table restauration are the result of many people's work. They thank God for the fishermen who work long hours at sea, the farmers who grow the fennels for fish stew, the cooks who sell *bohémienne* and couscous, the bakers who get out of bed to make baguettes—especially the bakers, for their workday begins before sunrise, God bless them. Christian pilgrims thank God for the bouquetière whose flowers bring outdoor beauty into the house, for artisans who crafted the cotton tablecloth with its printed pattern of sunflowers and lavender, for traders who brought that cotton from distant shores, and for faraway strangers from other lands who harvested the tea and coffee that accompany their lingering conversations in the quiet early evening hours.

The art of eating in season is less about becoming "foodies" and more about becoming mindful of the fact that it takes a marketplace to produce a good meal. Those who master the art come to see that eating in season is part of a bigger project: the art of making an organic living. *Organic* is not just a designer label associated with more expensive milk or produce. Nor does it refer to an isolated practice—a way of producing healthier juice or bread. *Organic* is not just a word but a world, an entire way of life that is in harmony with God's garden in our place (or our place in God's garden of earthly delights). *Organic*: a right place for every living thing, and every living thing in its rightful place.

WHAT'S AN EVERYDAY SAINT TO DO?

The santonnier is the mind behind the santons, the maker who casts them—literally—in their respective roles. The santons themselves are known as "the little clay ambassadors of Provence," and this was precisely the santonnier's intention: to capture and communicate the very soul of Provence through these clay figures. An author of one of the go-to books on santons makes a striking point: "The santonnier, in drawing out his creatures from the clay, repeats, albeit in a modest way, the act of the Creator."[11] Of course, he doesn't create them simply by speaking. Instead, he presses a lump of clay into a mold, fires it, and it emerges from the kiln fit for its part—just as the divine potter molds human clay and assigns his creatures roles in the story of salvation (Jeremiah 18).

Merchants in the manger scene are ambassadors not of Provence but of Christ (2 Corinthians 5:20). They play this most important role wherever they happen to be, including the workplace. Each everyday saint is part of the larger company all molded by the great Santonnier, who follows Jesus out of the manger, always waiting and watching for him—always Adventish!—and for ways to make their lives a suitable offering to him. In all that they do, they want to bring glory to God, honoring him who first cast us in our molds, assigned us roles, and set us in just these places to reflect his truth, goodness, and beauty.

"For we are his workmanship, created in Christ Jesus for good works, which God prepared beforehand, that we should walk in them" (Ephesians 2:10). As our fisherwoman understood, the Lord moves us from within like no earthly power or award can. We make a living to God by working in season for God's glory, ambassadors for Christ even in the marketplace, knowing that he has written our names, not on a shopfront plaque, but in bold letters in the book of life (Philippians 4:3; Revelation 21:27).

WEEK 4 — *Play Your Part*

"God chose . . . to wear that humanity as an ordinary working man . . . our ordinary existence is not so ordinary when we remember that God chose this existence to give us a true picture of the divine. Therefore there are no unimportant moments in any lifetime. All are precious gifts of opportunity to know and serve the One who made us and chose to stand with us and be like us in the gift of life."[12]

Mother Teresa writes, "The president of Mexico sent for me. I told him that he had to become holy as a president. . . . He looked at me a bit surprised, but it is like that: we have to become holy, each of us, in the place where God has put us."[13]

How might I play my part in the workplace? Consider these ideas:

- Churches have special dedication ceremonies for pastors, Sunday school teachers, elders, and missionaries. Can you imagine similar prayers or recognition services for white-collar and blue-collar and no-collar workers, for people who go off every morning to labor in fields, kitchens, gardens, art studios, and main street shops and offices—or stay at home as caregivers? Can you start your job each new day with the thought that your work—you—had been dedicated to God? Can you do this for yourself when you enter your place of work every morning this week?

- Is your church *organic*? Is it a part of the local life and businesses in its unique earthly place? Do our earthly dealings as Christians reflect God's goodness and justice, as far as we are able? To what extent do you think the local church should be a gathering of local peace- and placemakers? How might you help?

- Can you work in ways that facilitate your own participation as an everyday saint in an organic local community?

- How will you welcome Jesus into the world again—not in a manger, but in your workplace?

Chapter 12

WITH THE CHILDREN

THE ART OF SEEING AFRESH

Truly, I say to you, unless you turn and become like
children, you will never enter the kingdom of heaven.

MATTHEW 18:3

To be "lost in wonder, love and praise" when contemplating
what is in Christ is a far cry from losing touch with reality.
. . . Christian doctrine is for grown-ups who have childlike
imaginations, trusting stories in general only because one
story, the gospel of Jesus Christ, happens to be true.

KEVIN VANHOOZER, *FAITH SPEAKING UNDERSTANDING*

WHAT DOES THE NURSERY HAVE TO DO
WITH OUR EVERYDAY PILGRIMAGE?

We have accompanied many little saints on this seasons-of-life pilgrimage. Jesus invites everyone to follow him with no category left out: women and men, poor and rich, resident aliens in our land, wise men from afar, strangers and outsiders, and even the "simple-minded." All pilgrims were welcome to place their gifts at the feet of the baby Jesus on that miraculous night when our pilgrimage began, and all now can follow him out of the manger and seek to live out his life in them as they enter their everyday places—dwelling places, workplaces, or wherever.

Little children are there too—and why not, when our Lord came as a baby himself; when he, a grown man, rebuked his disciples for keeping the little children away from him? As one author of a book on santons puts it, the crèches "introduce us, like children, to the marvelous world of poetic time . . . [where] real time gains an elasticity that belongs to the world of dreams" characteristic of children.[1] As the little saints have shown us, in the crèche we exist in a time that is as much our own as it is that of the baby Jesus. It takes imagination, especially for adults, to see the whole of life as one long Advent night.

To this point, we have seen that santons have gifts related to their vocations to offer Christ. What can children bring to Jesus? What can a child have to contribute to the art of living in season, this story of continued pilgrimage in search of Christ in the everyday? Can a little child be a little saint?

A KEY TERM FOR EVERYDAY SAINTS:
LA TENDRE ENFANCE

In the land of the *santons*, there is yet another meaningful expression that is difficult to translate: *la tendre enfance*. The literal meaning is "tender childhood," yet something gets lost in translation. To the French, the expression brings to mind a sweet, safe, and affectionate place associated with childhood that endows our memories with a poetic, story-like quality and colors a child's early years with an endearing golden glow.

La tendre enfance has everything to do with *la tendresse maternelle* (maternal love) because one's mother is the principal source of a young child's comfort and joy. The gentle rocking rhythm and the cooing of lullabies provide a kind of arbor over mother and child. The mother orbits her little planet—or rather, the little planet orbits her sun— maintaining reassuring quotidian routines while letting the child explore the limits of her freedom and imagination in a safe place. Rachel Carson rightly captures that the mother is a necessary other: "If a child is to keep

Imagination in nature

alive his inborn sense of wonder without any . . . gift from the fairies, he
needs the companionship of at least one adult who can share it, rediscov-
ering with him the joy, excitement, and mystery of the world we live in."[2]

The ordinary season of childhood does not march but gently rocks
to the beat of a toy drummer: the dependable cadences of days, nights,
and quiet naps, of madeleines and hot cocoa, of warm pajamas and story
times. La tendre enfance is the season of classic stories in which fairies
are brought back to life by a handclap, little girls have tea parties with
fawns in three-piece suits, and "Expotitions" to the North Pole end with
everyone gathering for a table celebration.[3] It is a season in which the
child explores other worlds only to discover that her own world is marvelous. There will come a time for formal schooling, endless drives to
enrichment programs, and after-school clubs that teach important skills,
but this is not that time. For now, the real learning and most essential

skills are acquired at home: trusting that tender parental presence, exploring the great outdoors with all its wonders that do not yet have scientific names, and playing at stories that feed the mind and foster faith.[4]

Childhood can be a renaissance (a kind of rebirth) for the grown-up companion who lowers herself to see the world, once again, through the eyes of a little child. It is a time of wonder regained, bringing with it forgotten memories of a place one had once known or yearned for but

WEEK 1 ✍ *Pause*

Antoine de Saint-Exupéry is often cited as saying, "If you want to build a ship, don't drum up people to collect wood and don't assign them tasks and work; but rather teach them to long for the endless immensity of the sea."

Can you recall some instances when, as a child, you saw ordinary things in the world with wonder? Can you pause and dwell on these memories a while, then thank God for them and for the adult who shared these moments with you?

Can you reverse roles and think of times when you were the adult companion for a little child lost in wonder and imagination? Did you slow down your adult pace of life in order to enter this companionship? Did you have a sense of "pair-of-eyes regained" or a belief that anything can happen? If so, can you see these moments, then and now, as opportunities to come closer to the God of creation and re-creation? Could this be what it is to "long for the endless immensity of the sea"?

Some among us never had such a childhood, nor do we have children of our own to accompany us. Still, can you imagine what it might be like to look at the world through the eyes of a little child? Can you practice every day this week and try to marvel at the daily little miracles with fresh eyes as though you were seeing them for the first time? And can you try to think, again like a little child, that as long as Mother and Father are near—your heavenly Father—all shall be well? Might there be merit in trying to exercise this ability of a childlike imagination like a muscle throughout the seasons?

then forgotten, a place of tranquil serenity and simple faith. Through the eyes of the child, the grown-up parents travel back through time to that first season of life, where petits miracles happened on a regular basis, where, say, a hazelnut becomes an imaginary friend, who, when planted in the soil, turns into a giant! A mother (or father, or grandfather, or aunt) sees afresh what was forgotten when she entered the "real" world where incessant activities replace the circadian rhythms—*pair-of-eyes* lost, as it were. La tendre enfance is an essential season to discover (and rediscover) the marvelous in the mundane.

AN EVERYDAY VOCATION: AN AGE (AND EYES) OF INNOCENCE

Children also figure among the santons in the traditional crèche. The early carols give us charming ideas of what these children offer to Jesus: "What shall I bring [to Jesus] in my little bag? . . . Some honey, my toys, two pigeons, and a little *galette*. And then I shall cover him with kisses."[5] Most intriguing is the boy accompanying his blind father, a frequent pair in Provençal crèches. They walk hand in hand to the stable, prompting us to wonder who is leading whom. Surely the child would not set out on a pilgrimage in the middle of the night all by himself; but then neither could the blind man find his way without the seeing eyes of his son. It appears that both are on their respective pilgrimages to meet the child Christ *together*. And fittingly so because a patrimoine, one's local heritage, is passed on from parent to child. Indeed, what incentive would we have to preserve our local inheritance if there were no children to whom we could pass it on? Perhaps this is why the santonniers, themselves custodians of their patrimoine, have for centuries cast these little saints, the blind man and his son, standing *together*, two persons on *one* pedestal.

CHILDREN IN PROVENÇAL CULTURE

The children in the Provençal Christmas stories are often connected to stories of vision. The blind man and his son figure in a tale that ends in a miraculous healing, anticipating Jesus' ministry and the prophecies of old

L'homme aveugle avec son fils
(the blind man with his son)

that "the eyes of the blind shall be opened" (Isaiah 35:5). In the Maurel pastorale, Simon, the blind man's son, leads his father to the Holy Child: "Oh, if you could only see, father! His eyes sparkle, he looks at me and his mouth laughs." The blind man, "seeing" Jesus through his son's words, then addresses him: "My God, you have deprived me of admiring your Glory, but your Majesty blazes in my heart." And as he says this, he receives his sight—an event he calls not a petit miracle, but *un miracle admirable.*[6]

A noël tells the story from another angle. Now it is the child, a girl, who is physically blind from birth. As her mother prepares to set off on the pilgrimage to Bethlehem, the girl begs to come with her.[7] Her mother gives her a stinging retort: "What would you do there? You can't even see!" The girl responds, "I do not need eyes, mother dear, to believe or worship!" The message is clear: the blind girl, in her tendre enfance, sees better than her sighted mother. This puts an interesting spin on Jesus' words: "Blessed are those who have not seen and yet have believed" (John 20:29). In the end, her mother gives in and takes her along on her pilgrimage. When at last they arrive at the manger, the young girl takes Jesus' hand and places it on her heart—and she too regains her sight!

MY OWN PILGRIMAGE

No one led me to Jesus when I was a child, though I lived in a created order with plenty of opportunity for marvel—a good start. The beauty of nature brought me to see that there must be a God behind the world. And somehow—I don't know how; no one connected the dots for me—

I thought this same creator God must be related to the baby Jesus in the manger cradle and, through him, to the little saints crowding around him who were so like me.

The first question I asked when I finally came to Jesus myself was, Why did nobody tell me about this when I was younger? The second question was, How does one let the little children come to him? (Mark 10:13-14). These questions led me to enroll in Bible school (the European Bible Institute) where I could study Scripture to equip myself to minister to children. Over the years, I worked with all kinds of children of diverse social backgrounds: from North African Arabic immigrants in low-income French housing complexes and French children in Edinburgh trying to preserve their culture in the cold climes of Scotland to American children living in some of the most exclusive neighborhoods in the United States. I quickly saw that telling them the truth was not enough; they needed someone to *walk* that truth with them, every day of every season.

WEEK 2 ◆ *Ponder*

"Let the little children come to me and do not hinder them, for to such belongs the kingdom of heaven." MATTHEW 19:14

Could the season of tender childhood serve as a reminder that Jesus came into the world to restore our lost innocence and to refresh our vision of the heavenly Father?

Can you see how taking the time to walk with a companion child, who likes to stop and marvel every few steps, might be an opportunity to let them "come to him"?

What if trusting "blindly" in the goodness of God, like the sightless people in these noëls, were enough? Could this be what Jesus meant when he told his disciples they had to become like a little child, to whom the kingdom of God belongs? Until then, are we like these blind men in the stories?

Seasonal collections with a child

This is how I came to embark on the great pilgrimage: not a search for Christ but an attempt to walk with others through the seasons of nature, the church year, and life—and to do so in my place, one day at a time. I took the time to enfold my children into the story without which the pilgrimage made no sense. I became a *liturgiste du quotidien* (liturgist of the everyday). Isn't this, I asked myself, what the Lord asked of his pilgrim people Israel when he instructed them to talk about their Lord to their children throughout the rhythms of their lives, when they were seated in their houses, walking by the way, lying down, and getting up (Deuteronomy 11:18-19)? May we help the little children come to Christ at God's speed, at all times and in all seasons, along the endless acres of the Advent woods and beyond!

As a mother, I intentionally slowed down in order to live in my children's tendre enfance; and for a time I kept their tempo. I entered into their pretend games on the floor, and they entered into the seasons of Christ and of nature with me. It was, for me, a grace: the grace of reliving the beloved season of childhood but this time knowing Who was behind the wonder.

Advent walks invite quiet entry into the story of Jesus, even for a young child. I remember Advent walks on Blackford Hill, with a hazy Edinburgh in the distance, and how it provided two little girls with a treasure trove of decorations for the manger, including a half walnut that became Jesus' crib. This was the way they learned to welcome Jesus in their own place. If Jesus came to Bethlehem, or Provence, and even now to Edinburgh and its bonnie braes of heather, surely he could also come into our house. Our two-bedroom flat became a stage where ordinary time blended with the extraordinary, a space between worlds to treasure and explore.

"A little child shall lead them" (Isaiah 11:6). I was leading my little girls on the pilgrimage, teaching them about Jesus, but meanwhile they were giving me fresh vision. Could it be that the little child who comes alongside, rather than slowing down the adults he accompanies, in fact speeds them on the pilgrimage of faith by helping them walk at God's speed? Might God's speed, in fact, be child's speed? This is the gift of the child santon.

THE ART OF EATING IN SEASON

Children come to the table with their family because table fellowship is an integral part of the Christian pilgrimage, a place of nourishment and communion. Here, as elsewhere, children are neither the center nor on the margins of family life. There is no separate table for the children, for there is only one pilgrimage. The same fresh-grown local food nourishes adult and child alike. Attending to the seasons and the rhythms of the earth teaches youngsters about the rhythms of watching and waiting—for raspberries to become plump, for pumpkins to become as large as a fairy-tale carriage: a crucial life skill and discipline for those who wish to observe the "proper time" of things (Matthew 24:45). The land does not produce strawberries on demand. How much wiser it is to learn from a young age to wait for things at God's speed!

The table shows us not only the rhythms of nature but also the rhythms of human life. The table gathers young and old alike. The table is where we share hopes and hurts, where we learn to see the world through each other's eyes. Children contribute to the meal after their own fashion, according to their giftedness and capacity, be it picking wildflowers for a

WEEK 3 ∽ *Pray*

From "Be Thou My Vision," the beloved eighth-century Irish hymn, pray:

> "Be Thou my Vision, O Lord of my heart;
> Naught be all else to me, save that Thou art.
> Thou my best Thought, by day or by night,
> Waking or sleeping, Thy presence my light.

"Father, show me how to walk in your steps with the little children I live with, teach, babysit, or accompany; how to give them good reason to trust a caring parent or adult companion so they might trust their heavenly Father; how to help them marvel at the world around them so they might see you in and behind your handiwork.

"Help us, whether or not there are children around, through these reflections to see you and your wonderful world with a fresh vision of trust and wonder and, like little children, dare to imagine and believe in everyday miracles! Help us to discover (and rediscover) the marvelous in the mundane. Be Thou our vision!"

centerpiece, sweeping the floor, or saying grace. All these can be gifts for the child Christ, who is always there as a special guest.

In the land of my ancestors, there is a special meal that belongs to the season of childhood: *le goûter* (literally, "the tasting"). It is also called *le quatre-heure* (the four o'clock), that time for a little something to appease the growing pains of growing people, sandwiched in the middle of the long afternoon stretch between lunch and a dinner that may not be served until 8:00 p.m. Children typically eat their *goûter* at the table with Mother or Father and perhaps a sibling and a friend or two. They might take it outside on a nice day under a tree or by a riverbank.

The *goûter* is also the setting for madeleines, the little teacakes immortalized by Marcel Proust in his *Remembrance of Things Past*. In what is probably the book's best-known passage, the taste of a madeleine unexpectedly triggers a memory, instantly transporting the grown-up narrator back to a time and place of childhood felicity, conveying a palpable sense of both joy and longing. Although Proust does not put it in these terms, we might describe the experience as "a remembrance of la tendre enfance," particularly the weekly rhythm of visits to his aunt on Sundays punctuated with the unmistakable taste of a madeleine dipped in a cup of tea.[8]

Seasonal rituals, particularly table traditions with the children on our pilgrimage—the Thirteen Desserts (which we explored in chapter two), Sunday teas, and summer picnic breakfasts—remind us that there is a greater story that frames our lives. At the very least, as in my own tender childhood, the table rooted me in my family's and my region's story and terroir: we are home!

Everyday saints have their own special meal, of course, and their own special Table. The Lord's Supper, a tradition that is as precious as it is mysterious, serves as a means of remembering (and receiving) Christ's presence afresh. As such, it reminds us that we too are children—beloved and adopted children of God. It is by no means sacrilegious to say that the Lord's Supper is the everyday saints' madeleine, as it were, only it looks forward as well as back: "until he comes"

(1 Corinthians 11:26). This madeleine pulls in both directions because when Jesus entered the manger, he initiated our return home. We look forward to recovering the *tendre enfance* with God the Father that we once enjoyed. As Jen Pollock Michel says, "God put Adam and Eve in the garden much like a mother swaddles her newborn baby and puts the child in the cradle. *You're safe*, she shushes."[9]

WHAT'S AN EVERYDAY SAINT TO DO?

With or without children in tow, everyday saints do well to respond to Jesus' summons to become like a little child. It all starts with the Advent walk and continues through the joyful giving of Christmas, the welcoming of the stranger, the pruning of Lent, and not forgetting the

WEEK 4 ∾ *Play Your Part*

"Always, when he and his mother were alone, the library seemed intimate and familiar. . . . Around and through what they were doing, each of them was aware of the other's presence . . . all the lines and surfaces of the room bent toward his mother, so that when he looked at the pattern of the rug he saw it necessarily in relation to the toe of her shoe."[10]

Likewise, everyday saints see everything in God's household bent toward their Father, in whose story they travel. Try to cultivate the art of seeing afresh the toe of the Father's shoe this week:

- Think or speak with a friend or family member about a children's book that brought a sense of wonder in your childhood, or about a food that has a tender childhood story associated with it.[11] Spend some time at a child's speed, perhaps on your sabbath, paging through that book again. If you do this in a group, make it a *goûter* and have some madeleines to pass around and talk about the madeleine effect—and how we might be madeleines of God to others.
- If you organize a Christmas pageant annually and have more little actors than are needed, instead of casting extra children in hordes

occasional afternoon lézardage. We continue as children, pretending that we're in the Great Story (and, of course, we are!) through the ordinary seasons: when going to work; or looking for hidden blessings in winter gardens; or in reading books that transport us to imaginary places; or when lying down in beds, tents, or tree houses; or when waking to the smell of manna like fresh croissants. Your adventure begins with Advent. Better: every season of life, no matter how ordinary, has something Adventish about it, if only we could learn consistently to watch and wait for Christ's coming to us in everyday moments. Paying attention to the seasons through which we constantly live and move is a discipline that helps disciples stay alert and keep their vision fresh, like a little child eagerly anticipating Christmas morning.

of angels or shepherds (or sheep, as our children once were), ask the children what kind of little saint they'd like to be. What gift would they like to bring and why? Is there something they particularly love to do and are good at? Perhaps one might bake a batch of cookies, another might write a poem, and still another might bring a basket of homegrown carrots. Including everyday vocations in your Christmas pageant could be a compelling parable, a reminder that everyone can be a saint if they would only set apart their life and work as an offering to the Lord.

- Might these gifts be used for a Christmas party after the event or even for a Christmas food pantry? Expand your child's vision of how to be a little saint for the Lord! This is an excellent way of getting them—and the adults in the congregation—to rethink what discipleship means and looks like!
- Might "all the lines and surfaces of our world" bend toward our heavenly Father, so that when we gaze at the pattern of a flower or contemplate a line of ants on the pavement, we could see all these things in relation to our heavenly "Father of lights," the Giver of every good gift and perfect gift from above (James 1:17)?

Proust's narrator tries repeatedly to recapture his precious experience by dunking madeleine after madeleine; alas, the moment has passed. He ruefully realizes that one cannot manufacture these small moments of joy on demand. Everyday saints know that they come instead as gifts to those on pilgrimage, walking the Way with eyes (of faith) to see like a little child when they take time to stop and see the gifts. And there is more: everyday saints can be madeleines to one another, conveying not a memory of childhood past but a foretaste of childhood to come, an earnest hope for a future tendre enfance and for an eternal home where everyday saints, children of Abraham, will gather round the tree of life with the whole family of God and exclaim, "Abba, Father!"

Chapter 13

ALONGSIDE THE ELDERS

THE ART OF PASSING DOWN HEIRLOOMS

In him we have obtained an inheritance.

EPHESIANS 1:11

As long as we have stories to tell each other there is hope. As long
as we can remind each other of the lives of men and women
in whom the love of God becomes manifest, there is reason to
move forward to new land in which new stories are hidden.

HENRI J. M. NOUWEN, *THE LIVING REMINDER*

She had only to stand in the orchard . . . and look
up at the apples, to make you feel the goodness of
planting and tending and harvesting at last.

WILLA CATHER, *MY ÁNTONIA*

WHAT HAVE ELDERS TO DO WITH
OUR EVERYDAY PILGRIMAGE?

And so we arrive at autumn, the conclusion of our ordinary time in the land. The seeds planted at the start of our pilgrimage have produced a harvest in fields, homes, and towns. Farms display God's autumnal artistry on nature's canvas and his abundant provision in the land's last breath of generosity before its long winter rest. Autumn is a season of transition, a sunset with its poignant mix of changing hues, turning gradually from brilliance to enveloping dusk. Once the bright display of the scenery quiets down like a final sigh of worship, the country-side retreats into itself. It is time to put the garden to bed, to let the earth go under its cover of leaves as it retreats into its winter repose.

Our penultimate group of santons is the elders. It is fitting that they appear toward the end of ordinary time, for they are experiencing a transitional season in their own lives. Ordinary time slows as both nature and older saints gradually enter a season of what we might describe as hibernation.

Older characters figure prominently in the traditional crèche; they have their own roles to play. In stark contrast, elders are often invisible in contemporary society and are rarely seen in mixed company. Where are they? Their gait may have slowed, but are they no longer on the pilgrimage? Are they perhaps stuck in the backwaters or dead-end lanes, like withered heirloom apple trees? Can an elderly person be a santon, or is this a season to abandon the pilgrimage, to *retire* from discipleship?

KEY TERM FOR EVERYDAY SAINTS: *PLANTE PATRIMONIALE*

The idiomatic English equivalent for this term is *heirloom plant*. But the more literal *patrimonial plant* may be more fitting as we conclude our section on ordinary time. Remember that we began these reflections with the land (terroir) that grounds a patrimoine. Recall that a patrimoine is a common inheritance that includes both the material produce of a terroir (like heirloom tomatoes) and the cultural heritage growing out of it (like the *savoir-faire* of grafting fruit trees). A people must pass on a patrimoine from one generation to the next in order to maintain their sense of belonging, their particular identity and vital connection with their particular place. A functioning patrimoine requires both elders and children, both those who pass it on and those who receive it.

What is an heirloom plant? Simply put, to qualify as an heirloom a plant must be at least two generations old—and the older the better, for what heirloom enthusiasts love best is to know plant family history. Each heirloom has an individual story, an "intrinsic personality," often tied to a local terroir. Growers collect their seeds and cultivate an heirloom with the goal of preserving ancient genes for future generations. Heirlooms are the lifeblood of the local terroir and the patrimoine that has grown around it.

No heirloom produce is on more conspicuous display in my local farmers' markets during the autumn than apples. September marks the grand opening of this season of changes, and multiple varieties of heirloom apples begin to appear. The assortment is often astounding, though even this variety pales in comparison to the thousands of species of heirloom apples spread over myriad small family orchards across American and European countrysides. Many varieties come with names that are as colorful as the apples themselves. In my local market I have seen Bloody Ploughman and Esopus Spitzenburg, as well as my childhood favorite, Reine des Reinettes, to name but a few.

Where do they all come from? Heirloom orchardists are only too glad to share their knowledge of each specific apple. Each variety of heirloom apple has a narrative of its own that explains how it got its name, usually from some person, place, or event.[1] Settlers introduced apples to the United States beginning in the late sixteenth century: they came from Italy, France, Germany, Holland, England, and Scotland. In the words of Dan Bussey, the noted apple historian: "It was that little piece of home that you took with you."[2] These heirlooms have been passed down within families for generations with the intention of preserving what orchardists call a lineage. They contrast sharply with "Big Farma" (the agricultural industrial complex) and its predictable, commercially grown, mass-produced apples. Such industrial plants belong to a global market with no room for either personality or patrimoine.[3]

Isaac Newton discovered gravity by observing a falling apple. What we discover observing heirloom apples, however, is nothing less than a

fruit worth keeping, cultivating, and passing down—not only for its
juicy flesh but also for its cultured spirit.

AN EVERYDAY VOCATION

Old age eventually comes to every santon. These little saints are slightly
bent over, perhaps slower paced than when they were in their prime. Yet
they, too, have gifts to bring to the child Christ, so they persevere in their
pilgrimage. Many of these elder santons come as a couple linking arms
to support each other in their journey. Some of them travel alone, while
others have traveled the pilgrimage together for so long that they are
glued together on their stand.

Elders offer heirlooms: a piece of the past with meaning for the present,
symbols of a patrimoine that, if not handed down, would disappear. For
example, an elder's slower pace may itself represent a precious countercultural example to harried younger folks. Indeed, what the world calls
retirement can become for the elderly everyday saint an occasion for the

WEEK 1 ∽ *Pause*

Apple historian Dan Bussey described heirloom apples as a little piece of
home that you took with you.

Do you ever mark or celebrate the apple season (September all the way
through November)? Do you make a point of buying new kinds you've
never tasted before? Do you know which are better for eating, baking,
or storing?

Some varieties of apples are still harvested (depending on the weather
and region) just before the first frost. Investigate your area, talk with
orchardists, taste new kinds of apples, and find one species with which
you feel a particular affection. What is it that gives you that sense of
relatedness: its taste, coloring, odd shape, place of origin, or story?

Are there stories or objects other than apples in your life that connect
you with something from your past, a little piece of home that you take
with you?

reorientation necessary for living well—in time and in tune—in the season of sundown. As Vanessa Diffenbaugh notes about migrating birds: "Just when the sun drops beyond the horizon line, birds flying in the wrong direction correct their flight paths all at once."[4] Some elders in this sunset season try to fly high, pursuing "amortality" through various diets and

Les vieux (the elders)

exercises in a vain attempt to deny their finitude. [5] In contrast, everyday elder saints pursue spiritual exercises, walking in the measured steps of the Lord in whom they seek not amortality but immortality, the promise

A branch of bittersweet

of "an inheritance which is imperishable, undefiled, and unfading" (1 Peter 1:4). Older everyday saints have Adventish adventures too, watching and waiting in faith, the most precious heirloom they can pass on. For the inheritance that is theirs in Christ, whose guarantee is the Holy Spirit, lives even in older bodies and can vivify old bones.

My illustration depicts a branch of bittersweet. Its vivid colors convey the intense brilliance of the season while its name reminds us of the dusk that inevitably follows dawn. The autumn of our lives is a season to begin preparing to leave a place we love and know so well for a place we love and know by faith alone.

AUTUMN HEIRLOOMS IN PROVENÇAL CULTURE

The cultural heritage of my own birthplace presents both autumn's brilliant color and its fading sunset.

In the village of my ancestors nestled in the Rhône valley, there is still time in early autumn to harvest and preserve what we can in anticipation of the stark winter ahead. As long as the earth keeps producing bounties for pantries, those who live close

Black-eyed Susans in different stages

to the land continue to can vegetables and line them up on shelves, whence their vibrant and varied colors gleam through the glass. They hang bunches of aromatic herbs from rafters and spread fruit on wooden pallets where they dry out in the sun. Vintners and their crews frantically pick grapes before the late October rains spoil them: Grenache, Clairette, and Viognier, all of which eventually end up on the table one way or another, either fresh, dried, or pressed and bottled up.

The fields and vineyards slowly color the land in gold, copper, and bright russets until the leafy show ends in somber tones. Flowers go the way of all grass. The last black-eyed Susans, which in summer cast one dazzling ocher hue after another, are slowly turning into seedheads— food banks for the birds of the air.

As the dusk of autumn falls, the calendar becomes more and more meditative. On November 1, villages throughout the country observe *La Toussaint* (All Saints' Day) against a gloomy backdrop of overcast skies, constant drizzles, and brownish fluttering leaves. It is an important occasion to collect another kind of heirloom. The day typically begins with families visiting well-trodden cemeteries where young and old unite as they recall the melancholy lines of poems that we all learned in school. Paul Verlaine's "Chanson d'automne" is one: "The prolonged sobs / of autumn's violins / bruise my heart / with a monotonous / languor."[6] Here's one from Victor Hugo: "The fleeing summer is a departing friend."[7] Everyday saints should not shy away from this mournful mood. After all, Jesus himself paused in front of Lazarus's tomb and wept for the loss of his friend. Even he felt the bitterness of human loss, the passing of a season as it were, no matter how temporary.

In Provence, after depositing the customary *couronnes de toussaints* (a chrysanthemum "crown") on gravesites and paying their respects, people gather at the eldest member's home, perhaps to roast chestnuts around a crackling fire while pondering the passing of time. This is a moment for families to recall not the venerated "official" saints but all the saints, even the ordinary, unofficial ones: grandparents, parents, uncles, aunts, and others. They re-create the lives of their loved ones in bits and pieces, one anecdote or memory at a time. Through this process of communal storytelling, we construct a memory mosaic in which we see, in the words of Wendell Berry, that "the dead remain in thought as much alive as they ever were, yet increased in stature and remarkably near. . . . Our true home is not just this place, but it is also that company of immortals with whom we have lived here day by day."[8] We thus *re-member* or reconstitute our family thanks to the stories that have themselves become family heirlooms that sustain our identities and enrich our lives with each passing year. These stories become that little piece of home that we take with us.

Everyday saints aren't the only ones who practice remembering (and *re-membering*). Ancient Israel's family lists and genealogies figure prominently in Scripture—and they are essential to the story, not peripheral to it (e.g., 1 Chronicles 1:1-9:44). These genealogies reminded the children of Abraham where they had come from, how they had arrived at their present location, and where they were going. They are also God's way of reaffirming that he too remembered his people, and that he promised to lead them to a land where they would flourish. Recalling these genealogies provided an opportunity for resetting their trajectory, for remembering whose story they were enacting, and for giving thanks to God for his redemption. These stories are heirlooms, part of Israel's patrimoine, treasures to pass down to their children.

WEEK 2 ⁓ *Ponder*

"And now I am about to go the way of all the earth, and you know in your hearts and souls, all of you, that not one word has failed of all the good things that the LORD your God promised concerning you." JOSHUA 23:14

Have you ever considered the connection between autumn sunsets and the sunset of life? If you do not have a garden to put to bed, do you even notice the more reflective side of the season, or do you try to avoid thinking about it? How should an everyday saint think about this elegiac season?

What if the autumn season allows us time to process not just the sadness of departure, of missing absent friends, but also the thankfulness of looking back at what the departed ones have left us and the faithfulness of God in their lives and ours? Can we take time to recall our departed ones, bring up memories, share stories and photographs

So even to old age and gray hairs,
O God, do not forsake me,
until I proclaim your might to another generation,
your power to all those to come. (Psalm 71:18)

MY OWN PILGRIMAGE

I can still see them at the arrivals area of Chicago's O'Hare airport: my parents, two Hobbits stepping bravely outside their Shire for the first time, agape at the sheer size of the terminal, the cars and, yes, the Americans themselves, who towered over them. They had journeyed halfway around the world for their first grandchild's birth bringing gifts from afar, like mini-Magis. Among their bags was a box wrapped in string that I instantly recognized, for it used to appear every Christmastime: the family crèche. It was time to pass it down to the next generation.

The farther I am from my birthplace, the more I have come to see the crèche as a multi-faceted heirloom. On one level, it represents all the childhood Christmas stories that have been indelibly imprinted in my

with our children, our children's children, and a neighbor or two in this season?

How might you regain a sense of belonging to a greater story by remembering elders who have gone before you? Can you see how the elders who are still with us can help us to persevere and proclaim his might and faithfulness to the generations to come?

Where are our everyday elder saints, the ones we often overlook but who might have words of wisdom for us, holy heirlooms to pass down? Are they sitting out the final leg of the race set before them (Hebrews 12:1)? Or are they perhaps not made to feel welcome in our homes, neighborhoods, or—heaven forbid!—our churches? What would it take to accompany them in the final stages of their earthly pilgrimage, encourage them in their final season, and invite them to help us grow in our own discipleship?

memory, and now, on my children's. On another level, it represents the patrimoine of Provence, from the traditional architecture and métiers represented by the santons and the songs that tell their stories to the earth from which they are made. I still feel rooted in that land and family, despite being an ocean away. And on the deepest level, the crèche proclaims the underlying Great Story of God's grace made flesh, a story that it contextualizes in the noëls and pastorales of Provence, telling how God's son came to our sun-drenched lavender land. Like an heirloom apple, the crèche is, literally, a "little piece of home I take with me" wherever I go.

Clearly the crèche is an heirloom worth passing on. As I approach my own sunset years, I find myself revisiting conversations with orchardists about how to grow heirloom apples and asking: "What other heirlooms are worth cultivating and passing down?" One crisp October day a few years ago, as I was sketching my Spitzenberg apple in a small family-owned orchard, a helpful image came to mind. It had something to do with the age-old horticultural technique of grafting.

In grafting, the orchardist attaches a branch of a tree (the scion), say a Spitzenberg, to a rootstock in such a way that the new branch can grow from the older root. The scion must have proper contact with the root of the old trunk from whence nutrients come or the graft simply doesn't take. When the operation is successful, the graft and trunk eventually merge, becoming one, an apple tree in the Spitzenberg family: an heirloom with a lineage. Thanks be to God: some branches of Israel were broken off so that Gentiles like me could be grafted into the covenant people of God (Romans 11:17-24).

I realized that what an experienced orchardist passes down to the next generations is not just apples nor even apple trees, but the age-old practical wisdom of husbanding an heirloom. It struck me that this was precisely what my ancestors did when they grafted the story of the Christ child onto an ancient trunk, through the new branch of the crèche— complete with local stories, culture, and terroir of Provence. The heirloom, then, is not merely the object itself, no matter how precious, but everything it conveys: the spirit of its place and the stories that tie it to its people. There is nothing "sacred" about Provençal manger scenes. Possessions, treasures, events, even rites lose their value if they are devoid of the stories that give them meaning and bring them to life. Mere objects are empty things and may become idols. But if Christmas—nay, Christ—came to Provence to graft it and its land onto his Great Story, then the crèche and everyone connected with it indeed becomes holy: little saints.

And so in this season of my early autumn, I wonder: How can I continue to pass down, as did my ancestors, the art of grafting new life experiences onto old stories, prolonging their life by transplanting them into new contexts that they in turn enrich? This is what I was trying to do when I made my girls a family cookbook: next to each classic family recipe I included family stories and anecdotes, table graces we used to sing in rounds, and photos of our extended family at table in various places throughout the years. I see now that I was grafting new stories onto old recipes.

Everyday saints do something similar when they graft their own family stories into the larger story of Christ. This is what it means to belong to the company of pilgrims who are following Jesus out of the manger beyond Christmas and through the year. Moment by ordinary moment, season by season, we live out his life hidden in us. I want to inhabit his Great Story, whether in stingy winters or prodigal summers, in fields, homes, villages, or cityscapes—all the places I inhabit. I want to be a santon who presents gifts to Jesus, not only in the manger but also in ten thousand ordinary places.

The story of my pilgrimage is the story of an everyday Provençal saint trying to keep in step with Jesus, grafting everything I am and everything I do into Christ, now wrapped not in swaddling clothes but in my heart, memories, and personal stories, themselves planted in the physical world of my local terroir—wherever that happens to be. I want to grow his story that is that little bit of home I take with me from the sunrise to the sunset of my life.

THE ART OF EATING IN SEASON

The seasonal cycle in the kitchen garden ends on a high note with a rich harvest of produce, including apples, that will last months when stored

The seasons of a Spitzenburg apple

and preserved properly. Each breed of apple comes to fruition in its own time over a six-month span and has its own recipes for which it is most suited, from Normandy cider and southern French *clafoutis aux pommes* to simple dessert apples. One kind of apple can last up to two years in storage, hence its name, Deux Ans (Two Years). Another, the Calville Blanc, has a higher vitamin C content than an orange. Think of the apple as God's daily vitamin through the seasons. A petit miracle of its own!

WEEK 3 ⁓ *Pray*

Rueben Job, Norman Shawchuck, and John Mogabgab write, "Hold before my eyes, my Lord, the diminishing number of my fleeting days, that I may receive them as precious gifts and live them in faithfulness and fidelity to you."[9]

"Lord, thank you for the elder saints who have gone before me and passed down a heritage of true value: parents, pastors, friends, elder neighbors, and whoever helped me in my pilgrimage. Continue to place me in the path and writings of such people that I might grow more like you.

"Help me to graft my life into yours in such a way that my story draws strength from yours, that I might say with Paul: 'It is no longer I who live, but Christ who lives in me!' (Galatians 2:20). Help me to discern which are the heirlooms worth cultivating and passing down. Help me to let go of the ones that cannot be grafted onto you.

"Help me to welcome elders in my life, in my church, in my conversations, so I might learn from them, and appreciate that they still have a role to play in your Great Story—that they still have gifts to bring to Jesus!

"Help me, even in the season when I am bent over, to be an 'upright Christian.'"

Martin Luther writes in *Table Talk,* "Upright Christians pray without ceasing; though they pray not always with their mouths, yet their hearts pray continually, sleeping and waking; for the sigh of a true Christian is a prayer."[10]

Eventually autumn's dusk descends on elder pilgrims. Some grow confused, yet the rhythm of the seasonal table they have kept for a lifetime anchors them a while longer in the Great Story and in the earthly place that for a while longer, is still their home. When the routine culinary preparations become too challenging, it is time for a neighboring everyday saint with a soup kettle to drop by and leave restaurative stews or an invitation to share their own table. Gifts of seasonable heirloom foods such as pumpkin soups or age-old baked apples recall God's graciousness, the fleeting beauty of the passing seasons, and the honest goodness of saintly neighbors—simple truths an aging saint may occasionally forget.

Younger everyday saints who accompany the aged ought to invite them to the other Table they share weekly, in fellowship, where they might sing an heirloom hymn or two. For the elder saint, the words and tunes of classic hymns may be the last best means to remember the story in which they have journeyed, and for the young to walk in it with them. At this table, young and old alike are guests with their Lord as host, he who says to all, "Take, eat and drink, *in remembrance* of me." The Lord's Supper is the ultimate heirloom. It is an everyday meal at an everyday table where everyday saints remember the Great Story in which they are eternally remembered and *re-membered* (grafted into the body of Christ). This is the story that encompasses and completes all the meals, tables, and seasons that have anticipated the Lord's second Advent.

WHAT'S AN EVERYDAY SAINT TO DO?

Lineage matters, in and out of orchards. The Old Testament opens with the "generations / of the heavens and the earth" (Genesis 2:4), while the New Testament opens with the generations of Jesus, the genealogy of the long-awaited Messiah (Matthew 1:1-17). This is the background of the story of Christmas, a reminder that each person in the family tree had a role to play—even the obscure character of Azor (Matthew 1:13-14), mentioned nowhere else in the Bible. Everyday saints should recall their own genealogies in this remembrance season.

When human memories fade, it is comforting to know that God remembers everything perfectly. As God remembered Noah (Genesis 8:1),

WEEK 4 ∕ *Play Your Part*

"By the Holy Spirit who dwells within us, guard [and pass on] the good deposit entrusted to you." 2 TIMOTHY 1:14

Do you know elders who have learned the art of grafting their everyday lives onto the life of Christ, orchardists of the Lord with fruit worth passing down? What do they have that you find worth emulating and passing down? Can you start collecting words of wisdom from elders that can help you graft your own everyday life onto Christ?

Thank God for elder everyday saints. Send those who are still living a note or better yet give it to them in person, and—why not?—add a basket of heirloom apples, explaining to these elders how they have contributed to your own growth and fruition.

If your church segregates age groups, can you think of ways to bridge this generation gap, perhaps by organizing fellowship times for mixed ages? Can you imagine how this might be a blessing over time, fractured from extended families as we often are? Can you "adopt" an elder? Or, if you are one, can you "adopt" a younger person or young family? Doug Sweeney urges us: "Dear seniors, please show us how to live in light of eternity. Show us how to wean our affections from the world. Show us how to prepare for life in heaven and the new Jerusalem. We need you!"[11]

Be mindful, this week and forever more, of heirlooms in your life worth cherishing and passing down to those you love.

Perhaps you are in your sunset years and have never thought of heirlooms this way before. Not to worry. Today, if you hear his voice, follow him, enter his rest—and start grafting now (Hebrews 3:15). In this Great Story of good news and new things, every day holds the promise of a new Advent! Every day provides opportunities to cultivate heirlooms that are that little bit of him we take along.

Abraham (Genesis 19:29), and Rachel (Genesis 30:22), so he will *re-member* every believer, recreating each person, limb by limb and bone to bone (Ezekiel 37:7-14). To remember God's *re-membering*, as everyday saints need to do every day, is to sustain bright hope for tomorrow even as today fades away.

Every day elderly saints, whether they are literal orchardists or not, know that what matters most in one's pilgrimage is to graft oneself and one's vocation onto the true Vine, Jesus Christ, the origin of their new lineage. "I am the vine; you are the branches. Whoever abides in me and I in him, he it is that bears much fruit, for apart from me you can do nothing" (John 15:5).

The art of living in autumn means pausing a while, remembering one's lineage (where you've come from), destiny (where you're going), vocation (what your role is in the Great Story of which you are a part)— all of which is to say, your Lord (the trunk of the family tree onto which you have been grafted). The most precious heirloom everyday saints can pass on is the story of Christ. Call it heirloom faith. For when we are grafted into Christ, our lives and life stories pass on the Great Story that embraces, orients, and sustains us. In God's grace, our life stories become heirlooms themselves, not so much that little piece of home but rather that little piece of him to whose home we are traveling and hope to inherit, being "fellow heirs with Christ" (Romans 8:17).

Chapter 14

THE FEAST OF CHRIST
THE KING

THE ART OF COMING HOME

He shall build a house for my name, and I will
establish the throne of his kingdom forever.

2 SAMUEL 7:13

I have come home at last! This is my real country! I belong
here. This is the land I have been looking for all my life, though
I never knew it till now. The reason why we loved the old
Narnia is that it sometimes looked a little bit like this.

C. S. LEWIS, *THE LAST BATTLE*

WHERE SEASONS CONVERGE IN HOMELAND POETRY

The Christian year concludes with a unique date on the calendar, a crowning moment that embraces all the seasons, making it a fitting conclusion to our everyday saints' pilgrimage. This special season marks the reign of Christ and technically lasts only a single day—Christ the King Sunday. It is the final Sunday in Ordinary Time, typically landing toward the end of November, the last stop before Advent begins the new church year. (In this chapter I suggest spreading the reflections out over one week rather than four, until Advent.)

Our pilgrimage began quietly, seeking the baby Jesus. We have now traversed the whole of his life. Everyday saints have followed him as he left the confines of the manger, through the centuries and across continents. We no longer have to travel to Bethlehem: Jesus is in all four corners of the earth, for through his Spirit he now indwells everyday saints' ordinary times, places, and vocations. The babe born to be King of kings has been duly crowned "with glory and honor" (Hebrews 2:7, citing Psalm 8:5).

And here is the marvel, a wondrous exchange of place: in entering the lives of everyday saints in their everyday places, he has also made each everyday saint and place his home. Emmanuel: God with us. He is Lord over every square inch; he reigns in ten thousand places. He reigns already in our lives through his Spirit, and he will come again in his good time to reign in glory for all to see—his second Advent.

As the cold of the impending winter settles on a land yet warm from autumn, a mist rises from the ground, enveloping the village of my ancestors. It blurs the line between the heavens and the earth and makes the homes look like they float above the surface of the ground. This natural phenomenon left its mark on a short-lived French calendar of the late 1700s that assigned each month a seasonal name. *Novembre* became *brumaire*, the month of mist.[1] This gauzy season yet again matches its counterpart in the church calendar, for this time intimates the eschatological reign of Christ, which *already* envelops us faintly as we participate in his risen life—though we do *not yet* see the full glory of our reigning Lord. We are already and not yet home in the place Christ is preparing for us. Yet our pilgrimage has taught us to walk by faith, to "look not to the things that are seen but to the things that are unseen. For the things that are seen are transient, but the things that are unseen are eternal" (2 Corinthians 4:18).

The white oak provides a fitting botanical illustration for Christ's reign, as its stately appearance and strong wood traditionally connote majesty and strength. The Arbor Day Foundation even notes, "All oaks are considered America's national tree, but the white oak has been called the king of kings."[2] Yet in November, the oak's fresh green summer attire fades in memory and blends in with autumn's colors aided by the gentle mist. In this liminal season, when heaven and earth blur in a haze of tender hues, everyday saints might feel a restless longing for other places too poignant for words—call it an autumnal *frisson*—a tension between the love of their terroir and the glories of a promised land ahead, the home we are all seeking.

A liminal white oak branch

Wendy Miller reflects, "Perhaps, if we listen to Jesus, we will discover that these longings are the doorways through which we come to God and through which God comes to us."[3]

A KEY TERM FOR EVERYDAY SAINTS: *FÉLIBRIGE*

In the land of my ancestors, there is another important word without which perhaps none of the traditions described in this book would still be alive—and nor would this project have gotten off the ground. The *Félibrige* is a literary and cultural fellowship begun by seven writers (*félibres*) of Provence, the most famous being Frédéric Mistral.[4] It was founded in 1854 with the goal of guarding the language, literature, and culture of Provence—its historical traditions, its way of life, its very soul—which at the time were in danger of being overshadowed by the majority (French) language and culture.

The fellows who made up the Félibrige had a clear mission: to preserve in words the patrimoine of Provence, bringing the place and its people to speech in order to keep their spirit alive. Their life's goal was to articulate the spirit of their place in order to pass it on in generations to come, rooting their children and their children's children in their own terroir. This terroir, with its thyme- and rosemary-covered hills, cradles the crèche and its santons.

The Félibrige collected stories, songs, recipes—anything that made up their traditional way of life—and wrote them down in their own native tongue in their famous *Almanac Provençal*, published annually for decades. They preserved the culture by setting it not in stone but poetic stanza. The traditional noëls, pastorales, and the crèche were part and parcel of this cultural heritage. And the Christmas santons became so intricately and wonderfully woven into the cultural heritage that today they have come to represent everyday Provence in *all* seasons.

Pause

Ted Orland writes, "We become who we are by virtue of the choices we make—consciously or otherwise—about which parts belong to our story, and which parts can be left out."[5]

What might we learn from the félibre, the poet-guardian of a place's cultural heritage, its very soul? Is there something you value about your culture that is so dear to you that you would go to great lengths, perhaps even writing a poem, to preserve it? Does it have to do with your family? Your birth culture? Your present locale? What would you need to do in order to keep it from eroding or disappearing? Do you perhaps need to take charge and organize family reunions with intentional heirloom activities?

What about your cultural heritage? Think about what part you might play, what your own giftedness might contribute to preserve these endangered aspects of culture. How did Israel and the early church preserve their respective cultural heritages? Do you see any connection between what they did and the Félibrige?

AN EVERYDAY VOCATION

Our final santon is the félibre, whose ancestor might well be the thirteenth-century troubadour. The term *félibre* refers either to a Provençal poet who eulogizes her local place or to a Provençal person who devotes her life to preserving her cultural heritage, or both: call such a person a poet-trustee. A félibre preserves this trust both through words (poetry) and by adopting a way of life (practice) that is rooted in Provence.

Le félibre (the poet trustee)

This félibre santon comes to the crèche with a book under his arm: soothing rhymes for the baby Jesus. The presence of a félibre means that the baby will have a sense of place in which to root, dwell, and bear fruit. This little saint typically comes with a goatee and period attire that bear an unmistakable resemblance to Mistral; it's a simple homage to one of the original félibres. Mistral was the poet of Provence, a symbol of all those cultural trustees who have passed down the story of santons to me and countless other Provençaux.

Poets have a gift for calling our attention to important things that have somehow escaped our notice and for helping us to appreciate their significance by the beauty of the language with which they describe them. It is not unlike the way Jesus spoke in parables of the kingdom of heaven (*his* land and cultural heritage, as it were) for those who had ears to hear (Matthew 13:16). Poet-king David, himself a félibre of the Lord, excelled in calling attention to the splendor of God's world, its seasons, and the rhythms of life, in which everything has its own place. He also knew where his home was:

One thing have I asked of the LORD,
　　that will I seek after:
that I may dwell in the house of the LORD
　　all the days of my life,
to gaze upon the beauty of the LORD
　　and to inquire in his temple. (Psalm 27:4)

FÉLIBRIGE IN PROVENÇAL CULTURE

The fellowship of félibres persists to this day as a relatively small group meeting annually. It stands guard over the language and culture of Provence, the patrimoine handed down by their father's fathers, a homeland and heritage they in turn will entrust to future generations.[6]

Provence is not a holy nation, to be sure—although most Provençaux will try to convince you that it is. (This is the land of which Mistral said, no doubt playfully, "When the Good Lord gets discouraged with the world, he reminds himself that he created Provence."[7]) Yet like a nation (and the church), it preserves its traditions and way of life, not least by encouraging celebrations, special days that bring to mind the special seasons of the church, and by attending to and living in sync with their natural seasons too. No one thinks the félibres are divinely inspired, but we could with some justification describe them as evangelists for Provence or perhaps as reformers who insist on returning to the original languages not of the Bible but of the Languedoc (southern France).

By preserving and celebrating their patrimoine, the félibres were a major influence on what has come to be known as "the second renaissance of Provence."[8] At a time when the identity and integrity of their special place was threatened, this effort allowed them to reclaim their home and, in a sense, to return home.

The santons played a key role in this renaissance, communicating visually their place's local history and character: their cultural inheritance. It is telling that the French have nicknamed Provence "the land of the santons" (le pays des santons). Meanwhile, as figures in the story of Jesus, these same little clay figurines are imbued with the sacred as they busy themselves with their mundane vocations in the vicinity of Jesus. One has to ask: Am I looking at a slice of Provençal life or am I beholding the miracle of Christmas? Of course, the correct answer is *Oui!* There is no need for an either-or: the little saints are both ambassadors of Provence and ambassadors of Christ.

Everyday saints also have a homeland to represent: not Provence, but the kingdom of heaven, which Christians embody and bring to earth as the little saints do for Provence. Jesus used everyday people in his parables of the kingdom. I have tried to do something similar in this book, using the stories about the little saints surrounding the crèche as a parable for exploring the Christian pilgrimage. Provence is not heaven, but the way the little saints preserve their patrimoine is itself a parable of how everyday saints should seek to protect their cultural heritage and heavenly inheritance. For does not the kingdom of heaven on earth afford us a glimpse of our heavenly patrimoine? Could it be that, by keeping and observing the special seasons of Christ and living them out in our daily lives, we are poet-trustees here on earth of our patrimoine as it is in heaven?

Perhaps this way of living attentively in season—observing the special seasons of the church, the ordinary seasons of nature, and the varying seasons of life alike—is the highway of our pilgrimage that leads us home. Saint Augustine, a special everyday saint, spoke of Jesus as both our home and the way home: "though He Himself is our homeland, He made Himself the highway [*viam*] to that homeland [*patriam*]."[9] The art of living in season has everything to do with following Jesus out of the manger, onto the cross, and into our new life in Christ right here on earth in our everyday lives as his Spirit shows us the way.

There are "renaissance" stories in Scripture as well, in which the people of Israel recover their own cultural (i.e., covenantal) heritage. Perhaps the greatest of these recoveries began with the rediscovery of the book of the Law (probably Deuteronomy) under the reign of the boy-king Josiah. King Josiah realized that the Israelites were squandering their true inheritance, neglecting to worship the God that had brought them out of Egypt to the Promised Land and turning instead to the idols of the surrounding cultures (2 Chronicles 34).

In reading the book of the Law, Josiah remembered that the Lord had given the Promised Land to Israel, a land set apart so that Israel could be a set-apart people, "a kingdom of priests and a holy nation" (Exodus 19:6)—a gathering of little saints. Josiah rediscovered the word of God, delivered by Moses, that was to make Israel a great nation: "by this word you shall live long in the land that you are going over the Jordan to possess" (Deuteronomy 32:47). Josiah understood the Great Story to which his people belonged—and in telling it, he became a félibre of the Lord.

What Josiah recovered was not just a law textbook, but a treasure trove of stories of Israel's past complete with traditions to reenact, commandments to obey, foods to eat in their special seasons, songs to sing, and poems to recite. And this Book of the Law came with a promise: if the people kept these words and did what was required, they would

Ponder

Paul Ruat writes, "A félibre is a cultural advocate devoted to his local place who seeks to share his love of his homeland. He is an artisan of the written and spoken word who takes pleasure in the tongue of his ancestors; a félibre is one who makes it worth knowing local artists of the trowel, saw, and paintbrush, so that a ray of these homegrown glories might burst over France, for the greater benefit of the surrounding country."[10]

If the kingdom of heaven on earth is our Christian patrimoine, then shouldn't everyday saints be cultural advocates for our holy nation too? Think of ways that we can imbue our respective places with traces of Christ's kingdom, such that our places become, not the land of the santons but the land of everyday saints. What do Christians need to do and preserve in their respective places—home, workplace, neighborhood, local church—to become a ray of heaven's glories for the greater benefit of the surrounding country?

have a homeland forever, a divinely promised and prepared patrimoine. And the best blessing of all was that the Lord would meet and dwell with his people in the land as he had in the Garden of Eden.

MY OWN PILGRIMAGE

My own pilgrimage through the various seasons of life has led me, at last, to a wooded place. I like to think of it as a *sylvan* place (from Latin *silva*, "forest") because it

An oak leaf in its glories

describes both my own name and the places in which I first met the grandeur and glory of God: the evergreen forests of the Pyrénées and the lavender hills of the Luberon in Provence. God called me "Sylvie" in these sylvan places—a divine poetic touch!

In my current three-acre wood in the Midwest, I have learned to identify new trees not native to Provence: shagbark hickories, sugar maples, and the majestic white oaks. Botanists claim that "gardening with native plants perpetuates our region's unique natural heritage and creates a sense of place."[11] I have found this to be true. In learning about native roots, I put down roots of my own. I now belong to this new sylvan place, leaving my footprint in the soil, no longer simply a resident alien with a green card but a resident gardener with a green thumb in a green place: in a word, at home!

We live in an oak savanna, the sylvan patrimoine of the Midwest. Alas, the white oak is an endangered species. Without the diverse community of beneficial native plants that take shelter from its branches, rest in its shade, and attract pollinators, even the majestic oak becomes stressed. When the invasive hordes of European buckthorn turned out to be more than we could handle, arborists—call them félibres of the woods—came to our rescue, returning the oaks' ecosystem to its integrity in its original terroir. After months of diligent work, they scattered gallons of native seeds. A few seasons later, plants that belong to the region began to reappear, at home in the majestic oak understory designed by its original Gardener. It was a renaissance not of Provence but of the oak savanna.

I walk my sylvan paths in all seasons and find there a place to converse with my God. I agree with J. G. Millar that "the gift of the land was never intended to be an end in itself, but a means of developing the relationship between God and his people."[12] In late autumn, I glean branches and grasses that will go into my crèche, the better to root Jesus in my oak savanna. In the bleak midwinter, I find the promise of new life in the early buds on our hawthorns and wild blackberries. At Eastertime, I watch for spring beauties and trout lilies that, for a scant three weeks, transform the sylvan floor into a floral tapestry. In the long growing season of summer, I pause my stroll to contemplate the towering cup plants from which goldfinches sip rainwater, while monarch butterflies and hummingbirds flutter from black-eyed Susans to sneezeweeds.[13] For those who love oaks, all things work together for good in the savanna.

On these sylvan walks, I remember the félibres of old, those poet-trustees of Provence who in their own way (with words, not seeds) preserved what belonged to their place. Poet Christian Wiman could well be describing them when he says, "In the end we go to poetry for one reason, so that we might more fully inhabit our lives and the world in which we live them."[14] I have learned from the poet-trustees and from my own pilgrimage not to ask, "What do I *want* to grow in my garden?" but rather: "What *actually* belongs here?" And further: To which ecosystem do I belong? In what soil do I flourish? What story makes best sense of my pilgrimage through many earthly places? How can I find my true home (in Christ's kingdom) away from home?

I have come to realize that I belong not just to the oak understory but, more importantly, to Christ's overstory. The exalted Christ already reigns in heaven, but if I do not understand how to make my place on earth his home, how to graft things on earth onto his story, and how to clear away the invasive species that do not belong so that I can display his reign in my place, then I risk compromising his glory, much as the wrong understory weakens the mighty oak.

On my pilgrimage I have learned that I must make my place— wherever on earth it happens to be—a place to welcome Christ home by playing my role fittingly in God's good ecosystem, doing God's will on earth as it is in heaven. Living my citizenship of heaven on earth means engaging in a holy renaissance, like the félibres, though the realm I celebrate is not, after all, Provence, but the kingdom of God that has come "in Christ" to every place: where truth, goodness, and beauty are exhibited through his everyday saints in whom he dwells. And I am one of them: a little saint, an everyday saint, a little Christ.

THE ART OF EATING IN SEASON

In a happy coincidence of calendars, the feast of Christ the King usually falls in the week of American Thanksgiving. According to tradition, Thanksgiving commemorates the first Pilgrims who, thanks to their newfound

Pray

"Thy kingdom come; thy will be done, on earth as it is in heaven.

"God most high, you reign even now in earth and heaven. Help me to know what it looks like, in my place, to participate each day in your reign and to do your will on earth. Help me to remember the Great Story to which you have summoned me to become my true self. Help me to manifest your reign alive in all I do and say in my place, my work, my interactions, and my fellowship with your saints. Help me to discern how to preserve the integrity of your Greater Story and do only what is fitting as I continue my pilgrimage through it. Give me the courage to get rid of what does not fit and to keep growing all that belongs to your heavenly patrimoine here on earth!"

A colorful ear of Indian corn

neighbors' hospitality, eventually came to understand their new terroir. According to folklore, Native Americans shared turkey and succotash with the Pilgrims, causing them to thank God for the provisions of a new land. Although Thanksgiving is not part of the church calendar, a félibre of the Lord finds it fitting and poetically apt to graft it onto the greater story of divine providence: thanks be to God for gifts of food and drink!

Thanksgiving Day parallels the French *journées du patrimoine*, those cultural celebrations that take place at the end of harvest and focus on the provisions that grew out of a terroir (as we discussed in chapter eight). It is right and proper for everyday saints to give thanks for God's timely table provision throughout the seasons. In this particular season, the produce seems tailor-made—or rather, Creator-made—for the bare kitchen garden of the cold months ahead: pears and apples that can be stored for months, as can roots, nuts, and grains, not to mention the "hard" or winter squash. Indian corn contributes to the seasonal décor, feeds animals, and lifts the spirits of those who later will gather to pop corn on bleak midwinter nights.

Thanksgiving should remind everyday saints, present-day pilgrims, that the bounty they enjoy at their earthly table is merely a down payment of a banquet and a homeland yet to come. He also promises to "go to prepare a place for you" (John 14:2). Since Christ is king not merely for a day but forever, there is indeed a home ahead waiting for each one of us, to which all our longings point: a day when there will be no more pain, no more tears, and no more homesickness. On that day, Thanksgiving dinner will be a marriage supper of the Lamb (Revelation 19:9)—a thanksgiving banquet of another order—making our present Thanksgiving dinners an already and not-yet moment in the Great Story of Christ the King, in whom all the things and people we love have a place and are joined together in a superior and eternal patrimoine: that heavenly culture that even now is growing in our earthly terroir.

WHAT'S AN EVERYDAY SAINT TO DO?

This last santon, the poet-trustee, represents all everyday saints who want to play their parts well in the holy Pastorale of the Lord. The clay figurines matter not because they make a quaint appearance in Christ's manger, but because their stories make for everyday parables of the kingdom of God. Tish Harrison Warren puts it well: "The kingdom of God comes both through our gathered worship each week and our 'scattered' worship in our work each day."[15] Christ reigns when these everyday scenes become parables of the kingdom: stories of the extraordinary in the ordinary, of God transforming our daily prose into his royal poetry.

A Provençal writer observes: "each [santon] has a specific role to play in the motionless theatre of the crèche."[16] We living everyday saints have our own roles to play in Jesus' story, in the *living* theater of and outside the crèche. Whether in a small fishing village in Provence, the highlands of Scotland, a city neighborhood, or a prairie town, we pass on our saintly inheritance—our heavenly patrimoine—through our daily lives *on earth*. Is this not the very thing for which Jesus teaches us to pray?

Everyday saints are called to a holy Félibrige, to preserve the cultural heritage of King Jesus, the imperishable eternal *patrimoine* they have received in Christ. It is ultimately to the glories of this kingdom that we must bear witness, whatever the season in which we eat or drink, or do whatever it is we do. *This*, living in season to the glory of God, embodying Christ in our respective roles, must surely be our primary concern. As C. S. Lewis reminds us: "Considering the Christian idea of 'putting on Christ' . . . is not one among many jobs a Christian has to do. . . . It is the whole of Christianity. Christianity offers nothing else."[17]

We began our pilgrimage by looking for a way to welcome Jesus into our homes, in our crèches. But he was the one inviting us to his home all along. Listen to what New Testament scholar Robert Gundry says about homecoming: "God and Jesus abide in us just as we abide in

Play Your Part

Christina Rossetti writes in "In the Bleak Midwinter": "What can I give him, poor as I am? . . . If I were a Wise Man, I would do my part."[18]

Not all everyday saints are called to be poets, but each of us is called to be a félibre of the Lord, one who understands and sings the praises of her homeland and of the Author of everyday life (Acts 3:15). A félibre need not write poetry to proclaim the glories of her King. For it is through the little stories of little and everyday saints that we bear witness to the Great Story of the King whose name we bear. Every follower of Jesus, whether poet, arborist, ecologist, homemaker, teacher, engineer, or any other everyday saint, has to ask: How can I enact the reign of Christ today in my life, in my place, in my line of work?

The fact is, we are ambassadors of Christ, félibres of the Lord, and trustees of the gospel. Let us therefore play our part as an everyday saint and ambassador of Christ to the glory of God, and in so doing, pass on the precious patrimoine that belongs to all citizens of heaven.

We began our pilgrimage exclaiming with David: "I will not give sleep to my eyes / or slumber to my eyelids, / until I find a place for the LORD, / a dwelling place for the Mighty One of Jacob" (Psalm 132:4-5). We see now that he has found his place in us: in him, we are home!

them. We're their home just as they're our home—forever and ever. May this Homecoming remind us, then, of our home who has already come, and will yet come."[19] We have been preparing with our manger scenes a place for the One who is preparing a place for us (John 14:3).

The feast of Christ the King is homecoming season: we come home to him as we dwell in him not just for this one day but *throughout* our earthly pilgrimage. Everyday saints are wandering minstrels and faithful félibres, Renaissance women and men of God who practice the art of living in season by being attentive to Christ who comes, who advents through us, being "ready in season and out of season" (2 Timothy 4:2) to live his story and sing his praise.

EVERYDAY ADVENT:
THE ART OF REENGAGING

WHAT PILGRIMS NEED TO KNOW TO
CONTINUE THE PILGRIMAGE

Let us run with endurance the race that is set before us,
looking to Jesus, the founder and perfecter of our faith.

HEBREWS 12:1-2

WHAT'S AN EVERYDAY SAINT TO DO—
NOW AND IN THE YEAR AHEAD?

*A*nd so we return, a year later, to Advent. Everyday saints who have
kept in step with the santons traveling through the seasons now
revisit the quiet atmosphere of autumn's fading days and falling leaves—
but this time with a difference. We have learned to watch and wait. This
year we are better prepared to welcome the child Christ not simply in
the crèche or the church but in all the places we inhabit or pass through.

Why restart the journey? Haven't we been there, done that? Haven't
we already walked the Advent walk? Did we not welcome the Christ
child only twelve months ago? Do we really need to repeat our seasonal
pilgrimage, year after year?

Such questions evoke the anxiety of meaningless routines that my
angst-ridden generation dubbed *métro-boulot-dodo* (subway-work-
bedtime). Traveling with the santons through the seasons is not busy

Changing seasons of Virginia creeper

work, however, but something else altogether. My seasonal pilgrimage with these little saints helps me appreciate the goodness of the Creator and the created order, an order not of empty repetitions but of meaningful rhythms. I believe God gave us seasons not only to display the varied aspects of creation and keep us paying attention, but also to unsettle our inner landscapes to stop us from becoming too comfortable, too much at home, in any one place or time. For the changing seasons remind us that we are in transit, pilgrims on the way, and that we have not yet entered God's rest—which is precisely why we must reengage and prepare to embark on a new chapter in our pilgrimage. All our longings for the next season or the next big thing only point to our eternal home ahead. The art of living in season is learning to be at home in a place that is not home, waiting and watching for those Adventish moments when ordinary scenes become parables of the kingdom of God.

Our immortal God reigns over the constant ebb and flow of the seasons that shape our times and places. But this is not the meaningless cycle of Ecclesiastes, a vanity of vanities where there is nothing new under the sun. No, the art of living in season involves welcoming each new day, new fruit, new meal, new snowflake, and new face at the table as a seasonal gift. Pilgrims who follow Jesus out of the manger move from the season of Advent to seasonal *adventures*; they experience the constant flow of *petits miracles* that the divine Artist has never tired of producing. In the words of G. K. Chesterton: "It is possible that God says every morning, 'Do it again' to the sun; and every evening, 'Do it again' to the moon. It may not be automatic necessity that makes all daisies alike; it may be that God makes every daisy separately, but He has never got tired of making them."[1]

ADVENT, AGAIN (AND ALWAYS)

The pilgrimage through the seasons is ultimately a means of grace, of deep ongoing renewal: "So we do not lose heart. Though our outer self is wasting away, our inner self is being renewed day by day" (2 Corinthians 4:16). We can therefore ring in each new year with a sense of anticipation, not a fear of repetition. In Marcel Pagnol's words: "The pastorale is not some solemn text frozen for eternity; it is a canvas that is allowed to reinvent itself each year, according to the cultural mood and climate."[2] Yes, everyday saints may rehearse the same story that begins at Christmas, but the setting and cast are different each year. Some of the characters have grown, others have completed their journeys, and new ones have appeared onstage, where they will set off on their own pilgrimages and join the great cloud of witnesses. Everyday saints are not glued to little clay pedestals. Theirs is not a static story, nor is the gospel a tame tale. Everyday saints who follow the santons out of the crèche meet the same Lord, yet he is new every morning (Lamentations 3:23)—and every season.

Everyday saints therefore approach their new Advent season in a different place from the previous year. The challenge is to welcome the Christ who is the same yesterday, today, and forever (Hebrews 13:8) in *this* year in *this* place, and perchance to offer him a new gift under new circumstances. Some everyday saints will be richer, some poorer. Some will have lost their homes or farms. Yet they are still part of the Great Story, and they can still offer their time and energy as gifts to Christ. Others have lost loved ones. Their midwinter may be bleaker than usual. Yet our pilgrimage reminds us that these winters are indeed just that: seasons that last for a time only. It is not always, but *sometimes* winter. The art of living in season is about watching and waiting for Christ's Advent, and the petits miracles that accompany it, in all seasons, even as frosty wind makes moan and snow falls on snow.

The santonniers of Provence produce one or two new figurines every year. They're trying to maintain a delicate balance between preserving the culture of our ancestors while being relevant to the contemporary context, between welcoming the new without compromising the integrity of the past. For example, the celebrated Marcel Carbonel workshops introduced nurse figurines for Christmas 2020 in honor of their role in responding to Covid-19. In keeping with tradition, they wear nineteenth-century medical scrubs, yet we understand the reference: they too, can be everyday saints in the crèche scene. Many other santonniers take their contextualizing even further, producing figurines in contemporary clothes who carry briefcases or push strollers. This often gives rise to vigorous debates as social commentators worry about losing the original culture that the santons were meant to preserve on the one hand, or on the other hand losing touch with changing mores and contemporary life, rendering the santons irrelevant. These are discussions for the experts, the félibres of Provence. Yet we everyday saints face the same questions and concerns for handing on the gospel—how to be félibres of our holy nation.

MY OWN PILGRIMAGE

There is one more tradition in Provence that bears mentioning. Most households have a pair of larger santons sitting or standing in a prominent place in their homes not just at Christmas time but all year long. These larger figures (about ten inches tall) typically represent either a family trade or a personal interest. They celebrate local identity and signify that what we do as individuals fits into a larger tapestry, assuring us that we and our everyday lives have significance in our place and for our community. They are reminders of who we are and where we have come from.

My husband and I were given a pair as a wedding gift. The pair are an older couple; he is reading, she is knitting. My husband was (and still is) a theology student; I was (and still am) an enthusiast of the arts and crafts. The gift-givers knew us well. These medium-sized saints represent us even better now as we grow older together and continue to pursue our vocations—and come physically to resemble them! Like all pilgrims, this pair too bears the marks of their journey: *he* has a broken leg which won't stay glued; *she* has a broken needle, and her knitting has become unraveled. Things—and people—fall apart. This too is a season of life.

Traditions are living things that can stay the same even as they change. Remember, for instance, the thirteen desserts we discussed in chapter two, which accompany Christmas dinner and continue to tell the sweet story of Jesus and his twelve disciples. Papa and Maman, now departed, no longer send us the candied chestnuts and other regional specialties that are supposed to adorn the tray. I now include heirlooms picked up elsewhere over the years in our family pilgrimage: mince pies from Britain and heirloom American cookies replace the missing French items. More recently, I invited our son-in-law to add a Central American specialty of his choice in memory of his childhood in Guatemala. Adding such non-traditional ingredients might be anathema to the Provençaux, yet it works for us, reflecting the largeness of the family of God. Including new things in this traditional dessert passes on both the story of the grown Christ and his twelve disciples and landmarks in our own family story. There are still thirteen desserts; we have simply grafted some new branches onto an old Provençal tradition and the story of Christ.

There is always another season to come. What will happen to my little saints this year, I wonder, as I unwrap the precious santons once more, just as Maman did years ago while I watched her with rapt attention. This is when I discover which figurines are still in good shape, which now need a touch of glue, and which just need replacing. This year's crèche will not look the same as last year's. There is greenery to be collected outdoors, but winter came early this year, and I may not find thyme buried under that foot of snow. I shall have to improvise. This year, the little saints will be positioned by little hands that have grown bigger or more wrinkled, or by new visitors to the crèche.

Learning the art of living in season has helped me see that the Christian pilgrimage or journey through life is about enfolding our everyday lives into the life of Christ, season by season. It is the art of making my place—home, church, workplace, and elsewhere—a living crèche with Jesus in the center. It is the art of doing my part, wherever I happen to be and whatever I happen to be doing. It is the art of following Christ out of the manger, continuing to bring such gifts as I have to offer: my skills, my time, my energy, my possessions, my creativity, my very self.

THE ART OF REENGAGING—TODAY

Advent is a time of watchful waiting, yet everyday saints continue their journey with God throughout the seasons. *Today* is the day to work the garden in whatever place he has seen fit to plant us. *Today* is the day to reengage our place and time, to embrace the call to be holy, to live as everyday saints in the everyday. Dietrich Bonhoeffer knew this and did it: "What is important is not that God is a spectator and participant in our life today, but that we are attentive listeners and participants in God's action in the sacred story, the story of Christ on earth."[3] *Today* is the day to give our hearts to him, for "by a single offering he has perfected for all time those who are being sanctified"—everyday saints (Hebrews 10:14).

What can I give him, poor as I am? What I can, I give him: my part, my art, my heart!

ACKNOWLEDGMENTS

Every good gift and every perfect gift is from above,
coming down from the Father of lights, with whom
there is no variation or shadow due to change.

JAMES 1:17

I f I have gifts to offer in this book, it is because others have gifted to me in the first place, and for those, I am thankful—first of all to God, then to the people he placed around me—for those gifts.

Maman was a bottomless resource of all things *Provençal*: she is the one who set out the crèche in my tender childhood, greeting each new santon as though it were a well-known family member. Papa taught me the rhythms of his garden in his terroir, where he sat contemplatively on his bench at dusk unwittingly passing down a love for my *patrimoine*.

My teachers at the Chicago Botanic Garden taught me introductory botany (Rich Hyerczyk), horticulture (Tim Johnson), Midwest gardening (Sharon Yiesla), and eventually what ended up captivating me: botanic art. Thanks to Marlene Hill Donnelly, Heeyoung Kim, Nancy Halliday, and Claudia Lane for their dedication to their craft and their efforts at passing it down. My fellow botanic artists in the Reed-Turner Botanical Artist Circle and the American Association of Botanic Artist continue to inspire and challenge.

My local farmers, Radical Roots and Prairie Wind, provided most of the produce in my illustrations. As I tell them at the end of each growing year, they have helped this pilgrim plant healthy roots in this land.

My friends listened to my stories over the years, watched me live in season, and encouraged me to write about it, thus sowing seeds in my heart for this book. Linda McCullough Moore said, "I think you have a book in you" soon after we first met and dared me to articulate my thoughts about what that book might be. Susan Kadera introduced me to the beauty of the prairie in conversations about Willa Cather, read some sample writing, and encouraged me to pursue publication. Susan Watts prayed for the book to appear even before it was a twinkle in my eye. My son-in-law Josh Rodriguez has been an eager, supportive, and thorough proofreader.

Others never saw one bit of my writing, yet they still believed. Thank you to Philip Clayton, Russ and Kay Howell, Tom Schwanda, Dan and Amy Treier, and Doug and Wilma Sweeney. I'm also grateful to those in my husband's PhD seminar who came to pay their respects to the crèche at our annual Advent at home and suggested that I write something about it. Voilà!

My editor, Ethan McCarthy, saw the potential of this book and believed in the integrity of the project: text, art, French vocabulary, culture, and all. His encouraging and penetrating suggestions throughout the process, and sensitivity to the organic nature of the project, made revising a delight. This book is much better because of his input. The entire InterVarsity Press team provided just the support and guidance a brand-new writer and illustrator like me needed. I always trusted my manuscript was in good hands!

My daughters, Mary and Emma, have been enthusiastic supporters and have contributed to this project's growth from the start each in their own way, reflecting their distinct gifts and personalities. This book is my heirloom gift to them, a reminder of both their earthly roots and heavenly inheritance that gives them and me "a future and a hope" (Jeremiah 29:11). They have listened to the stories over the years, sung the songs, and each has a crèche of their own. More importantly still, each is an everyday saint and fellow pilgrim.

Kevin, companion santon, first encouraged me to write about the santons three decades ago, long before I began working on the present book. Eventually, date nights became dates every night at the computer poring over my first draft. That he knows me and my mother tongue so well, appreciates Provençal culture, and believed in this project from the first enabled him to guide me along, fixing my occasional *franglais* while preserving my voice. God has promised: "I will give you shepherds after my own heart, who will feed you with knowledge and understanding" (Jeremiah 3:15). Kevin has been the shepherd-friend who has accompanied and, well, husbanded me. He has been feeding me knowledge and understanding about theology and culture since our first conversations before we were married. *The Art of Living in Season* is my gift to him too, and comes with all my love and gratitude as we celebrate forty-three years of living in season and common pilgrimage in four different countries. We may have been away from our respective homelands but we have been at home with one another as we are at home with the Lord. Merci!

GLOSSARY OF FRENCH TERMS

agriculteur—Farmer; one who cultivates the land.

crèche—French word for the manger scene. In contemporary usage, also a term for infant daycare.

félibre—A writer, especially an author or poet writing in Provençal; coined by Frédéric Mistral to describe poets trying to preserve Provençal language and culture (see *Félibrige*).

Félibrige—A literary association founded in 1854 by seven *félibres* in Avignon for the preservation of the Provençal language and culture. An important factor in the "second renaissance" of Provence and, to some extent, of the retrieval of the Provençal Christmas.

goûter—An "afternoon bite," primarily for children (*goûter* means "to taste"); the French equivalent of an afternoon snack or afternoon tea.

lézardage—Literally "lizarding," the state of resting a few minutes in the sun like a lizard on a warm stone wall. By extension, a condition of the soul, an appreciation of the present moment as a time to rest—with or without sun.

métier—A trade, profession, or occupation.

métro-boulot-dodo—Literally "subway-work-bedtime"; a French idiom from the 1960s expressing the doldrums of quotidian routines (the final "t" in *boulot* is silent, so the three words rhyme).

Noël—The word both for "Christmas" and (when not capitalized) for traditional Christmas carols; from Old French *nael* meaning birth (or, by extension, something new); derived from Latin *natalis* ("birth," hence "nativity").

pastorale—A creative retelling of the nativity story featuring shepherds (see *pastre*) and other figures from a traditional nineteenth-century Provençal village.

pastre—Provençal for "shepherd" (see *pastorale*).

patrimoine—The cultural inheritance tied to a local place; its material (castles, churches, museums, etc.) and immaterial (stories, traditions, etc.) value. A heritage to be preserved and passed down, unchanged or possibly enriched; closely linked to *terroir* (see below).

promenade de l'Avent—The "Advent stroll" is a traditional Provençal family walk in the countryside before Christmas for the sake of collecting local herbs with which to deck the crèche and the home.

Provençal(e)—Adjective for all things from Provence, including the language, an Occitan dialect still spoken by a small minority with interest in preserving their *patrimoine* (some preschools reintroduced it in the 1980s) despite the use of French as the official language. "Provence" itself was named by the Romans as a "province" of Gaul.

quotidien—"Daily"; derived from Latin *quoti* + *dies* "each day"; more frequent in French than its English equivalent ("quotidian") in expressions such as *le journal quotidien* (the daily paper) and *notre pain quotidien* (our daily bread).

santon—A small clay figurine that is part of the Provençal manger scene (see *santonnier*).

santonnier—Artisan who makes *santons*.

tambourinaire—Traditional Provençal musician who plays fife and drum.

terroir—A cultivated place (derived from *terre*, the French word for "earth") with special reference to its soil conditions and what grows there. More broadly, the local culture and way of life that a particular place may be said to cultivate such that land (terroir) and culture (patrimoine) are inextricably linked.

NOTES

INTRODUCTION

[1]C. S. Lewis, *The Lion, The Witch and the Wardrobe* (London: Geoffrey Bles, 1950).

1. ADVENT

[1]While the Advent Walk remains a cherished tradition, a time to "plant" the crèche in the terroir of one's ancestors, it is largely a cultural tradition. The spiritual dimension, and the discipline of solitude in particular, reflects my own experience and perspective.

[2]*Terre*, the French word for "earth," gives us the term *terroir*—local earth.

[3]Wendell Berry, *Fidelity* (New York: Pantheon, 1992), 20.

[4]Mary Oliver, "Sometimes," in *Red Bird: Poems* (Boston: Beacon Press, 2008).

[5]I recommend listening to The Terra Nova Consort, *Renaissance en Provence* (Dorian Recordings, 1998). It is not officially a Christmas collection, yet most of the songs are noëls. For more details about the origins of the noëls, see "The Book/The History of Noëls," on my website www.theartoflivinginseason.com.

[6]Nicolas Saboly, *Li Pastourèu*—a classic noël (my translation).

[7]Blaise Pascal, *Pensées*, 139.

[8]Jan Johnson, *Spiritual Disciplines Companion* (Downers Grove, IL: InterVarsity Press, 2009), 12.

[9]C. Galtier and E. Cattin, *Les Santons de Provence* (Rennes: Éditions Ouest-France, 1996), 4 (my translation).

[10]Swiss chard is no more Swiss than french fries are French. The chard is an ancient Mediterranean vegetable, related to the beet. As for french fries, they are originally Belgian!

[11]Yvan Audouard, *La Pastorale des Santons de Provence* (Éditions du Gulf Stream, 2001), 3 (my translation).

[12]Ron DelBene, "A Simple Way to Pray," from *Weavings*, cited in Rueben P. Job, Norman Shawchuck, John S. Mogabgab, *A Guide to Prayer for All Who Walk with God* (Nashville: Upper Room Books, 2013), 192.

2. CHRISTMAS

[1]C. S. Lewis, *Mere Christianity* (Glasgow: William Collins & Sons Ltd., 1977), 47.

[2]See the traditional folk English carol "The Holly and the Ivy."

[3]I am referring to Yvan Audounard, *Pastorale des Santons de Provence* (Éditions du Gulf Stream, 2001), 3 (my translation).

[4]I highly recommend a book by luthier Martin Schleske, *The Sound of Life's Unspeakable Beauty* (Grand Rapids, MI: Eerdmans, 2020). He is not from Provence, but he is a little saint, and he has written a profoundly spiritual book about his vocation.

[5]Henri Moucadel, *Noëls Provençaux* (Avignon: Librairie contemporaine, 1995).

[6]Christina Rossetti, "In the Bleak Midwinter," first published as "A Christmas Carol" in *Scribner's Monthly*, January 1872, Poetry Foundation, www.poetryfoundation.org/poems/53216/in-the-bleak-midwinter.

[7]Moucadel, *Noëls Provençaux*, 14.

[8]Nicholas Saboly, *Pèr noun langui*, 1699 (my translation).

[9]Rossetti, "In the Bleak Midwinter."

[10]Reuben P. Job and Marjorie J. Thompson, *Embracing the Journey* (Nashville: Upper Room Books, 2006), 29.

[11]C. S. Lewis, "On Church Music," in *Christian Reflections* (Grand Rapids, MI: Eerdmans, 1967), 99.

[12]This, along with the *santons*, is one of the most cherished of the Christmas traditions in the land, known all over France.

[13]Yvan Audouard, *Pastorale des Santons de Provence* (Éditions du Gulf Stream, 2001), 7. The French often refer to unexpected happy events as *des petits miracles*.

[14]Rossetti, "In the Bleak Midwinter."

[15]Moucadel, *Noëls Provençaux*.

3. EPIPHANY

[1]Ash Wednesday comes forty weekdays before Easter, whose date is determined according to the first full moon after March 21, making it a variable feast from year to year.

[2]See Vincent van Gogh's 1888 painting of "Caravans Encampment of Gypsies" for a contemporary rendering.

[3]"Soun tres rèi en campagno," usually attributed to Nicolas Saboly (my translation). The interpretation by the *Corou de Berra* ensemble is particularly recommended.

[4]Andrew F. Walls, *The Missionary Movement in Christian History: Studies in the Transmission of the Faith* (Maryknoll, NY: Orbis, 1996), xvii.

[5]The "strangers" were an international team from Operation Mobilization, and later, Pastor Tom Harris and his wife, Gay, from the United States. I am eternally

grateful to the Operation Mobilization team for giving me the gift of the gospel, and to Tom and Gay for helping me unwrap it. (I read a few years later in a newsletter that, through them, Christians all over Europe had been praying for me and my brother!)

[6]See Karl Barth's essay, "The Strange New World of the Bible," in *The Word of God and the Word of Man* (Gloucester, MA: Peter Smith, 1978), 28-50.

[7]For more on this tradition, see my website www.theartoflivinginseason.com.

[8]This is my own free interpretation of the *fève* tradition.

[9]Thomas A. Tarrants, *Consumed by Hate, Redeemed by Love* (Nashville: Nelson Books, 2019), 194.

[10]David I. Smith and Barbara Carvill, *The Gift of the Stranger Faith, Hospitality, and Foreign Language Learning* (Grand Rapids, MI: Eerdmans, 2000), 102.

[11]French bakeries are often happy to make a *Galette des Rois* for you, particularly if you ask ahead of time. Or you might prefer to check online for pictures and recipes.

4. CANDLEMAS

[1]I recommend the King's College choir rendition, arranged by Gustav Holst.

[2]Marcel Pagnol adapted the play from his screenplay for *La femme du boulanger* (*The Baker's Wife*), directed by Marcel Pagnol (Paris: Les Films Marcel Pagnol, 1938).

[3]From the Latin *com* + *panis*: "with bread." A *companion* is literally a "bread-fellow."

[4]Eugene H. Peterson, *Run with the Horses* (Downers Grove, IL: InterVarsity Press, 1983), 74.

[5]Yvan Audouard, *Pastorale des Santons de Provence* (Éditions du Gulf Stream, 2001), 7 (my translation).

[6]C. S. Lewis, *Mere Christianity* (Glasgow: William Collins Sons & Co., 1977), 122.

[7]William Shakespeare, *Much Ado About Nothing* (Clayton, DE: Prestwick House Literary Touchstone Classics, 2007) act v, scene 4.

[8]Paul Verlaine, "Dans l'interminable": "*Dans l'interminable ennui de la plaine, la neige, incertaine, luit comme du sable*" (my translation).

[9]William Willams (1717-1791), "Guide Me, O Thou Great Jehovah."

[10]Augustine, Letter 130, to Proba (2, 5).

[11]See Augustine, *Confessions*, tr. Henry Chadwick, book 1 (Oxford: Oxford University Press, 1991), 3.

5. LENT

[1]"*Taille tôt, taille tard, rien ne vaut la taille de mars.*" (Technically speaking, not all pruning takes place in March. Consult your local arborist!)

[2]The opening words of the Heidelberg Catechism, question 1.

[3]Maurel, *La Pastorale Maurel, ou Le Mystère de la Naissance de Notre Seigneur Jésus-Christ* (Marseille: P. Tacussel Editeur, 1978), 42 (my translation and emphasis).

[4]John Baillie, *A Diary of Private Prayer* (New York: Scribner, 1936).

[5]I owe this point to Linda McCullough Moore, *The Book of Not So Common Prayer* (Nashville: Abingdon Press, 2014), 6.

[6]From Peter Jackson's film adaptation of *The Lord of the Rings: The Fellowship of the Rings* (Burbank, CA: New Line Cinema and Wellington, NZ: Wingnut Films, 2001). The original quote, from the prologue of J. R. R. Tolkien's book, says only, "As for the Hobbits of the Shire . . . laugh they did, and eat, and drink, often and heartily, being fond of simple jests at all times, and of six meals a day (when they could get them)," J. R. R. Tolkien, *The Fellowship of the Ring* (London: George Allen & Unwin, 1954), 12.

[7]Rueben P. Job, Norman Shawchuck, John S. Mogabgab, *A Guide to Prayer For All who Seek God* (Nashville: Upper Room Books, 2003), 15.

[8]Job, Shawchuck, and Mogabgab, *Guide to Prayer*, 342.

6. EASTER

[1]Emily Dickinson, "A Little Madness in Spring," *The Complete Poems of Emily Dickinson*, Thomas H. Johnson, ed. (Boston: Little, Brown and Company, 1960).

[2]Willa Cather, *My Ántonia* (New York: W. W. Norton & Company, 2015), 65.

[3]Translated as: "*Adam e sa Coumpagno.*"

[4]Yvan Audouard, *Pastorale des Santons de Provence* (Éditions du Gulf Stream, 2001), 23 (my translation).

[5]The lavoirs were built around the time the santons themselves came into existence. They were a modern invention of sorts, in an age when the fear of epidemics, such as cholera and typhoid, made hygiene a top government priority.

[6]Kathleen Norris, *The Quotidian Mysteries—Laundry, Liturgy and "Women's Work"* (Mahwah, NJ: Paulist Press, 1998), 15.

[7]Audouard, *Pastorale des Santons de Provence.*

[8]Ralph Earle, note on Matthew 26:23 in *The NIV Study Bible*, ed. Kenneth Barker (Grand Rapids, MI: Zondervan, 1985), 1,484.

[9]Ann Voskamp, *One Thousand Gifts: A Dare to Live Fully Right where you Are* (Grand Rapids, MI: Zondervan, 2010), 32, 45.

[10]Voskamp, *One Thousand Gifts.*

[11]From notes to members of my CSA (community shared agriculture), by our providing farmer and certified herbalist.

[12]Elizabeth Ehrlich, *Miriam's Kitchen, A Memoir* (New York: Penguin, 1997), xi.

[13]Gerard Manley Hopkins, "The Wreck of the Deutschland," first published 1918.

[14]From Peter Jackson's film adaptation of *The Lord of the Rings: The Two Towers* (Burbank, CA: New Line Cinema and Wellington, NZ: Wingnut Films, 2002).

7. PENTECOST

[1]C. S. Lewis, *Mere Christianity* (Glasgow: William Collins & Sons Ltd., 1977), 47.

[2]This is my loose translation of the original French: *En avril, ne quitte pas un fil, en mai, fais ce qui te plaît.*

[3]For more information, see Sarah Rutherford, *Botanic Gardens* (Oxford, England: Shire Publications, 2015).

[4]*Les Herbes de Provence* (Septèmes-les-Vallons: Editoriale, Marseille, 2001), 2 (my translation).

[5]*Domestic* has intriguing connotations, pertaining not only to home but also to home country. In this book, it is therefore closely related to *terroir*.

[6]Dorothy Sayers, *Creed or Chaos?* (Manchester, NH: Sophia Institute Press, 1949), 78.

[7]Julie Canlis, *The Theology of the Ordinary* (Wenatchee, WA: Godspeed Press 2017), 50.

[8]Elisabeth Lambert Ortiz, *The Encyclopedia of Herbs, Spices and Flavorings* (London: Dorling Kindersley, 1992), 9.

[9]Canlis, *Theology of the Ordinary*, 51.

[10]Canlis, *Theology of the Ordinary*, 19.

PART TWO: EVERYDAY SAINTS IN ORDINARY TIME

[1]Laurence Hull Stookey, *Calendar: Christ's Time for the Church* (Nashville: Abbington Press, 1996), 133.

[2]Julie Canlis, *The Theology of the Ordinary* (Wenatchee, WA: Godspeed Press, 2017), 30.

8. ON THE LAND

[1]This usage goes back to Roman times, when an inheritance was passed down from the father's side: *pater* = "father."

[2]These days were instituted by the French Ministry of Culture in 1982 as an effort to preserve regional diversity within a growing global Europe (several European countries have since followed suit, around the same date).

[3]Leonard Hjalmarson, *No Home Like Place A Christian Theology of Place* (Portland, OR: Urban Loft Publishers, 2014).

[4]George Monbiot, *Regenesis: Feeding the World without Devouring the Planet,* New York: Penguin, 2022).

[5]This is not an essay on ecology. For further reading on this important topic, see Wendell Berry's agrarian essays in *The Art of the Commonplace* (Washington, DC:

Shoemaker and Hoard, 2002), and Ellen Davis, *Scripture, Culture, and Agriculture* (Cambridge, England: Cambridge University Press, 2008).

[6]Alan P. F. Sell, "The Reformed Family Today: Some Theological Reflections," in *Major Themes in the Reformed Tradition*, ed. Donald K. McKim (Eugene, OR: Wipf & Stock, 1998), 438.

[7]Jean Giono, *Regain* (Paris: Librairie Générale Française, 1995), 94 (my translation and emphasis).

[8]The French term *regain* refers to the grass that grows again after the first cut. It therefore carries a connotation of revival or renewal.

[9]Charles Dudley Warner, "My Summer in a Garden" *The American Botanist*, vol. 17 no. 4, Nov. 1911, 119.

[10]From Elizabeth J. Canham, *Weavings*, in Rueben P. Job, Norman Shawchuck, John S. Mogabgab, *A Guide to Prayer for All Who Walk with God* (Nashville: Upper Room Press, 2014), 372.

[11]Rachel Peden, *Speak to the Earth: Pages from a Farmwife's Journal* (New York: Alfred A. Knopf, Inc., 1974), 5.

[12]*CSA* stands for community shared agriculture. Subscribers pay an annual sum to a local farmer and then collect a share of his produce, all local and mostly organic, as well as eggs and dairy throughout the growing season, and root vegetables in the winter.

[13]All farm notes are taken from Radical Root (www.radicalrootfarm.com) and Prairie Wind (www.prairiewindfamilyfarm.com) farms.

[14]Inspired by the opening paragraphs of Isak Dinesen, *Out of Africa* (New York: Modern Library, 1992), 3.

[15]Dan Guenthner, *Simply in Season* (Waterloo, Ontario Scottsdale: Herald Press, 2005), 67.

[16]Diane Morgan, *Roots, the Definitive Compendium* (San Francisco: Chronicle Books, 2012).

[17]Barbara Kingsolver, *Animal, Vegetable, Miracle* (New York: Harper Perennial, 2007), 205.

[18]Wendell Berry, *A World Lost* (Washington, DC: Counterpoint, 1996), 139.

9. AT THE TABLE

[1]Wendell Berry, *The Art of the Commonplace* (New York: Counterpoint, 2003), 321.

[2]The term *carbon footprint* refers to the amount of carbon dioxide emissions required to transport, say, fruit from other countries. The larger the carbon footprint, the greater the cost to the environment.

[3]See, for example, Andrea Michelson, "Toxic Chemicals Linked to Infertility Found in Big Macs and Taco Bell Burritos," *Insider*, October 27, 2021, www.insider.com/big-macs-taco-bell-burritos-found-to-contain-harmful-chemmicals-2021-10; and Vanessa Glavinskas, "Chemicals Linked to Infertility and Birth Defects also Linked to Preterm Birth, Study Says, Environmental Defense Fund," Environmental Defense Fund, September 23, 2022, www.edf.org/article/chemicals-linked-infertility-and-birth-defects-also-linked-preterm-birth.

[4]The English language uses the modern French spelling for the term *restaurant*, as is often the case for French food vocabulary: *cuisine, casserole, menu*, etc.

[5]For more on this subject, see Mary Beth Lind and Cathleen Hockman-Wert, *Simply in Season* (Scottdale, PA: Herald Press, 2005).

[6]Jean Giono, *Regain* (Paris: Librairie Générale Française, 1995), 140.

[7]Anne-Marie Marina Mediavilla, "Pour mieux comprendre Regain," in *Regain*, 169 (my translation).

[8]Nicolas Saboly, *Que disès, mei bon fraire.*

[9]Reuben P. Job, Norman Shawchuck, and John S. Mogabgab, *A Guide to Prayer for All God's People* (Nashville: Upper Room Books, 1990), 214.

[10]Mireille Guiliano, *French Women Don't Get Fat: The Secret of Eating for Pleasure* (New York: Alfred A. Knopf, 2005), 65-66.

[11]Taken from my Botany 101 notes course at Chicago Botanic Garden.

[12]Norman Wirzba, *Food and Faith* (Cambridge, England: Cambridge University Press, 2012), 28.

[13]Jan Karon, *These High, Green Hills* (New York: Penguin Group, 1998), 43.

[14]*Cuisine* in French, means both the kitchen and the prepared food, giving us another interesting example of an ethnobotanical relationship.

10. ROUND THE GARDEN

[1]Sarah Orne Jewett, "From a Mournful Villager," *Selected Stories Novels and Stories* (New York: The Library of America, 1994), 592.

[2]Note that it is unclear what Jesus' "lilies" really were, and if they even were "lilies" such as we know. They may well have been some other kind of wildflower than the lilies we have in mind (most of which actually originated in Asia—not Palestine, Europe, or America).

[3]Bérengère Desmettre, *Le mouchoir de la duchesse* (Paris: Riveneuve Éditions, 2016), 21 (my translation).

[4]For more on this constant watchfulness in the flower garden, even in the middle of the night, read Celia Thaxter, *An Island Garden* (Cambridge, MA: Riverside Press, 1894).

[5]E. M. Forster, *Howards End* (London: Edward Arnold, 1910).

[6]Beverley Nichols, *Merry Hall* (Portland, OR: Timber Press, 1951), 115.

[7]Julie Canlis, *The Theology of the Ordinary* (Wenatchee, WA: Godspeed Press, 2017), 18.

[8]The city of Grasse has long been considered the "world capital of perfumes."

[9]From the classic folk song, *Auprès de ma blonde*, that starts with the words: "*Dans le jardin d'mon père, les lilas sont fleuris.*"

[10]*Helleborus niger*, also known as Lenten rose, because it grows well in the cold season.

[11]Peter J. Leithart, "Quodlibet," *Touchstone Magazine*, May/June 2010.

[12]Emily Dickinson, "To Make a Prairie," 1779, www.emilydickinsonmuseum.org /to-make-a-prairie-1755/, accessed October 19, 2023.

[13]Botanic art is technically a form of scientific illustration, a mixture of science and art—another example of joining the useful and the beautiful. Centuries ago, it played an integral role in voyages of discovery. It remains the principal way of recording the various seasonal changes and parts of a newfound plant's life (the useful) and presenting it pictorially, where rules of composition and color wheels apply (the art).

[14]Antoine de Saint-Exupéry, *The Little Prince* (New York: Clarion Books, 2000), 64.

[15]G. K. Chesterton, as quoted by James M. Houston, *Joyful Exiles: Life in Christ on the Dangerous Edge of Things* (Downers Grove, IL: InterVarsity Press, 2006), 140.

[16]N. T. Wright, *Simply Christian: Why Christianity Makes Sense* (San Francisco: Harper Collins, 2006), 235.

[17]Ted Orland, *The View from the Studio Door: How Artists Find Their Way in an Uncertain World* (Santa Cruz, CA, and Eugene, OR: Image Continuum Press, 2006), 39.

[18]Celia Thaxter, *An Island Garden* (Boston: Houghton Mifflin, 2001), 71. Her island flower garden (fifty by fifteen feet all told) in Appledore, Maine, became known as "America's first artists' colony." Her summer garden attracted the likes of Childe Hassam, Sarah Orne Jewett, Nathaniel Hawthorne, and many others during the last couple of decades of the nineteenth century.

11. IN THE MARKETPLACE

[1]See my website for further details, www.theartoflivinginseason.com.

[2]The honor is awarded every year by the combined French ministries of Agriculture, Education, Labor, Artisanat, and Economy to workers in various trades, such as food production, building construction, domestic arts and furnishing, metal work, ceramic, china and clay work (including *santonnerie*), clothes, jewelry, surgical tools, clockwork, graphic design, printing, musical instruments, and more. There is no monetary prize. The honor (complete with tricolor ribbon and medal), including a reception offered by the French president at the Palais de l'Elysée, is enough. Prospective customers know that they offer top quality products, set apart not simply because of the materials

used but because they have *soul*, namely, a respect for tradition and a recognition of the terroir that gave rise to it.

[3]Keith Van Sickle, "Meilleur Ouvrier de France: The Finest Craftsmen of France," in *France Today* (February 8, 2021). *France Today* is the leading website (www.france today.com) and print magazine for an international Francophile audience interested in French travel, culture, entertainment, art and design, society, and history.

[4]Rueben P. Job, Norman Shawchuck, and John S. Mogabgab, *A Guide to Prayer for All Who Walk with God* (Nashville: Upper Room Books, 2013).

[5]Martin Luther, *Exposition of Psalm 147*, quoted in Gustav Wingren, *Luther on Vocation* (Evansville, IN: Ballast Press, 1994), 138.

[6]Yvan Audouard, *Pastorale des Santons de Provence* (Éditions du Gulf Stream, 2001), 11 (my translation).

[7]Tim Keller, *Every Good Endeavor: Connecting your Work to God's Work* (New York: Riverhead Books, 2014), 45.

[8]Tish Harrison Warren, *Liturgy of the Ordinary* (Downers Grove, IL: InterVarsity Press, 2016), 94, 80-81. This is a reference to the sugar boycott initiated by William Wilberforce as a protest against the slave-trade in 1791.

[9]James K.A. Smith, *You Are What You Love: The Spiritual Power of Habit* (Grand Rapids, MI: Brazos Press: 2016), 174.

[10]John Baillie, *A Diary of Private Prayer* (New York: Scribner, 1936).

[11]Jean-Max Tixier, *La Crèche et les Santons de Provence* (Genève: éditions Aubanel, 2000), 69 and 152 (my translation).

[12]Job, Shawchuck, and Mogabgab, *Guide to Prayer*, 50.

[13]Mother Teresa, *My Life for the Poor* (New York: Ballantine Books, 1987).

12. WITH THE CHILDREN

[1]Marthe Seguin-Fontes, *Santons et Traditions en Provence* (Paris: Flammarion, 2001), 82 (my translation).

[2]Rachel Carson, *The Sense of Wonder: A Celebration of Nature for Parents and Children* (New York: Harper Collins, 1956), 48-49.

[3]Allusions to J. M. Barrie, *The Adventures of Peter Pan*; C. S. Lewis, *The Lion, the Witch and the Wardrobe*; and E. H. Shepard, *Winnie the Pooh*.

[4]For more on children's stories, see Gladys Hunt, *Honey for a Child's Heart: The Imaginative Use of Books in Family Life* (Grand Rapids, MI: Zondervan, 1969).

[5]Joseph Roumanille, "Li dous pijoun," *Noëls Provençaux*, 70.

[6]Maurel, *La Pastorale Maurel, ou Le Mystère de la Naissance de Notre Seigneur Jésus-Christ* (Marseille: P. Tacussel Editeur, 1978), 204 (my translation).

[7]Joseph Roumanille, "*La Chato Avuglo*," *Noëls Provençaux*, 70.

[8]Marcel Proust, *Swann's Way: In Search of Lost Time*, vol. 1. (New York: Penguin Books, 2000), 45-47. The *madeleine* is an everyday child's afternoon tea item; this story is known to most French adults, even if they have not read Proust. The "madeleine effect," that transports one back to childhood through association, is often called *la madeleine de Proust.*

[9]Jen Pollock Michel, *Keeping Places: Reflections on the Meaning of Home* (Downers Grove, IL: InterVarsity Press, 2017), 66.

[10]William Maxwell, *They Came Like Swallows* (New York: Vintage International, 1997), 11.

[11]Here are suggestions for the magic of the childhood vision and imagination: Shirley Hughes, *Alfie's World*; Kenneth Grahame, *The Wind in the Willows*; Tove Jansson, *The Finn Family Moomintroll*; Antoine de Saint-Exupéry, *The Little Prince*; J. M. Barrie, *The Adventures of Peter Pan*; C. S. Lewis, The Chronicles of Narnia seres.

13. ALONGSIDE THE ELDERS

[1]Reine des Reinettes, an ancient French apple that figures in children's folk songs, means "Queen of queens." The Bloody Ploughman got its name after the story of a ploughman who was shot while stealing apples near Megginch Castle in Scotland. His wife threw the stolen bag of apples on the compost heap and a seedling grew out of it, giving the apple this name. The Esopus Spitzenburg apple (the botanical illustration in this chapter) is a very old species that was discovered around 1700 in the Dutch settlement of Esopus, New York, hence its name. It was a favorite of Thomas Jefferson, who grew several in his own orchard.

[2]Notes on heirloom apples come from a lecture at the Chicago Botanic Garden, October 6, 2018, by apple historian Dan Bussey of the Seed Savers Exchange. In his thirty years of research, he has cataloged several thousand heirloom apples, all of which he discovered in the United States and Canada alone. See Dan Bussey's seven-volume work *The Illustrated History of Apples in the United States and Canada* (Mount Horeb, WI: Jak Kaw Press, 2015), which contains fourteen hundred botanical illustrations of heirloom apple species.

[3]Growers value these varieties for their ability to withstand mechanical picking and cross-country shipping, and for their tolerance to pesticides. Dan Bussey says that every decade or so, a new apple appears on the market, but only to satisfy consumers' need for change. For example, at present the Honeycrisp is everywhere, whereas the Red Delicious is in decline, making a quiet exit.

[4]Vanessa Diffenbaugh, *We Never Asked for Wings* (New York: Ballantine Books, 2016), 50.

[5]For the "amortality" trend, by which older people "rely on exercise, diet and cosmetic procedures to remain transcendentally youthful," see Catherine Mayer, "Forever Young," *Time* April 25, 2011, vol. 177, no. 16.

[6]Paul Verlaine, "Chanson d'automne": *"Les sanglots longs/Des violons/De l'automne/ Blessent mon coeur/ D'une langueur/Monotone,"* (my translation).

[7]Victor Hugo, "L'aube est moins claire": *"L'été qui s'enfuit est un ami qui part,"* (my translation).

[8]Wendell Berry, *A World Lost* (Washington, DC: Counterpoint, 1996), 151.

[9]Rueben P. Job, Norman Shawchuck, and John S. Mogabgab, *A Guide to Prayer for All God's People* (Nashville: Upper Room Books, 1990), 286.

[10]Martin Luther, *Table Talk,* tr. William Hazlitt (London: H. H. Bohn, 1857), 159.

[11]Douglas A. Sweeney, "Senior Saints, We Need You: Why the Church Needs Seniors," Gospel Coalition, August 14, 2022, www.thegospelcoalition.org/article/senior-saints -we-need-you.

14. THE FEAST OF CHRIST THE KING

[1]During the French revolution, the government implemented a secularized calendar, from late 1793 to 1805, which included the seasons of nature but not the seasons of the church.

[2]"White Oak," *Arbor Day Newsletter*, July/August 2018, 8.

[3]Wendy Miller, *Learning to Listen: A Guide for Spiritual Friends,* quoted in Rueben P. Job, Norman Shawchuck, and John S. Mogabgab, *A Guide to Prayer for All Who Seek God* (Nashville: Upper Room Books, 2003), 120.

[4] Frédéric Mistral won the 1904 Nobel Prize for Literature in recognition of his body of work: original poems, a dictionary of Provençal, a translation of the book of Genesis in Provençal, written transcripts of troubadour songs, and more, all forming a contri- bution to his *patrimoine.*

[5]Ted Orland, *The View from the Studio Door* (Santa Cruz, CA, and Eugene, OR: Image Continuum Press, 2006), 12.

[6]France now has laws to protect its cultural diversity, part of a larger European concern for "the right by every country to protect its national culture . . . and to promote a dialogue of cultures that respect all," Ross Steele, *The French Way* (New York: McGraw-Hill, 2006), 122.

[7] *"Quand le Bon Dieu en vient à douter du monde, il se rappelle qu'il a créé la Provence."* This is the oral version of a well-known quote, generally attributed to Mistral (my translation).

[8]The "first renaissance" was influenced by Nicolas Saboly, who sought to preserve the everyday life and culture of the 1600s in the music and lyrics of his noëls.

Notes to Pages 221-236

[9]Augustine, *On Christian Doctrine* 1.11.11, quoted in and translated by William Harmless in *Augustine in His Own Words* (Washington, DC: Catholic University of America Press, 2010), 168.

[10]Paul Ruat, *Charradisso sus Calendau* (Marseille, 1909), 14. My translation and emphasis.

[11]Charlotte Adelman and Bernard L. Schwartz, *The Midwestern Native Garden, An Illustrated Guide* (Athens: Ohio University Press, 2011), 2.

[12]J. G. Millar, "Land," in *New Dictionary of Biblical Theology*, T. D. Alexander and Brian S. Rosner eds. (Downers Grove, IL: InterVarsity Press, 2000), 627.

[13]All the illustrations of native plants in this book come from our own restored native woods, including the oak in this chapter.

[14]Christian Wiman, *Ambition and Survival: Becoming a Poet* (Port Townsend, WA: Copper Canyon Press, 2007), 120.

[15]Tish Harrison Warren, *Liturgy of the Ordinary* (Downers Grove: IL, InterVarsity Press, 2016), 92.

[16]Jean-Max Tixier, *La Crèche et les Santons de Provence* (Genève: Éditions Aubanel, 2000), 91 (my translation).

[17]C. S. Lewis, *Mere Christianity* (Glasgow: William Collins & Sons Ltd., 1977), 163.

[18]Christina Rossetti, "In the Bleak Midwinter," first published as "A Christmas Carol" in *Scribner's Monthly*, January 1872, Poetry Foundation, www.poetryfoundation .org/poems/53216/in-the-bleak-midwinter.

[19]Robert H. Gundry, "Coming Home," in *Extracurriculars, Teaching Christianly Outside Class* (Eugene, OR: Wipf & Stock, 2012), 122. The quote comes from a homecoming speech given at Westmont College in 2003, when my husband, Kevin, was alumnus of the year, by his mentor, Robert Gundry.

EPILOGUE: EVERYDAY ADVENT

[1]G. K. Chesterton, *Orthodoxy*, in *The Collected Works of G.K. Chesterton*, vol. 1 (San Francisco: Ignatius Press, 1986), 100.

[2]Marcel Pagnol, preface to Yvan Audouard, *Pastorale des Santons de Provence* (Éditions du Gulf Stream, 2001), (my translation).

[3]*Dietrich Bonhoeffer's Works*, ed. Victoria J. Barnett, *Life Together and Prayerbook of the Bible*, vol. 5 (Minneapolis: Fortress Press, 1996), 62.

FURTHER READING

*O gracious Presence . . . Guide my mind to choose the right books
and, having chosen them, to read them in the right way. When I
read for profit, grant that all I read lead me nearer to thyself. When
I read for recreation, grant that what I read may not lead me away
from thee. Let all my reading so refresh my mind that I may the more
eagerly seek after whatsoever things are pure and fair and true.*

JOHN BAILLIE, *A DIARY OF PRIVATE PRAYER*

For the art of walking daily with saints throughout the ages and attending to the seasons of the church year

Bobby Gross, *Living the Christian Year* (Downers Grove, IL: InterVarsity Press, 2009).

Malcolm Guite, *Sounding the Seasons* (Norwich: Canterbury Press, 2012).

Rueben P. Job, Norman Shawchuck, and John S. Mogabgab, *A Guide to Prayer for All Who Seek God* (Nashville: Upper Room Books, 2006)—and the other books in this collection.

For the art of attending to the seasons of nature

Hannah Anderson, *Turning of Days* (Chicago: Moody Publishers, 2021).

Clare Walker Leslie and Charles E. Roth, *Keeping a Nature Journal* (North Adams, MA: Storey Publishing, 2000).

For the art of watching the seasonal cycle of English wildlife, with personal notes, illustrations, and poetry quotes

Edith Holden, *The Country Diary of an Edwardian Lady* (New York: Holt, Rinehart and Winston, 1977, 1982).

For the art of observing the changing seasons on a Midwest farm through the year

Rachel Peden, *Rural Free* (Bloomington, IN: Indiana University Press, 1961).

For the art of eating in season

Brother Victor-Antoine d'Avila-Latourrette, *Twelve Months of Monastery Soups* (New York: Broadway Books, 1998).

Mary Beth Lind and Cathleen Hockman-Wert, *Simply in Season*, A World Community Cookbook (Scottdale, PA: Herald Press, 2005).

For the art of walking the seasons with a child and through the eyes of a child

Shirley Hughes, *Out and About* (London: Walker Books, 1998).